'A very readable, deeply reported examination of what could be the next great political upheaval to hit the West. Mallet understands the centuries-old history of the French far right, arguably dating back to its "defeat" of 1789, but he is also on top of the present, and has spoken to today's most important actors. Read it to avoid future shocks.'

Simon Kuper, author of *Impossible City: Paris in the Twenty-First Century*

'Après Macron... Marine? With the next French political revolution predicted to come from the radical right, this is a smart, timely and clear-eyed guide to how the party founded by Jean-Marie Le Pen shed its pariah status, won over middle France and placed itself in pole position to claim the presidency.'

James Coomarasamy, BBC radio and TV presenter

'A compelling, vivid and indispensable account of one of the most consequential political developments for Europe in the twenty-first century: the inexorable rise of the French populist far right.'

Sylvie Kauffmann, lead writer and columnist, *Le Monde*

'Victor Mallet combines deep reporting and historical perspective to chart the National Rally's move from the fringes to the very centre of French politics. Venturing far beyond Paris, Mallet delves into the anger and alienation of the provinces that drive the far right's rise. A window into the political shifts transforming the country, this is the book that no one interested in the future of Europe can afford to ignore.'

Saskya Vandoorne, Paris Bureau Chief, CNN

'Victor Mallet deftly traces the origins of the French far right and lays out the stakes for the movement's continuing rise. A must for anyone who cares about France and its future.'

Lauren Collins, staff writer, *The New Yorker*, and author of *When in French*

'An acute, punchy account of how the far right has taken the lead in French politics—and of the dangers that represents. A penetrating panorama, melding political analysis and grassroots reporting.'

Jonathan Fenby, author of *The History of Modern France*

'An indispensable and accessible introduction to the seemingly inexorable rise of the extreme right in contemporary France. It is entirely plausible that the Rassemblement National of Marine Le Pen will come to power in France in 2027. This lively and well-informed book by a seasoned observer of French politics explains why France finds itself in this situation and what it portends for the future.'

Julian Jackson, author of *France on Trial*

'For anyone interested in France as well as the future of Europe, Mallet's book is essential reading. The urgency of his warnings is perfectly balanced with understanding and compassion.'

Ruth Harris, author of *Dreyfus: Politics, Emotion, and the Scandal of the Century*

FAR-RIGHT FRANCE

VICTOR MALLET

Far-Right France

*Le Pen, Bardella
and the Future of Europe*

HURST & COMPANY, LONDON

First published in the United Kingdom in 2026 by
C. Hurst & Co. (Publishers) Ltd.,
New Wing, Somerset House, Strand, London, WC2R 1LA
© Victor Mallet, 2026
All rights reserved.

Distributed in the United States, Canada and Latin America by
Oxford University Press, 546 Fifth Avenue, New York, NY 10036,
United States of America.

The right of Victor Mallet to be identified as the author of
this publication is asserted by him in accordance with the
Copyright, Designs and Patents Act, 1988.

A Cataloguing-in-Publication data record for this book
is available from the British Library.

ISBN: 9781805264132

EU GPSR Authorised Representative
Easy Access System Europe Oü, 16879218
Address: Mustamäe tee 50, 10621, Tallinn, Estonia
Contact Details: gpsr.requests@easproject.com, +358 40 500 3575

This book is printed using paper from registered sustainable
and managed sources.

www.hurstpublishers.com

Printed and bound in Great Britain by Bell & Bain Ltd, Glasgow

For N and G,
who make the world a better place

CONTENTS

Preface: *Why We Failed to See It Coming*   xi

Introduction: After Emmanuel Macron   1

PART I
GOODBYE TO THE OLD ORDER

1. Yellow-Vest Rebellion   23
2. The Trump Effect   33
3. In the Beginning Was the Father   47
4. Political Patricide   69

PART II
RISE OF THE RASSEMBLEMENT NATIONAL

5. The Road to Power   93
6. Who Is Jordan Bardella?   105
7. North and South   121
8. Far-Right Fiefdom   137

CONTENTS

PART III
THE NEW FRANCE

9. The Big Issues: Immigration and the Economy	149
10. Environmental Battles and Culture Wars	175
11. France's Fox News and the Battle for Public Opinion	185

PART IV
EXIT MARINE?

12. To Russia With Love	197
13. Embezzlement: "Unbelievable"—But True	207
Conclusion: Far-Right Future	219
Acknowledgements	229
Notes	231
Select Bibliography	275
Index	279

PREFACE

WHY WE FAILED TO SEE IT COMING

"Our victory is only postponed," said Marine Le Pen after her party was excluded from government despite winning the most votes in the 2024 general election. This book is about the rise of the far right in France, past, present and future. It focuses on the leaders and the millions of supporters of one of the most successful far-right movements in Europe: Jean-Marie Le Pen helped found the Front National (FN) in 1972, his daughter Marine Le Pen inherited it in 2011, she renamed it as the less aggressive-sounding Rassemblement National (RN) seven years later and then handed the party's presidency to her young protégé Jordan Bardella. At the time of writing, the RN is the most popular party in France, although it is not (yet) in government. My argument is that the far right is likely to come to power in France in one way or another in the years ahead, with consequences as profound for France and the European Union as Donald Trump's rise has been for the US and the world, and as important politically and economically as the Brexit vote to leave the EU has been for the UK.

Far-Right France, however, is not a polemic. I am a journalist rather than a historian or a political scientist, but I rejected the advice of friends and colleagues who thought I should use this

PREFACE

book to campaign against extremism, fascism and racism. Many such books already exist. Instead, I wanted to understand and explain why the Le Pens and their successors are so popular, why their voters are so angry and why French society is so divided between working-class and middle-class citizens in the provinces on one side and the intellectual and political elite in Paris on the other.

Liberals might interpret this book as a timely warning. Right-wingers might see it as an affirmation of their views. But my aim is simply to tell a story that I believe is not well enough understood either in France or abroad: there are obvious parallels between the unrest in France and the economic, social and political upheavals in the US and the UK that have already brought Trump, Brexit and the right-wing British populist Nigel Farage into the spotlight. We in the "mainstream" media, we in the metropolises of Washington and London, notoriously failed—for the most part—to comprehend what voters were thinking in 2016 in Oklahoma or Great Yarmouth, and so we failed—for the most part—to see what was coming in the form of Trump's first presidency and the vote in favour of the UK leaving the European Union. I did not want to make the same mistake in France: Paris and its suburbs are home to the country's powerful elected president, the parliament and most big businesses, and the capital has an exceptionally strong grip on the nation's cultural, economic and political life, but the views of the Parisian elite rarely reflect those of the country as a whole. I have therefore tried to get out of Paris as often as possible to report the news from provincial France and urged my colleagues to do the same. This book is the result.

PREFACE

Who's an extremist? A note on political labels

Politicians and voters on the far right hate being called "far right" or "extreme", and often they do not even accept the "right-wing" label either. "Extreme" in English is indeed seen as pejorative: my newspaper's style guide for writers and editors says the word should be applied to "parties or politicians that have anti-democratic views and promote or use violence to accomplish goals", and the RN today does not fit that definition. This creates a dilemma in French because there is no obvious French translation for "far" in this context, other than *extrême*, unless one opts for *radical*. Jean-Marie Le Pen, Marine Le Pen and Jordan Bardella each denied in their autobiographies that they were of the *extrême droite*. Jean-Marie Le Pen, the most eloquent of the three, explained it best:

> The epithet "extreme-right" was very useful in France after the second world war: fascist, colonialist, imperialist, racist, fundamentalist or reactionary, "extreme-right" always designated the bad guy in political life, the one you could not associate with, the one who should not gain power. The adjective "extreme" is negative, it suggests an excess, and all excess is a failing in relation to the ideal of balance. By convention, it targets the right more than the left: one says "leftist" but "right-wing extremist", not "rightist".[1]

In this book, I call the RN party and its leaders "far right" because they are objectively on the far right of the political spectrum, in the same way that Jean-Luc Mélenchon and La France Insoumise (LFI, France Unbowed) are on the far left. This is illustrated in the seating arrangements in the *hémicycle* of the National Assembly, where centrist parties such as Emmanuel Macron's are in the middle with the Socialists and the centre-right Republicans, while the more radical parties are on the periphery.[2] The RN's policies, furthermore, include the far-right traits of vigorous nationalism, fierce opposition to immigration and resentment of "woke" attitudes. The French philosopher Pierre-Henri Tavoillot has argued that the RN is "a party of the radical, populist and illiberal right" but not *d'extrême droite* because it is neither anti-parliamentary nor fanatical, while Marine Le Pen abandoned the provocative antisemitism of her father and prefers to keep religion out of politics rather than pander to Catholic traditionalists.[3]

As to the matter of whether the RN is the "right" at all, Marine Le Pen has asserted that the political battle is no longer between left and right but between nationalists and globalists. From her father's time onwards, the movement's leaders have always insisted they are "neither right nor left", but then other politicians have said much the same, all the way back to the current Republic's founder, the imperious post-war president Charles de Gaulle. "There is almost no populist party in Europe that hasn't at one point adopted the slogan 'neither right nor left—for the people'," says the political scientist Catherine Fieschi.[4]

That brings us to other labels. Apart from being far right, the RN is also radical (sometimes), hard right (usually), populist (frequently) and nationalist (always), although its own leaders sometimes prefer the words sovereigntist (an awkward way of saying you want to "take back control"), or patriotic, which does not so much describe a policy as try to define the user as being on the side of the angels, rather like the word progressive when used by the left. Labels are useful as long as one recognises that they are shorthand pointers rather than comprehensive descriptions, and I have used them in what I hope are the appropriate contexts. So if Le Pen is championing France against the so-called Eurocrats in Brussels, I might call her a nationalist, and if Bardella is rousing a crowd to anger against the abuse of welfare by illegal immigrants, I might label him a populist, bearing in mind Fieschi's definition of populism as "a politics of the gut"

PREFACE

with the aim of pursuing "a sense of community through outrage".[5] I have also tried to be consistent when applying the same labels in countries other than France, though it can be difficult given how reluctant many people are in the UK or the US to accept that Brexit was a populist, nationalist project or that Trump and Elon Musk act and speak like far-right extremists.

There remains the question of how to translate the name of the main political party of the far right. Jean-Marie Le Pen's original FN was the exact linguistic equivalent of the neo-fascist National Front in the UK, although the French party quickly evolved into a more successful and less extreme movement than its fringe British counterpart. Since Marine Le Pen "detoxified" the party and renamed it the RN in 2018, it has often been translated into English as the National Rally. I have opted to use the French name of the RN throughout because "rally" has distracting and irrelevant connotations in English, while Rassemblement successfully evokes the intended meaning of a reunion or gathering of the forces of the right. I have used the French names for the other parties as well.

INTRODUCTION

AFTER EMMANUEL MACRON

"Unbelievable!" exclaimed Marine Le Pen and walked out of the courtroom. She had just learned that she was banned from competing for elected office for five years. She would almost certainly be unable to compete in the 2027 presidential election and would therefore never fulfil her ambition to become France's first woman president. Not for the first time, her political career seemed to be over. Not for the first time, she vowed to fight on.

Until that ruling on 31 March 2025, Marine Le Pen and the far-right RN party were on course to win the next round of French presidential elections, installing her in the eighteenth-century Élysée palace in Paris, giving her members of parliament control of the National Assembly and turning France over to the rule of the far right for the first time since the Nazi occupation and the Vichy regime. Nothing is certain in politics, especially in today's febrile geopolitical climate, but in the first half of 2025, Le Pen was leading in the opinion polls for the next presidential race and would almost certainly have qualified for the second-round runoff (effectively a final between the two leading candidates), as she did in the previous two such elections in 2017 and 2022. In both those elections, she was beaten by Macron, but after two terms Macron cannot stand again, and Le Pen's popularity had been on the rise.

FAR-RIGHT FRANCE

The combination of a far-right president in the Élysée and a far-right prime minister in the Hôtel de Matignon on the other side of the Seine would revolutionise France and its relations with its neighbours. Le Pen or her appointees would drastically reduce immigration, discriminate against foreigners with a policy of "national priority", challenge the EU's powers over its twenty-seven member states in every area from agriculture to defence, reverse renewable energy projects and environmental policies designed to tackle climate change and adopt a hands-off approach to the Russia–Ukraine conflict that would appal most other west European members of Nato. "I don't think the British will ever recover from Brexit, and the election of Trump has polarised Americans like never before," confided one of Macron's cabinet ministers after the first Trump administration and before the second. "I don't want the same thing to happen in France: if France switches [to the far right] it's the whole European continent that switches."[1]

Like the British populist-nationalists who promoted Brexit, the leaders of the French far right are nostalgic about their imperial and colonial past and have an exaggerated view of France's global importance in the twenty-first century, but in Europe at least France does remain a significant power. With a population of 68 million, France is the second most populous EU nation after Germany; and the two countries were founders of the EU and its forerunners and remain the bedrock of what is now the world's largest trading bloc. Like the UK, France is a permanent member of the UN Security Council, which gives it the right of veto over binding resolutions, and the two neighbours across the Channel have the most effective armed forces in western Europe. France also has its own, small, nuclear deterrence forces, which unlike the UK's are entirely independent of US supply and technical support.

On that fateful Monday in March 2025, however, all this sovereign power suddenly seemed out of reach for the French far

INTRODUCTION

right when Bénédicte de Perthuis, one of the three judges handling the case, read out the ruling on how the late Jean-Marie Le Pen, his daughter Marine and their colleagues misappropriated government money in the tawdry way that has become typical of French politicians. The Paris criminal court convicted Marine Le Pen and twenty-three others for embezzlement, or concealment or complicity in the crime, over a long-running scheme in which millions of euros to pay for assistants in the European Parliament (she was an MEP, a member of the parliament, at the time) were systematically diverted to finance work for the RN's domestic political operations. She was sentenced to four years in jail (two suspended, two commuted to surveillance at home with an electronic ankle bracelet), fined and—more importantly for her political future—disqualified from standing in an election for five years, a disqualification that was applied, unlike the jail term and the fine, even during her appeal against the conviction. Marine Le Pen, the favourite at the time, could not stand in 2027 or in an earlier contest if Macron decided to resign before the end of his second term.

Le Pen and the French far right can nevertheless recover from this judicial disaster, and they probably will. Aged fifty-six at the time of the judgment, she is one of France's wiliest, most determined and most experienced politicians and was able to continue leading the party in the National Assembly despite her conviction and until the next parliamentary election. Even if constitutional appeals fail and she is conclusively eliminated from electoral politics for the next few years, she has nurtured a charismatic young successor—Jordan Bardella—who is adept on social media and as popular as she is across the country. The RN has become not only a respectable and electable party but is the most deep-rooted and popular political movement in France today. At the time of writing, it had more seats than any other in the National Assembly. (In the first round of the 2024 French general election, the RN got almost exactly the same share of the vote—over 33 per cent—as Keir Starmer's Labour Party did in its landslide victory in the UK election the same year, but the French system allowed the other parties of left and right to gang up on Le Pen in the second round and keep the RN out of government and prevent Bardella from becoming prime minister.)

Today's combination of a struggling French economy and a sour mood among voters about their centrist government is highly favourable to the country's far-right opposition, and Le Pen is further encouraged by similar anti-establishment anger around the world all the way from Javier Milei's Argentina to Germany and eastern Europe.

At home, President Macron has been the quintessential liberal internationalist—the ideal establishment figurehead to be hated by the ordinary working people who increasingly look to the RN to protect them from the baneful effects of globalisation and mass immigration. No matter that Macron, a self-styled revolutionary and economic reformer, has been proved right on many important issues since he stunned France in 2017 by beating the traditional politicians of left and right to become the youngest president in the country's history at the age of thirty-nine.

Shortly after taking office, three years before the Covid-19 pandemic and five years before Putin launched his full-scale invasion of Ukraine, Macron declared in a prescient speech at the Sorbonne University that Europe would have to develop joint budgeting to protect itself from economic shocks and collaborate more closely on military matters. His freelance approach to policymaking infuriated Angela Merkel, the German chancellor at the time, but the pandemic and the Ukraine war ensured that both these ideas were indeed put into practice by the EU. He quickly became the West's most prominent champion of democracy, multilateralism and the "rules-based international order" even as Trump was trying to wreck all three and the UK was obsessed by Brexit.

INTRODUCTION

One thing Macron is definitely not, however, is a man of the people. On the left and on the populist far right, he is mocked as a "president of the rich", a former Rothschild banker who abolished the country's wealth tax. Even among the centre-right voters who initially supported him, he is criticised for failing to curb immigration, tackle crime or bring growing public debt and budget deficits under control. And there is one Macronian fault on which almost everyone seems to agree: arrogance and *mépris*, or contempt for ordinary people. As one French banker put it: "Macron does have a tendency to lecture. You can admire him without loving him."[2] Le Pen, by contrast, is the grand-daughter of a Breton fisherman who engages easily with working-class voters, while her protégé Bardella likes to talk about his early life in one of the tougher neighbourhoods of the northern Paris suburbs. People call them "Marine" and "Jordan", but when they shout at the president, they call him "Macron!"; one unfortunate teenager who greeted him with "Ça va, Manu?" (the nickname for Emmanuel) was told firmly "You call me Mr President, or Sir."[3]

In the autumn of 2018, a year and a half into his first term, Macron was confronted with one of those popular uprisings that periodically shake France: this time, it was the *gilets jaunes* protests, which are covered in the chapter that follows. The protests began with motorists in their yellow safety vests—hence the moniker *gilets jaunes*—demonstrating at suburban roundabouts and soon swelled into a series of increasingly violent marches through city streets across the nation. The confrontations were a very French illustration of a phenomenon affecting liberal democracies around the world: ordinary people rooted in their communities outside the big cities—the British writer David Goodhart called them the "Somewheres"—were fed up with being told what to do by the privileged, metropolitan, globalised elite (the "Anywheres", or, in former British prime minister Theresa May's words, the citizens of "nowhere").

This is why the motivations of the French *gilets jaunes* marchers were at first quite unlike those in Communist-led trade union demonstrations of old even if the banners and the anti-government chants were similar. It is also why France's traditional centre-left and centre-right parties have done so badly in recent elections (in 2022, the Socialist candidate got less than 2 per cent of the vote in the first round of the presidential election, and the candidate for Les Républicains less than 5 per cent), leaving the RN stronger than ever. Like Trump and Farage, the leaders of the French far right have understood that politics in the twenty-first century is more about nationalists versus globalists, the people against the elite or us against them, than it is about left versus right.

Macron understands this—like Le Pen, he says he is "neither right nor left" and won his first election in 2017 on that slogan—but he is inescapably a member of the economic, social and intellectual elite. When I first interviewed him at the Élysée along with *Financial Times* editor Roula Khalaf, the books piled haphazardly—or perhaps artfully—behind his desk included works by the late Socialist president François Mitterrand and Pope Francis, the letters exchanged by Flaubert and Turgenev, and a few copies of his autobiography, *Révolution: C'est notre combat pour la France* (Revolution: This is our fight for France).[4] He has been much mocked for talking of the need for a "Jupiterian" presidency, and he characteristically likened the *gilets jaunes* protests to the peasant *jacqueries* of the Middle Ages, an uprising so named because peasants were known to their masters as Jacques or Jacques Bonhomme, rather like an ordinary person is sometimes referred to in English as Jack or Joe.

During the worst of Covid, Macron also recognised that the globalisation he championed was gravely threatened not just by the pandemic but also by de-industrialisation and rising inequality in western societies. "I think it's a profound anthropological shock," he said of Covid-19 and the lockdowns:

INTRODUCTION

> We have stopped half the planet to save lives, there are no precedents for that in our history. But it will change the nature of globalisation, with which we have lived for the past 40 years ... We had the impression there were no more borders. It was all about faster and faster circulation and accumulation ... There were real successes. It got rid of totalitarians, there was the fall of the Berlin Wall 30 years ago and with ups and downs it brought hundreds of millions of people out of poverty. But particularly in recent years it increased inequalities in developed countries. And it was clear that this kind of globalisation was reaching the end of its cycle, it was undermining democracy.[5]

Yet Macron continued to insist that globalism was the only way to solve global problems such as pandemics and the existential threat of climate change. With Covid-19 still raging less than a year later, he laid out a characteristically ambitious international agenda to improve supplies of western vaccines to Africa, revive the UN and the World Trade Organization by re-engaging with China and Russia, combat climate change and control "the globalisation of hate" through social media. It was also essential, he said, to engage the US to achieve global carbon neutrality by 2050. In an interview with me and my colleagues in 2021, Macron also said he was struck in his conversations with then US president Joe Biden and his vice-president Kamala Harris by how they spent a third of their time discussing threats to democracy, whether from rival autocratic systems or domestically. He presciently called for transatlantic cooperation on regulating the big technology companies in order to protect democracy:

> These big networks, I'm convinced, have clearly allowed an acceleration of innovation and an acceleration of transparency, which are good. It is a formidable innovation, but at the same time it is a globalisation of emotions. It is a globalisation of hate. It is also a globalisation of the worst [of everything].

With the expansion of vast technology platforms, "we have for the first time created a public space, an agora where there are no rules". Online anonymity coupled with the "virality of emotions" was changing the way people behaved, Macron said, describing it as a form of "anthropological metabolisation".[6]

Macron lost full control of parliament after the legislative elections in 2022 and made a politically disastrous decision two years later to call a snap election that lost his centrist alliance eighty-six seats, leaving him powerless in the National Assembly. By September 2025, two of his prime ministers had been toppled in no-confidence votes, and he was on to his third in nine months. In France and abroad, he was losing the argument. Neither Le Pen nor Trump use phrases like "anthropological metabolisation". Nor do they want to curb the social media platforms that transmit their messages so effectively or plead for urgent international action on climate change. Instead, Le Pen and Bardella promise to remove wind turbines and have joined the centre-right in voting to abolish low-emission zones, which are designed to curb pollution but inconvenience the owners of diesel- and petrol-driven cars, while Trump mocks climate scientists and urges Americans to "drill, baby, drill!" for oil and gas.

Trump's return to the White House in 2025 will have a profound if as yet incalculable impact on France and Europe, as discussed in Chapter 2. Some of it will be good for the far right, and some of it will be bad. His unpopularity in Canada and Australia has already won elections for liberal and left-leaning parties in those two countries, although the Trump effect on European politics is harder to judge and depends on the mood in each country: the vocal support for neo-Nazis, extremists and nationalists from Trump, his vice-president J.D. Vance and his tech-bro hatchet man Elon Musk did no harm to the far-right Alternative for Germany (Alternative für Deutschland, AfD) in the Bundestag elections in early 2025, nor to the Romanian far right in the presidential election in May 2025, even though the pro-EU candidate eventually won. But Trump and his return to

INTRODUCTION

power are not the original cause of the populist far right's recent extraordinary surge in the liberal democracies of the UK and continental Europe: Trump's triumph is simply one more example of a global twenty-first-century phenomenon, even if the fact that he runs the world's pre-eminent superpower gives him greater influence than his peers over what happens in the rest of the world. Nor has Trump been the first populist-nationalist rabble-rouser since the second world war to make his mark on a western liberal democracy. He was preceded, among others, by the late Jean-Marie Le Pen, who shared Trump's gifts for provocation, antagonising the left and inviting criminal prosecutions.

When I first conceived this book a few years ago, Marine Le Pen and the RN party seemed to be unusual among far-right movements in western Europe in the way they were gathering influence and threatening the established political parties to the extent that power finally seemed to be within their grasp, although the nationalist, populist right was already on the rise in Italy and Giorgia Meloni of the Brothers of Italy party had become prime minister in 2022. In eastern and central Europe, Hungary's increasingly authoritarian Viktor Orbán had begun his second stint as prime minister back in 2010, and Poland's Law and Justice (PiS) party lost its parliamentary majority only in 2023. In the first half of the 2020s, the mood of electorates across Europe changed dramatically in favour of the far right, particularly in Germany, Austria and the Netherlands but also to an extent in Spain and Portugal, two countries supposedly inoculated against right-wing extremism by the post-war fascist dictatorships of Francisco Franco and António Salazar that ended only in the mid-1970s.

Many of the world's beleaguered liberals would be delighted if Trump messes up so much this time that he discredits right-wing populism and nationalism for a generation. His second term would then be remembered as a time of "peak populism" and would usher in a return to normality and sensible government by wise internationalists and prudent economists. Ben Ansell, the Oxford University political scientist, recently suggested that Trump's unusual combination of authoritarianism and chaos in government, and his friendliness towards the West's declared enemy Vladimir Putin, might have brought us to this peak already. To be sure, the peak was pretty high, Ansell argued,

> [b]ut I think something is shifting now. The mainstream is getting another chance, just as it did after World War Two. And like then, it is the common enemy that unites and inspires ... That enemy is most clearly Vladimir Putin. But we have had Putin for almost [a] quarter-century. So it's not him alone. No, it is the Trump–Putin quasi-alliance that has done the trick. It is the fateful decision of chaotic, populist authoritarianism to sidle up to stable, deep, old-school authoritarianism.[7]

Liberals, however, should beware of wishful thinking. This is not the first time we thought we had seen peak populism. Think of Biden's defeat of Trump in 2020: Trump returned four years later, re-energised and more disruptive and vengeful than ever. Or consider Starmer's Labour Party election landslide in 2024, which has been followed by a surge in support for Farage's populist-nationalist Reform UK and local election victories for the party in 2025. Or the successful combined efforts of the French political establishment, including the far left, also in 2024, to stop the French far right winning control of the National Assembly and the government that its electoral success had earned it: the year of chaos and dysfunction that followed only appeared to increase the popularity of Bardella and Le Pen.[8]

France today—with its hung parliament, its lame-duck president and a succession of prime ministers appointed by him who are vulnerable to no-confidence votes—has been particularly unstable since the National Assembly elections of mid-2024, a situation that has parallels with the political instability of the

INTRODUCTION

1930s before the war and the late 1940s and 1950s that heralded the ends of both the Third and the Fourth Republics. Before the outbreak of war and Hitler's occupation of France, the left-wing Front Populaire with the Socialist Léon Blum as prime minister was in power from 1936 until 1938, but it was divided over economic policy and how to handle the Great Depression and confronted by violent fascist opponents.[9] Post-war governments also grappled with shortages, inflation and strikes. "In one form or another the economic problem destroyed most governments in the first seven years of the Fourth Republic," wrote the historian Philip Williams;[10] in the twelve years of that republic, France was run by twenty-five governments. With the far right again on the rise around the world, France could be the next domino to fall.

* * *

Jean-Marie Le Pen (Chapter 3), his daughter Marine Le Pen (Chapters 4 and 5) and Jordan Bardella (Chapter 6) have for years understood and exploited popular grievances that are in many cases identical to those that have generated votes for other populists and far-right parties across the West. Speak to a French white man or woman, young or old, in any town or village outside Paris, and they are likely to tell you they are struggling to make ends meet by the end of the month, worried about mass immigration of Muslims, bitter about what they say are declining public services and resentful of Macron and the Paris elite. Many of these citizens are quoted in this book. They will often see themselves as victims of an uncaring establishment. They will be nostalgic about the past (if they are older) and pessimistic about the future (if they are younger). They will complain, with some justification, about French bureaucracy, and if they are farmers or fishermen, they may tell you how much they hate EU regulations such as those restricting the use of pesticides. A common complaint in the countryside—and one that triggered the *gilets jaunes* protests—is about the burden of the environmental rules and taxes necessary for the "ecological transition" to a zero-carbon economy.

In the land of Voltaire, Jean-Jacques Rousseau, Louis Pasteur and Marie Curie, a surprising number of people have also begun to doubt the findings of science, question whether "experts" should be trusted and subscribe to conspiracy theories about vaccines or the supposedly harmful effects of smart electricity meters. As in other countries, the influence of traditional newspapers and television stations (and their websites and apps) is in decline, and the French are increasingly getting their news and views from unregulated or barely regulated social media platforms.[11] It would be wrong to oversimplify or deny the wide range of individual views that fall between the two extremes, but France is a divided country, split broadly between liberal internationalists, represented in politics by the parties of left, right and centre, and the anti-establishment nationalists represented almost exclusively in politics by the RN. Asked a few months before her embezzlement conviction how she saw her relationship with the French people, Le Pen said she considered herself to be among them. "I am them," she said. "I often think I am feeling the same as the French are feeling. I react like the average French person. I share their outrage when they are outraged ... I have the same bursts of enthusiasm, the same worries. And above all the same hopes."[12]

Many French writers of the past fifty years have analysed or fictionalised the crumbling of the institutions of the Roman Catholic Church, the Communist Party and the trade unions that once framed the lives of the French and have described the resulting deep divisions in society that have energised the far right. Perhaps none has done this better than the novelist Michel Houellebecq and his depressed, misanthropic and cynical protagonists. In non-fiction, the best-known example is the political scientist Jérôme Fourquet's self-explanatory title *L'Archipel fran-*

INTRODUCTION

çais: Naissance d'une nation multiple et divisée* (The French archipelago: Birth of a multifaceted and divided nation).[13] The geographer Christophe Guilluy coined the phrase "La France périphérique" in a book that was subtitled *Comment on a sacrifié les classes populaires* (How the working class was sacrificed).[14] The Belgian philosopher Michel Feher has artfully applied "producerist" theory to French politics, arguing that the RN represents the hard-working "middle" of French society that is victimised by parasites both from above (the privileged elite) and below (immigrant labour); the RN therefore succeed in winning a mass of votes from the middle because they can kick up at the elites and down at the immigrants simultaneously, whereas the left gets its support from below and cannot afford to kick down, and the traditional right does not want to attack its wealthy supporters above.[15]

Journalists have criss-crossed the country in search of the human stories behind these theoretical constructs and have found, as I did, that there is a smouldering resentment of the Paris establishment and a widespread conviction that things are getting worse even at those times when the economic statistics say they are getting better. The photojournalist Vincent Jarousseau met far-right voters during his research across France in the decade to 2025 and concluded that economic concerns were paramount. "In fifty years, we have seen enormous economic upheavals: there are sections of the population that have never been included in the process of globalisation, who for years have felt left out of this new world, and who in any case don't necessarily want to be a part of it."[16] In recent years, we have also witnessed the political consequences of such feelings: a surge of support for Le Pen, Bardella and the RN. As Fourquet said after the presidential election in 2022, Le Pen won as many votes in numerous *départements* in western France—previously a political desert for the far right—as she or her father used to win in their strongholds in the south, which meant the party's earlier vote ceiling was now the floor. That meant an RN victory in 2027 could not simply be brushed aside, he said.[17]

One striking change is that supporters of the far right have come out of the shadows: except perhaps in Parisian *bobo* society (a *bobo* is a bourgeois-bohemian and the equivalent of a Champagne socialist), RN voters are rarely embarrassed to express their support in public for the party or its leaders, as they would have been thirty or twenty or even ten years ago. Nor are they as likely to fear the taunts of left-wingers abusing them as *fachos* (fascists). The boot these days is on the other foot. It is the far left, not the far right, that frequently finds itself outnumbered on the streets, as I found in the far right's fiefdoms in both the north and the south of France in the 2020s (Chapter 7). And it is Jean-Luc Mélenchon, veteran leader of the far-left LFI party, who is accused these days of antisemitism, not the RN's leaders, who have renounced the antisemitism of the late Jean-Marie Le Pen, expressed whole-hearted support for Israel and successfully courted French Jewish voters. Even Serge Klarsfeld, the Holocaust survivor and Nazi hunter, said he would vote for the RN if it was a choice between them and the left.[18] The charge of generalised racism against the RN and its supporters does not stick as well as it used to either. It is true that few black faces or people of Arab origin are visible at RN rallies, but then Le Pen won more than 60 per cent of the votes in the predominantly black French Caribbean islands of Guadeloupe and Martinique in the second round of the last presidential election in 2022, albeit in votes marked by low turnouts; she would have replaced Macron as French president had that score been replicated nationwide.[19]

Business organisations and entrepreneurs who might previously have shunned a meeting with Jean-Marie or Marine Le Pen on the grounds that they were too toxic—shareholders would have been nervous, unionised employees horrified and the left-wing media outraged—have now cautiously opened up to

RN officials, MPs and MEPs, particularly the young party president Jordan Bardella. The reasons for this have little to do with any newfound admiration for the policies of the far right: corporate bosses simply realise that the RN now has power within its reach, and they want to persuade the party to make its policies more business- and investor-friendly. After Patrick Martin, the head of the employers' federation Medef, said the RN's policies were "dangerous for the economy", Bardella tried to reassure a Medef panel that his party's aim was "a responsible break with the past" that would respect employers and employees and foster "the stability of institutions".[20]

A previously secretive far-right thinktank called Les Horaces has also stepped into the limelight as a result of the RN's increasing prominence in French life.[21] Les Horaces—the classical allusion is not to the poet but to a family of ancient Roman heroes—was established in 2014 to provide the economically inexperienced Marine Le Pen with discreet policy advice from top civil servants, industrialists, academics, military officers and others; defence advice is still provided by an anonymous General X, according to the group's website.[22] Its meetings and members were not publicised in the days when the far right had to hide its face, according to RN MP Guillaume Bigot, because lots of people said "[w]e agree with you, but there's always the problem that we don't want to come out of the shadows because we don't want to be stigmatised".[23] A crucial goal of Les Horaces was to give some economic credibility to a presidential candidate and a political party that were and still are badly in need of it, and the organisation gives itself credit for persuading Le Pen to jettison her unpopular plan to abandon the euro currency and return to the French franc.[24] In an interview for the launch of Les Horaces's public website, Le Pen talked about public debt, high energy prices and EU bureaucracy, as well as immigration and foreign policy.[25] RN policies on migration, the economy, climate change and the environment, as well as culture wars and so-called *wokisme*, are examined in Chapters 9, 10 and 11.

None of Le Pen's increasingly strong performances in French presidential races over the years nor the RN's successes in elections to the National Assembly and the European Parliament would have been possible without the party activists on the ground in French cities, towns and villages. Le Pen and Bardella now have a formidable party machine at their disposal, just as the traditional parties—Socialists, Communists and centre-right Les Républicains—seem to have lost their way, a failure reflected in their declining vote shares in recent elections. The French Greens remain a minority party. Macron's centrist Renaissance party—previously En marche! (On the move!) and then La République en marche—was a vehicle for himself, founded the year before his first election victory in 2017 and probably destined to wither away once he leaves the Élysée at the end of his second term. In 2024, the main political party that mounted a serious challenge to the rising RN was Mélenchon's far-left LFI, and by 2025 even the LFI was weakened by internal divisions and disagreements with the other leftist parties in the Nouveau Front Populaire that had blocked the RN from taking control of the National Assembly.

Even when there is no election looming, the RN's hundreds of municipal councillors and MPs and its few town mayors attend local wine fairs, sports competitions and saints' day celebrations to show their faces and shake hands. They diligently scan the provincial press—still strong across France—for news of shop openings, football club victories, factory disputes or deaths and then send emails to offer congratulations, assistance or condolences to those concerned. Edwige Diaz, an MP in the Gironde in the south-west who is in her thirties and among the RN's rising stars, recalls the delighted reaction from the owners of a country restaurant with whom she had commiserated over flood damage.

INTRODUCTION

"They said 'we didn't think the RN had people like you'," said Diaz, adding that the couple felt ignored by other politicians.[26]

Far-right activists, for so long excluded from power, feel the winds of change blowing in their favour, and they are preparing for what they say will be the first significant change of political regime in France since the Socialist François Mitterrand deposed the republican right in 1981. Their methods are the tried and tested tools of local democratic politics anywhere in the world, and much the same as those of the old French left. "They have a real talent for understanding local pride, traditional festivals and anything that illustrates how they are grounded in a community," according to Thierry Pech, an expert on the RN who heads the political thinktank Terra Nova.[27]

Can an RN candidate finally win the presidency? Can the far right really end up in control of France? For years, the left has comforted itself that it can lure back discontented FN/RN voters on the assumption that they are, in Mélenchon's words, "fâchés pas fachos"—that is, angry rather than fascist—but the reality is that the RN and its leaders have enduring support. It is not a mere protest movement. More than 13 million votes were cast for Le Pen in the second round of the presidential election in 2022, and French commentators have started to point out that it is awkward to label politicians or their supporters "extremists" when they represent between a third and a half of the country's voters. "She's the new mainstream," one senior government MP admitted to me ruefully. "She's the favourite. She's the only one who's got a party that actually looks like one. She's got the biggest presence in parliament ... The question is, who can be anti-mainstream?" It will not be easy for the RN to increase the second-round vote share of 41.5 per cent that Le Pen achieved in 2022 to the more than 50 per cent needed to win, according to Jean-Yves Camus, an expert on the far right, but it is no longer unthinkable. "In 2002, it was very clear, except to the left-wing anti-fascists, that Le Pen senior had no chance of winning," he said. "And ten years ago, no colleague of mine or myself would have said she [Le Pen] will win. It was an impossibility. There were still more than 50 per cent of the French who said the party and Marine Le Pen herself were a threat to democracy." Today, according to Camus, it is Mélenchon and the far left who are seen as the greater threat.[28]

The nationalist ideas of the RN are now widely accepted in French society, increasingly represented in traditional media and supercharged by the explosion of digital social media. (These media phenomena are the subject of Chapter 11.) French institutions and the media have until recently leaned largely to the left, but sympathetic French tycoons have taken control of key newspapers and TV channels, just as Rupert Murdoch did long ago in the US, the UK and Australia, giving valuable airtime and column inches to Le Pen and Bardella in the same way that Murdoch's outlets did for Trump and the promoters of Brexit. Some French commentators had so much distaste for the far right and were so detached from the concerns of *la France profonde*, the country beyond Paris, that they criticised and mocked Marine Le Pen and the RN without understanding the extent of their growing popularity and influence. Just as liberal Britons or Americans were appalled by Brexiters and Trump before 2016 but failed to realise they could actually win, so French intellectuals have been slow to grasp the real possibility of a Le Pen presidency and a far-right government.

That began to change in France as Macron's popularity collapsed in the middle of his first term. The liberal news magazine *L'Express* put Marine Le Pen on its front cover in January 2020 standing at her future desk in the Élysée surrounded by shards of shattered glass, over the headline "The end of the glass ceiling". In the same issue, the sociologist Jean-Pierre Le Goff was asked whether France would ever accept being ruled by a Le Pen

INTRODUCTION

given that voters would always behave sensibly. "I'm wondering to what extent this isn't just a way for some of the elites to give themselves some easy reassurance," he replied:

> Remember what intellectuals and journalists used to say before Trump's victory—"The country will never elect an idiot like him." We have to pay attention to the illusions of the inward-looking world of media and politics. This world has been so discredited that I think a part of the population has switched into a chaotic rejection of everything, a meltdown that no one can control. I believe lots of people can no longer tolerate politicians, especially when they are lecturing from on high, because they don't trust them and are so utterly fed up.[29]

Even so, the road to power for the French far right is not without obstacles. Marine Le Pen's earlier financial dependence on Russia and its allies and her support for Putin before his full-scale invasion of Ukraine in 2022 (the subject of Chapter 12) means that her political fate may depend partly on the progress of the war and the level of threat posed by Putin to west European democracies, given that the French have generally supported Ukraine and Volodymyr Zelenskyy. Another problem for Le Pen and Bardella, neither of whom has held high office or has a deep understanding of foreign affairs, is that French voters tend to turn to the experienced policymakers they trust when confronted with this kind of grave international crisis: they may not like how Macron handles the French economy, but they appreciate his sure-handed leadership as an international statesman, and his approval ratings tend to rise during global crises. Another obstacle is Le Pen's continuing battle in the courts over her embezzlement conviction and five-year disqualification from standing for election, the details of which are dealt with in Chapter 13. While the judges' sentence applies only to her and some other RN MPs, MEPs and employees, the case indirectly affects the whole far-right movement because she is the candidate from that camp who would have the best chance of winning the presidency if she were allowed to stand. Even a Bardella presidential campaign as a Le Pen substitute could be called into question if another investigation into the party's finances—highlighted by a raid on the RN's Paris headquarters in July 2025—were to lead to further action from the French authorities.

Le Pen, however, is a thick-skinned politician who has recovered from setbacks before to pursue her lifelong ambition of seizing the levers of French power for the far right. In one way or another, the far right has a good chance of winning France, either through outright election victories or by co-opting the forces of the traditional right, a process already begun in 2024 with the defection of former Les Républicains leader Éric Ciotti to the far-right camp. The question raised in my final chapter, therefore, is whether a far-right administration in France would be as bad as many liberals fear, or as successful as many nationalists hope. The answer is: probably neither, but it would nevertheless shatter long-held assumptions about western European democracies and mark the beginning of a radically different phase of French post-war history. The early signs were there in October 2018, when angry French motorists donned their fluorescent yellow safety jackets and launched the first of the protests that would soon swell into the nationwide uprising of the *gilets jaunes*.

PART I

GOODBYE TO THE OLD ORDER

1

YELLOW-VEST REBELLION

It seemed like the old days, like the Paris demonstrations of the twentieth century: people marching through the capital to vilify the president or the government or wealthy employers until the protest broke up and ended with a fight between stone-throwing youths and riot police firing tear gas and rubber bullets. But for all the similarities, these marches in 2018 and 2019 were not the same as those earlier events—at least not to begin with—and they had a very different origin.

For a start, the marchers wore the high-visibility yellow jackets that all French motorists must keep in their cars in case of accidents, a distinctive new uniform that gave the movement its name of *gilets jaunes*, the yellow vests. The demonstrators, furthermore, were in the early weeks mostly neither students nor trade unionists nor political activists nor from the big cities as in previous protests. Instead, many were conservative and came from the suburbs and from rural areas. Many were also motorists, because the first protests—at suburban roundabouts in the autumn of 2018—had been triggered by a rise in fuel prices following the imposition of a green tax by the government of President Macron. Above all, the *gilets jaunes* uprising—which became serious enough to threaten the stability of Macron's administration—never had a national figurehead or a coherent leadership.

The *gilets jaunes* movement and its successful challenge to the establishment—Macron was forced to back down on the green fuel tax and make other costly financial concessions—were a political gift to the far right, as the FN founder Jean-Marie Le Pen, who was writing his memoirs at the time, noted with satisfaction in his assessment of the 2019 European elections. "Macronism has lashed out at public enemy number one—populism and the nationalism it loathes: without the contribution of the *gilets jaunes*, the RN would have been done for."[1] (The RN emerged as the winning French party in the election, narrowly beating Macron's alliance.) The *gilets jaunes*, Jean-Marie Le Pen said, had seemed for a moment to show that "the people can still rise up", even if "the boys in blue with their truncheons" always managed to prevail in the end.[2]

The RN's leaders, however, had not launched the protests—like the French left and the trade unions, they were taken by surprise—and it took time for them to realise the significance of a movement that was not at first left-wing or right-wing but pitted ordinary working people against the establishment, against the metropolitan elite. This was exactly the way Marine Le Pen, still party president at the time, framed the RN's political struggle, and its anti-tax element even echoed the Poujadist days of her father's politics in the 1950s when shopkeepers and other small business owners rebelled against government tax inspections. The images of mayhem in Paris in the later stages of the 2018–19 protests, when they reverted to the traditional French template of street-fighting, should not obscure the fact that this began as a set of peaceful protests by motorists, by people who needed to use their cars every day to get to work. Polling showed that people who depended heavily on their cars were more than three times as likely to identify as *gilets jaunes* as those who did not.[3] Rural commuters were incensed not only by the fuel tax but also by a reduction in the rural speed limit from 90 to 80 km/h, which might not seem a lot but gave the authorities a chance to levy more speeding fines: the impression was that Macron's foppish officials flitting to and from work on their electric scooters in Paris were making life impossible for hardworking country folk or suburbanites in their cars.

But the feeling of alienation was not limited to transport or tax: it was a much broader feeling of anger at the establishment, the government, the elite—in short, "them". There was a strong popular urge to give the finger to the overbearing, interfering and bureaucratic yet simultaneously uncaring authorities and their figurehead, the president (in this case Macron). It was a French version of the populist politician Beppe Grillo's *Vaffanculo* (Go fuck yourself) heyday in Italy, and the sentiments expressed were sometimes reminiscent of those of the English voters who supported Brexit precisely because much of the British establishment and the Tory prime minister David Cameron wanted the UK to remain in the EU. People living in depopulated rural and suburban France—memorably described by Guilluy as *La France périphérique* (peripheral France)—complained of poor transport links and inadequate health and other public services. They had lost control of their lives and felt that all the wealth and power was being sucked up by the cities.

"The *gilets jaunes* movement is anti-urban, anti-elite, anti-intellectual, anti-parliamentary, anti-globalisation, anti-liberal and occasionally antisemitic (which goes with the others, but the RN was smart enough not to let that develop too far)," wrote the authors of a wry political analysis in 2025 of a dystopian future imagining what would happen if Marine Le Pen became president, recalling how the RN had benefitted from the *gilets jaunes* protests. "The fact is that the leaders of the movement who subsequently went into politics—with the notable exception of Priscillia Ludosky and one or two lesser known [far-left] Mélenchonistes—all sided with the extreme right."[4]

By the time I returned from several years working in Asia to report from France again at the start of 2019, the *gilets jaunes* protests were in full swing but still had no coherent message or recognised leadership, and so seemed more like the 1968 demonstrations that shook de Gaulle's second presidency than the traditional marches by trade unionists or students over specific complaints such as wages, pension reform or education policy. Indeed, the first demonstrator I happened to meet in January 2019 was Bernadette Noël, a seventy-three-year-old retired nurse and great-grandmother who told me this was the first time she had taken part in a protest since 1968; this time, she had come into Paris from suburban Seine-et-Marne to complain about the increase in her tax bill as a pensioner. Two months later, I came across Laurence Gonzalvo, a fifty-nine-year-old social security administrator from Pigalle in Paris, and asked her why she had "unhappy granny" written on the back of her yellow vest. She replied that she was afraid for her children's future and was demanding a greater share of the country's wealth for people like her. "Many people live worse than four or five years ago," she said.

Other marchers were environmental activists who grew their own vegetables, and some even supported the Macron carbon taxes that had triggered the demonstrations in the first place. Many wanted direct democracy, demanding that all big decisions be put to referendums rather than being taken by elected politicians. Some waved Corsican, Catalan, Breton or Algerian flags or the French *tricolore*. Some wanted Frexit, insisting that France should follow the UK and leave the EU. Some were *casseurs* (wreckers) who took advantage of the marches to loot shops, burn cars and attack the police. Hélène was a forty-five-year-old music festival organiser who said she was "against the neoliberal system" and the euro and appalled that an investment banker such as Macron had become president of France. Yves Grare, a retired sixty-one-year-old sign painter, said he had voted for an anarchist in the first round of the 2017 election and for the late comedian Coluche (a French way of spoiling your ballot) in the second round because he liked neither Macron nor Le Pen.[5] In general, the early *gilets jaunes* marchers were not only older but also more right wing than those of 1968. Often they were middle-aged white conservatives from country towns who wanted lower taxes, disliked immigrants, were suspicious of globalisation and felt they were despised by an out-of-touch metropolitan elite exemplified by the haughty Macron.[6]

The leaders of the *gilets jaunes*, whether self-appointed or chosen by others, were very diverse. They included Ghislain Coutard, a mechanic from Narbonne who was credited with suggesting the use of the yellow vest as the demonstrators' symbol; Éric Drouet, a truck driver from Seine-et-Marne who described himself as an "angry *gilet jaune*", launched a Facebook appeal with Priscillia Ludosky for a national blockade against rising fuel prices in November 2018 and was twice arrested and charged over the protests (but ultimately exonerated on appeal); Christophe Dettinger, a former French boxing champion convicted and jailed for hitting and kicking gendarmes blocking a footbridge over the Seine; Maxime Nicolle, a transport worker known on social media as Fly Rider who claimed the government initiated what was actually an Islamist terror attack on a Christmas market in Strasbourg to divert attention from the *gilets jaunes*; Ingrid Levavasseur, a health worker and single mother from Normandy; Benjamin Cauchy, a commercial manager from Toulouse and former right-wing student leader; Jacline Mouraud, a hypnotherapist and spiritualist from Brittany; and above all Priscilla

Ludosky, whose online petition for a reduction in fuel prices was seen as the start of the whole movement.

I went to interview Ludosky in the outskirts of Paris and as a carless Parisian had an immediate lesson in the importance of vehicles for the inhabitants of rural and suburban France: at the railway station, there was no chance of a taxi and no obvious way to reach the shopping centre where we had agreed to meet, so I walked through a litter-strewn wood and across a deserted industrial estate to get there. Ludosky, a black woman whose parents came to mainland France from Martinique and who used to be a back-office bank worker at BNP Paribas preparing letters of credit, was far from politically radical and had little in common with the far-right and far-left *gilets jaunes* marchers she and Drouet had inspired. "At the beginning, when people shouted 'Macron resign!' and told me, 'We don't hear you shouting with us,' I said, 'I'm not out here particularly so that Macron resigns, I'm here to condemn the problems I've been talking about, whether it's him or someone else in charge.'" Later, she decided she did want Macron to go, but only because of the way he responded to the protests and the violent methods used by the police to suppress them. While the new fuel tax was the trigger, the underlying problem, she said, was economic hardship and government neglect. When she launched her petition, she was deluged with emails and messages on Facebook complaining about the cost of living:

> People said, "We've got to the stage where even if you earn €2,000 a month you can't make ends meet because there are too many taxes, too many expenses, we're completely crushed, and when you do the shopping or go to the doctor you have to pay in instalments." Eventually, people said, "We can't take it any more."

One characteristic of the earlier protests noted by reporters and commentators, and by Ludosky, is that they brought together people—even people from different social classes—who felt isolated in their daily lives and depended heavily on social media. "I wouldn't call it a success, but it's changed quite a lot of things," Ludosky said:

> What's changed is that people have come out of solitude and isolation to share their problems. And they have helped each other, there has been a great movement of solidarity and fraternity which basically didn't exist in France because people are so tied up in their daily lives, their worries and then their work, work, work that people don't talk to each other any more.

She hoped the movement would help people to mobilise on neglected issues all over France, whether the problem was unemployment or air pollution, and she said she had been contacted by people from other countries, including Hong Kong, who were eager to learn how the whole thing started. "Things are boiling over everywhere," she said.[7]

The protests did have international repercussions. They confirmed foreign perceptions that the rebellious French were always eager to take to the streets to challenge their governments, while Russian media in French and other western European languages, such as Sputnik and RT (previously Russia Today), relentlessly amplified reports of violence and disorder and the demonstrators' defiance of Macron and the establishment. The nationalist Italian governing duo at the time, Matteo Salvini of the anti-immigrant League and Luigi Di Maio of the populist Five Star movement, relished Macron's discomfort. Salvini was already an ally of Le Pen, while Di Maio provocatively met some of the *gilets jaunes* in France and declared that "[t]he wind of change has crossed the Alps," prompting Macron to recall the French ambassador from Rome in protest.

After a year, however, the *gilets jaunes* protests faded away. One reason was that Macron helped to defuse them by launching a "great national debate" in which the public and local elected representatives discussed the issues raised by the demonstrators, and by encouraging the French to air their grievances in *cahiers de doléance*, suggestion books on paper and online modelled on the historical royal and revolutionary complaints system of the same name. (Eventually, a million and a half such contributions were made online, and more than 200,000 on paper in 19,900 *cahiers* at town halls, although not much came of them in terms of policies or projects.)[8] Macron had already backed down on the fuel tax and released billions of euros of government money to increase the income of low-paid workers. Macron's popularity recovered, and in later demonstrations the *gilets jaunes* were confronted by rival *foulards rouges*, "red scarves" who supported Macron. Another reason for the end of the movement was that it became less popular once it was hijacked by violent *casseurs* and young *black bloc* anarchists who attacked the police and the banks. One of the worst days was on Saturday, 16 March 2019, when demonstrators daubed the Arc de Triomphe with graffiti, set fire to a bank and news kiosks and ransacked more than ninety shops and restaurants, including the famous brasserie Fouquet's on the Champs-Élysées.[9]

The *gilets jaunes* left their mark on French society, and not simply because of the violence and the human toll. (Some 2,500 demonstrators and 1,800 police officers were injured, with more than forty protesters suffering serious eye injuries from police weapons, and over 3,000 people were convicted of various offences.) According to the sociologist Michel Wieviorka, the *gilets jaunes* combined the use of social media with on-the-ground action in "an exceptional, very spectacular, very media-savvy" way that bypassed the trade unions and political parties that had dominated anti-government protests since the second world war. "The *gilets jaunes* told the government not to forget the poor, the social injustices—and the government listened and understood. The government was not deaf."[10] The pollster and political analyst Jérôme Fourquet also concluded the movement was exceptional because of the way it worked outside the normal French political and social framework. Research showed that the protests were both geographically spread (there were protests in around 2,000 different places on 17 November 2018 across the whole of metropolitan France) and socially diverse (nearly a third of *gilets jaunes* were workers, a quarter were self-employed, nearly a quarter were employees, another quarter were middle-level or senior professionals and 15 per cent were retired).[11] The movement's visceral but ill-defined hostility towards the establishment is one reason why few conventional politicians or commentators saw it coming. Only the preternaturally perceptive writer and misanthrope Michel Houellebecq seems to have foreseen how such widespread resentment might play out in practice. His seventh novel *Serotonin*, published in France in January 2019, includes scenes of a rural road blockade that turns to violence, although the protagonists in the book were angry farmers rather than angry motorists.[12]

In retrospect, the *gilets jaunes* movement was a good sign for the French far right because it highlighted the strength of popular grievances and demands that the RN had been voicing for years and continued to champion in the elections that followed. However, given that Le Pen and Bardella have tried to show that they play by the rules as responsible republicans, they remain at risk of being overtaken by a hitherto unknown populist who will, like Trump, ignore all political conventions and amass public support at the expense of established political parties, including those on the extremes of left and right. In discussing the *gilets jaunes*, the political analyst Giuliano da Empoli recalls that the liberal internationalist Macron stunned France by transcending left–right politics and winning the 2017 election despite never having held elected office before, and wonders whether there might not be a mirror-image Macron waiting in the wings, "a leader who would have the ability to overcome the left–right split to unite the populist-nationalists of both sides". Macron's trajectory "proves that a figure of this type can emerge very rapidly when the circumstances are right".[13] She may have been born into politics and practised it for most of her adult life, but Le Pen would like to be that mirror-image Macron, the populist-nationalist disruptor rather than the liberal-internationalist one that he was, and would try to crush any external rival who tried to seize the presidency she thinks she deserves.

As the *gilets jaunes* demonstrations faded and the Covid-19 pandemic spread from China to the outside world in early 2020, just such a populist disruptor had narrowly failed to win a second term as US president. No one knew it then, but Trump would be back four years later with even more disturbing consequences for France and Europe.

2

THE TRUMP EFFECT

Trump's triumphant return to the White House in January 2025 reminded the world that populists and nationalists could win elections in hitherto liberal democracies—even in the most powerful democracy of them all, and even with a candidate who was a convicted criminal and had campaigned on an extremist agenda. On the face of it, this was welcome news for the French far right, and for its allies across Europe from the UK to Romania. The far right was on a roll, and, as the US historian Hal Brands wrote the day after Trump's inauguration, the world was less horrified by Trump than it was at the start of his first term because it had become more like him since 2017. "The ideas that Trump rode to power—hostility to migration and globalization, an emphasis on national identity and sovereignty—now animate political debates and political disrupters across multiple continents. Populists and strongmen are enjoying a global moment," he wrote, noting that Trump already had counterparts in India's Narendra Modi, Saudi Arabia's Mohammed bin Salman, Russia's Vladimir Putin, China's Xi Jinping, Italy's Giorgia Meloni and Hungary's Viktor Orbán. Le

Pen and Bardella, however, were cautious, formally congratulating Trump on his re-election but ordering their MPs and MEPs to avoid effusive praise for the US president.

Why were they cautious? Because Le Pen, a battle-hardened campaigner with a lifetime of election experience, and Bardella were aware of the risks for a European politician of being associated too closely with the unpredictable Trump. Of course, many of Trump's policies match those of the far right in Europe: deporting immigrants, nationalism, economic protectionism, contempt for multilateral institutions, the dismantling of environmental regulations and the war on "wokeness" in the workplace and public life. But Trump himself is not popular among Europeans, even on the right, and he presents two obvious dangers for those who emulate him. First, he could make a mess of his second term, demonstrating to the world that populists may be fun to support in opposition but can inflict severe damage on their own economies and societies once they gain power. Second, he could inflict direct pain on Europe and its inhabitants, either through his trade wars or by cosying up to an aggressive Putin in Russia, or by some other as yet undreamed-of behaviour on the world stage.

The potential for such a backlash against Trump was evident in the early months of 2025. While autocrats and right-wing leaders already established in power—including Israel's Benjamin Netanyahu, Turkey's Recep Tayyip Erdoğan and Rwanda's Paul Kagame—took immediate advantage of Trump's presence in the White House to crack down on their opponents and attack their enemies with impunity, right-wing opposition politicians seeking power in western democratic elections did not have it so easy, especially if they had echoed Trump's policies in the past. They found that Trump's actions undermined their popularity with voters and hampered their campaigns: that was particularly the case for Canadian Conservative Pierre Poilievre after Trump threatened to make Canada the fifty-first US state, and the "anti-woke" Australian right-wing opposition leader Peter Dutton, both of whom lost elections soon after Trump returned to office.

Among the global stars of the far right, Le Pen had a particularly acute Trump dilemma because she had smoothed down the FN's extremist edges since taking over from her father and renaming it the RN. Trump is by European standards on the extreme right of the political spectrum, and it is presumably only out of habit that the media do not often refer to Trump Republicans as extremists. "Trump's America is a stark outlier from western Europe and the rest of the Anglosphere. In many cases, the Maga [Make America Great Again] mindset is much closer to that of Vladimir Putin's Russia or Recep Tayyip Erdoğan's Turkey," wrote John Burn-Murdoch in an analysis of the World Values Survey. "The stark divide remains even when we compare US Republicans with their conservative counterparts elsewhere in the west. On the key policy issues defining the 2020s, Trump-era Republicans are a different breed from the British, French or German right."[1]

This marks a big change from the twentieth century, because while the US Republicans have since moved sharply to the right, the French far right has moved in the other direction, edging away from the antisemitism and provocative extremism that was prevalent under the FN's founder Jean-Marie Le Pen. From his semi-retirement outside Paris, he claimed during Trump's first term that he had been told he had fans in America who saw him as "Trump's big brother, as the father of populism." And he cited Trump's success as one reason to criticise his daughter's policy of *dédiabolisation* or detoxifying the RN in an attempt to win votes in France. Trump, he said, had succeeded by radicalising himself, "by becoming the very devil he was accused of being". Swedish nationalists, on the other hand, had been kept out of power because they had watered down their policy wine, whereas "the Chianti Classico of Salvini is working wonders for him" in Italy.[2]

FAR-RIGHT FRANCE

After Trump's re-election in November 2024, Marine Le Pen, Bardella and their party colleagues sought to portray the US vote as a vindication of their policies while distancing themselves from a personality typically described in the French media as "sulphurous", in other words one that reeked of the devil. "I have a lot of respect and admiration for the patriotism of Donald Trump, for his will to defend the interests of his country first and above all," Bardella said diplomatically at his New Year press conference in Paris at the start of 2025. He praised Trump's expulsion of migrants and said the RN was now a "privileged interlocutor" in international relations because like the US under Trump and other superpowers it favoured "economic patriotism" and "the control of frontiers". Philippe Olivier, a senior member of the RN and husband of Marine Le Pen's sister Marie-Caroline, also emphasised that RN leaders could talk to people in the Trump administration in a way that was impossible for the French left or even President Emmanuel Macron. "We don't lecture people," he said. Olivier also stressed the global significance of Trump's second term. "What is happening now and what has happened in the United States is for the West what the Iranian revolution was to Islam. It was a wake-up call."[3]

Bardella, however, took pains to say that he was not "a little brother" of Trump and that France should stand up for itself and not be in the shadow of any great power, which was why neither he nor Le Pen had attended the inauguration. (In fact, they were not invited, unlike the rival French far-right leader Éric Zemmour and his partner Sarah Knafo, though three lesser RN figures did go to Washington.)[4] A few weeks later, Bardella abruptly cancelled a speech he was due to make at the Conservative Political Action Conference (CPAC) in Washington after Trump's adviser Steve Bannon—who has actively promoted far-right causes in Europe—raised his arm there in a Nazi salute. "One of the participants made a provocative gesture linked to

Nazi ideology," Bardella said. "I therefore took the immediate decision to cancel my appearance." Bannon retorted that Bardella obviously had not listened to his speech and was not worthy to govern France. "He's a little boy, not a man," Bannon said.[5]

This exchange underlines the point that the Franco-US unease in the Trump era is mutual—that while Trump may be too extreme for the RN, the RN is not extreme enough for Trump, who might be tempted to throw his weight behind another rightist such as Knafo or Marion Maréchal, Marine Le Pen's niece and a past Bannon favourite. Another senior RN politician said the party loved Trump's anti-woke crusade and supported his attempts to make peace between Russia and Ukraine but was worried by the possible negative impact of his trade wars. His political style also did not go down well in France. The RN promoted "France first" just as Trump wanted "America first", and Trump spoke to voters in a language they could understand, this politician told me, but "the exuberant, the outrageous thing doesn't work in France".[6]

The views of Le Pen and Trump did converge briefly over her conviction by a French court for embezzlement of EU funds intended for European parliamentary assistants in March 2025. She was not only sentenced to jail but also disqualified from standing for elections for five years. She appealed, but the disqualification remained pending the outcome of the appeal, prompting her to launch an unusually bitter, almost Trumpian attack on what she claimed was the politicisation and left-wing bias of the French justice system. Trump weighed in on his Truth Social media platform, praising Le Pen, comparing her judicial fate to his and saying the "Witch Hunt against Marine Le Pen is another example of European Leftists using Lawfare to silence Free Speech, and censor their Political Opponent, this time going so far as to put that Opponent in prison ... FREE MARINE LE PEN!"[7] Aside from the fact that she was not in jail and probably never would be—like other French politicians, if her conviction is upheld she would probably be under a form of house arrest with an electronic ankle bracelet—Trump's public championing of Le Pen was more of an embarrassment than a comfort given widespread French mockery of the US president. "She does not want to be associated with a guy who is, to put it mildly, a little bit weird," I was told by Jean-Yves Camus:

> She wants to be the one who embodies common sense. Trump is the opposite of common sense. And besides, in France, we have a long tradition, including in the policies of General de Gaulle, of being very sceptical about America ... And the extreme right has always been very sceptical about the United States, which embodies, in their opinion, everything they despise. It's a country of a melting pot, it's a country of big finance, the country of Wall Street and big companies. It's a superpower; they do not respect the independence of other countries. Donald Trump himself, he wants to take over Greenland, Canada and maybe someday he will say, "I also want to grab this or that."[8]

The early months of the second Trump administration seemed to confirm the wisdom of RN leaders' caution about Trump. Although Bardella had proposed the creation of a "ministry of government efficiency" along the lines of Musk's department of government efficiency (DOGE) in the US, and although RN supporters enjoyed watching Trump deporting migrants and discomfiting liberal universities and the liberal media, the chaotic rollout of Trump's trade tariffs, the initial near-panic in financial markets, the haphazard firings of government employees and the risk that such measures would anger poorer Americans suggested the RN had little to gain from a closer association with Trump. "Donald Trump is putting populism in a negative light," Jean-Philippe Tanguy, the RN's economic and financial expert told *Le Monde*, even if he confessed his views were not shared by most of his party colleagues. "I've always thought he was toxic and that we should keep our distance, and explain how we're different."[9] Unlike Trump, who encouraged the violent assault on the US Capitol in January 2021 to try to overturn Joe Biden's election victory the previous November, Le Pen has for years insisted that she and her followers show themselves to be loyal citizens who respect the French Republic and abide by its laws—which is one reason why the court case over RN officials' embezzlement of EU funds was so embarrassing. The international context is important here: European far-right parties are campaigning and in some cases governing in a region where both domestic and international law still largely apply, whereas neither China, nor Russia nor the US under Trump show much respect for either.

* * *

Trump's return to power, along with the war waged by Russia in Ukraine and the conflicts in the Middle East, presented another political problem for French far-right leaders: international turmoil played to the strengths of their political rivals, especially President Macron, who had been a lame duck in domestic politics since the National Assembly elections in mid-2024. Le Pen had never paid much attention to foreign affairs, an attitude that did no harm when French voters were mainly worrying about reaching the end of the month with enough money to pay the bills but was less of an advantage when the world was threatened with global financial and security crises. It was scant comfort that the extreme-left party led by Mélenchon had much the same problem. Macron, who had called for Europe to take more responsibility for its defence when he first took office back in 2017, saw his popularity rise in the opinion polls, although he cannot stand again for president, and Le Pen–Bardella maintained their lead in polling predictions for 2027. French presidential hopefuls such as Dominique de Villepin—the former centre-right foreign minister and prime minister under Jacques Chirac who eloquently opposed George W. Bush's invasion of Iraq in 2003—re-emerged on to the political scene.

De Villepin, whose flamboyant foreign policy style in the run-up to the Iraq war was immortalised in the graphic novel *Quai d'Orsay* (the address of the ministry in Paris),[10] not only criticised Trump's populism and belief in "illiberal democracy" but predicted that his radical approach would prove unworkable and undermine European nationalists and populists by association. The world would soon see that "populism is completely fake," de Villepin told the Anglo-American Press Association in Paris:

> The idea [of having] a leader saying "I'm going to act, I'm going to decide without limit, without any rules"—this can only bring chaos ... [T]here are a lot of similarities between the neoconservatives and the populist attitude of the Trump administration. The consequences will be the same: chaos, disorder and violence. Everybody will see that. Does France want to have the same [thing] in France? Does Germany want to have the same in Germany? I don't believe so. So they have a problem because of the principle of reality, which is the biggest enemy of populism.

As for Le Pen, de Villepin acknowledged that she was an experienced politician who had wisely kept her distance from Trump, but he predicted that her past closeness to Putin's Russia and the similarity of her policies to those of the Trump administration—"anti-immigration, anti-globalisation, anti-multiculturalism"—would work against her:

> The populist parties in Europe are completely linked to the proposals of Donald Trump. And they have this in common: they are not practical; they cannot change anything; you can apply the full programme of any of these parties and it won't change anything. This is pure illusion, delusion, not looking at the realities, because to be effective in today's world you have to go through processes.

THE TRUMP EFFECT

De Villepin, who also criticised President Javier Milei's "chainsaw" approach to reforming Argentina, might have been underestimating Trump's ability to ignore due process and the rule of law and ride roughshod over American institutions, but he insisted that populists were deluding themselves if they thought the business of government was simple. "You need to have a knowledge of the complexity and who is going to gain and who is going to win. You need to have the leadership to explain all that." The French, like the Americans, were full of "fear and anger" about the state of the world, de Villepin argued, but eventually would have to make decisions about their future. "I don't see ... any kind of doubt about the fact that everybody will stand up and be ready to fight for our own liberty and our own values."[11]

Back in 2003, de Villepin turned out to have been right about the hard realities of the US invasion of Iraq, but two decades later the hopeful liberals who appreciated his analysis about the downside of Trumpism for European populists needed to be wary of wishful thinking—the same kind of wishful thinking that had afflicted British and American liberals in 2016. After Trump's re-election eight years later, there were two prominent aspects to this continued liberal optimism in France. First there was the idea that France and Europe were more resistant than the US to authoritarian populism because liberalism and tolerance were more entrenched in Europe. Second, there was de Villepin's prediction that the chaos and economic pain unleashed by Trump's rule would discredit Trumpism for a generation.

On the first matter of Europe's supposed exceptionalism, the historian Mark Mazower argued in late 2024 that Europe remained chastened by its experiences under fascism in the second world war and was a less polarised society than the US. "Europe inhabits a post-fascist universe," he wrote:

> This has not prevented the rise of parties that would once have been considered far-right. Several of those who are descended from out-

right neo-fascist movements in the past are now in power or close to it. But in no case have their leaders been able to act as if fascism and the war did not happen: the common historical memory is an inhibitor, if a waning one.

Even far-right parties in Europe had women as leaders, and the issue of abortion was largely settled in the EU. Nor did the capture of the US Republicans, one of the country's two main political parties, by an extremist movement have a parallel in western Europe. "The right is on the rise in Europe, but still operates within a broadly accepted institutional setting shaped by common recent experiences," Mazower wrote.[12]

Others agreed that Europe was different, seeing the continent as perhaps the last bastion for liberal democracy. "Europe," French centrist politician and Macron ally Roland Lescure told me in 2025, "is becoming the Maginot Line for global democracy", a haven for scientists and liberals and minorities. However, he added: "The main problem is that Europe is out of cash."[13] The fact that the Maginot Line of defences invoked by Lescure notoriously failed to stop Hitler's invasion of France in 1940, and Mazower's admission that the memory of fascism was a "waning" inhibitor for Europe's far right, suggested to me that even the proponents of European exceptionalism were not confident that it would be enough to prevent the further rise of extremism. Polling and reporting by YouGov and *The Economist* in the spring of 2025 showed that Trump's return had alienated voters in Canada, France and the UK from the US and made them more supportive of centrist and centre-left leaders in their own countries. But voters on the European hard right, in parties such as the RN in France, the AfD in Germany and Giorgia Meloni's Brothers of Italy, had become more favourably disposed towards America since Trump's victory.[14]

The second reason for liberal optimism—the notion that Trump would be mugged by reality and that his mistakes would

THE TRUMP EFFECT

discredit the far right globally—was still being tested in the early months of his second administration, but some European nationalists were much less shy than the RN about welcoming the Trump revolution. Hungarian prime minister Viktor Orbán, the doyen of governing far-right nationalists in the EU, had promised to open several bottles of Champagne if Trump returned to office but ended up drinking vodka to "share our joy at this fantastic result" because he was on a visit to Kyrgyzstan. "History has accelerated," he said. "The world is going to change." Geert Wilders in the Netherlands and Serbian president Aleksandar Vučić were equally enthusiastic, with Wilders rejoicing that "patriots are winning elections all over the world".[15] Less than a month into Trump's new term of office, European far-right leaders gathered in Madrid, hosted by Spain's anti-immigrant Vox party, and celebrated again under a "Make Europe Great Again" banner echoing Trump's MAGA slogan. Spain's ruling Socialists dismissed the gathering as "a coven of ultras", echoing Hillary Clinton's notorious description of half of Trump's supporters as a "basket of deplorables", but the participants were jubilant. "The Trump tornado has changed the world in just a few weeks," said Orbán. "Yesterday we were heretics, today we're mainstream."[16]

Trump, his adviser Elon Musk and his vice-president J.D. Vance were meanwhile returning the compliment, singing the praises of Europe's extreme-right politicians from Romania to Spain. Musk said on his social media platform X that "Vox will win the next [Spanish] election."[17] Vance shocked European liberals by telling the Munich Security Conference that the biggest threat to Europe was not Russia but "the threat from within"—by which he meant the liberal establishment and its reluctance to accept the views of opposition voters who wanted an end to "uncontrolled migration". Vance pointedly met Alice Weidel, leader of the extreme-right AfD party.[18]

FAR-RIGHT FRANCE

Each country, of course, has its own history, its own political system and its version of far-right populism, and nationalists by definition find it harder than internationalists to cooperate with other countries. A shared aversion to immigration or gender-neutral pronouns, therefore, does not mean an automatic affinity between two movements if some other issue sets them apart. So while Hungary's Orbán ticks most of Trump's boxes, and Trump ticks most of Orbán's, the same across-the-board Trumpism might not be true for Le Pen and Bardella in France or Poland's Jarosław Kaczyński, leader of the nationalist PiS party. Poland is an important US ally, but its history means that its people, including PiS voters, are deeply suspicious of Putin and Russia and have strongly supported Ukraine: many Poles were particularly shocked by Trump's cosying up to Putin at the start of his second term and his overt hostility towards Zelenskyy in Ukraine.[19]

Trump's return to power was at best a mixed blessing for the European far right. He had shown that a revolutionary, far-right candidate could win an election in a liberal democracy and start implementing radical economic and social policies, but the early results also showed the limits of such an approach and its disadvantages. Among other effects, Trump's radicalism energised the traditional European parties of left, right and centre at the expense of the far right. "[T]he European political scene has been transformed into a clash between Trump-allied revolutionaries and Trump-resisting 'do not bully us' liberal nationalists," wrote Bulgarian political scientist Ivan Krastev less than two months into Trump's new administration:

> Now it is for the far right to justify Trump's anticipated tariffs on Europe ... and to ask Europeans to follow Washington's leadership in foreign policy. By contrast, mainstream parties are acting as defenders of national sovereignty who hope to mobilise support by appealing to national interest and national dignity.[20]

France, the only nuclear power in the EU, was no exception to this rule.

Yet Trump's re-election was also a brutal reminder to French liberals that their country was subject to the same divisions and disinformation campaigns as the US and might go the same way. "As in the United States, all the ingredients for an extreme-right victory are present in our country, from the establishment of a sympathetic media empire to the feeling of abandonment among a growing share of the population and the obsession with immigration," wrote Cécile Prieur, editor of *Le Nouvel Obs* magazine. "Without yet officially being in power, populist nationalism, fuelled by the extreme polarisation of our public debate, has already conquered hearts and minds."[21]

The history of how the RN increased its influence under Jean-Marie Le Pen, Marine Le Pen and Jordan Bardella to reach its goal of becoming the most popular party in France is the subject of the following chapters.

3

IN THE BEGINNING WAS THE FATHER

Like many other French politicians of left and right, Marine Le Pen and Jordan Bardella like to quote General Charles de Gaulle, the man who led the free French from exile during the second world war and established the current Fifth Republic in 1958, to justify whatever policy they are defending at that moment. Marine's father and party co-founder Jean-Marie Le Pen, on the other hand, detested de Gaulle for abandoning French Algeria and was more of an admirer of Marshal Philippe Pétain, the first world war hero who accepted an armistice with the Nazi invaders in 1940, headed the collaborationist Vichy government and was convicted of treason after the second world war.

To some extent, this was a generational difference: Le Pen was at school during the war, and his childhood home in Brittany was not unusual in displaying a photograph of Pétain until 1945, next to an image of Joan of Arc.[1] Many of those who lived through Vichy and the occupation, and wanted to shake off the charge of collaboration, later subscribed to the idea that the liberator de Gaulle was the "sword" of France while Pétain was the "shield" protecting the French at home, a view that conveniently ignores the 75,000 Jews deported from France to Nazi death camps. To this day, the party's ideology and methods bear traces of this and other convulsive moments of French history.

The very terms "right" and "left" in politics have their origins in the French Revolution of 1789, during which the monarchist sympathisers with the *ancien régime* sat on the right of the president in the constituent assembly in the Tuileries Palace, while the democrats who demanded universal suffrage were on the left. Until the Second Empire of Napoleon III in the second half of the nineteenth century, a mixed bag of counter-revolutionaries embodied what would become the far right, and they were lampooned on one occasion as a group "hostile to the status quo and the ruling elites, skeptical, in favour of starting all over from scratch in order to reestablish order, contemptuous of politicians but laudatory of action and force"—a reasonably prophetic description of some of the twentieth-century fascist regimes to come in Europe.[2]

A hundred years after the Revolution, there was a resurgence of what would today be called nationalist, populist, far-right sentiment in the form of *boulangisme*, when Georges Ernest Boulanger, a general and politician sometimes known as *Général Revanche* (General Revenge), whipped up a frenzied hostility to neighbouring Germany among conservative Catholics, royalists and the French working class and came close to staging a *coup d'état* before his movement was suppressed and he fled the country in 1889. Racism, hatred of foreigners and a sense of victimhood were to become characteristics of the French extreme right, and of the far right everywhere.

With nationalism and antisemitism on the rise in Europe, the next defining historical moment in the structuring of French politics was the Dreyfus affair that shook the French Third Republic for twelve years from 1894, although its echoes are heard in French life and politics to this day. (Roman Polanski's

IN THE BEGINNING WAS THE FATHER

film about Dreyfus, *J'accuse*—its English title is *An Officer and a Spy*—came out in 2019, and in mid-2025 the French National Assembly passed a law to rehabilitate Dreyfus and promote him posthumously to brigadier-general.) Captain Alfred Dreyfus was a French Jewish artillery officer wrongly accused of spying for Germany, convicted of treason and jailed on Devil's Island off the coast of French Guiana. He was eventually exonerated in 1906. French society was passionately divided between *dreyfusards* and *antidreyfusards*, the latter including Édouard Drumont, an antisemitic author and newspaper publisher.

The French far right's support for the persecution of Jews and admiration for fascism reached its apogee during the second world war, when police in Nazi-occupied northern France, and Pétain's government in the rump state ruled from Vichy, collaborated in the rounding up of Jews, Roma, Communists and other political prisoners in concentration camps set up in France, as well as the deportation and slaughter of tens of thousands of these detainees sent to death camps in eastern Europe. Far-right thinkers and movements such as François de La Rocque's Croix de Feu, originally for veterans, had flourished after the first world war. Charles Maurras (1868–1952), a prominent intellectual who despised Hitler but was openly antisemitic, anti-Protestant and anti-freemason and supported the reactionary policies of Pétain's Vichy, once said that "to hate Jews and immigrants is to love France". When he was convicted in 1945 for collaborating with the enemy, he said: "It's the revenge of Dreyfus."[3]

Despite his wartime record, Maurras and his Action française movement continue to inspire French politicians of the right and the far right, including Éric Zemmour, a television talk show personality and far-right presidential candidate in 2022 who is himself of north African Jewish origin. While some in France continue to defend Pétain, the historian Zeev Sternhell has lambasted those who argued that the French were never really inclined towards fascism. "One can never emphasise enough the importance of the fascistisation of the intellectual right, starting at its Maurrasian core, as well as the role of intellectuals in creating a climate that allowed fascism to get a grip," he wrote. "The men who came to power in the summer of 1940 were as morally and intellectually ready to get to work as the Nazis were in 1933, and perhaps more than the Italian fascists in 1922." As for the racial laws, the roundups and the deportations to the death camps, "Neither Franco, nor Salazar, nor Mussolini went so far."[4]

Even in this very brief survey of the post-revolutionary origins of the French far right, it is worth remarking that its various parties have often drawn ideas and activists from the far left, including Communists. It is not just that far-right activists sing the revolutionary national anthem the Marseillaise as lustily as anyone (the song is in any case an anti-Prussian war chant that champions French racial purity rather than a celebration of the Revolution): Georges Sorel (1847–1922), the Marxist philosopher, shifted towards the nationalist, antisemitic Action française and was eventually dubbed "the intellectual father of fascism";[5] and Jacques Doriot (1898–1945), after being pushed out of the French Communist Party, veered to the right, founded a new party and fought in German uniform on the side of the Nazis on their eastern front. The far left and far right often hold similarly anti-liberal views about the primacy of community over the individual and the importance of state management of the economy.

"A number of the ideas that currently constitute the foundation of far-right ideology (nationalism, populism, and antisemitism in particular) were defended at that time [the so-called first globalisation period of 1840–1940] by the revolutionary left," wrote Jean-Yves Camus and Nicolas Lebourg in their study of the far right in Europe.[6]

Indeed, the FN flourished from the mid-1970s when the *trente glorieuses*, the three decades of post-war industrial and eco-

IN THE BEGINNING WAS THE FATHER

nomic growth, gave way to crisis, stagnation, globalisation and working-class resentment of immigrants. "Over the last two centuries, we have seen the gradual rise of a multifaceted far right," political scientist Pascal Perrineau told *Le Monde* in 2021:

> Today there remains a reactionary branch, the Action Française [Maurras was a leading light], which is probably the most intellectually coherent; a neo-fascist far right; and a nationalist-populist far right embodied by the Rassemblement National ... It's above all an anti-immigrant party, that's how it was born and how it succeeded. Since then it's become a truly populist organisation.[7]

After the second world war, the French far right had taken years to regroup and fully recover from its association with Hitler, the Holocaust and Vichy, but its historic support for Pétain himself did not disqualify it permanently from public support given how widely the marshal's wartime rule was accepted in France. "Most of the people who had applauded de Gaulle when he was the winner had applauded Pétain three or six months earlier," Camus told me when I asked why the French far right had been so strong for so long; in the post-war UK, by contrast, the extreme right survived at first only on the fringes of politics, and the British fascist Oswald Mosley retired to France to write his autobiography.[8]

* * *

After the war, the French far right also began to draw inspiration from the new trauma of French decolonisation, including the 1954 defeat in Vietnam, which resulted in the withdrawal from all of Indochina, and the doomed war to keep Algeria French (1954–62). It was no coincidence that the man who became the unquestioned figurehead for the far right from the 1970s onwards was Jean-Marie Le Pen, who had been deployed as a paratrooper to both of those conflicts as well as serving in the humiliating postcolonial fiasco of the 1956 operation to seize the Suez Canal.

Marine Le Pen inherited in the FN a family business created and developed by her father. Jean-Marie, a boisterous, provocative campaigner and a gifted orator, was arguably the most successful far-right politician in the democracies of western Europe of his generation, in part because of his own skills and in part because of the particular conditions in France after the second world war and France's abandonment of most of its overseas colonies in the 1950s and 1960s. His pugnacity and determination never won him the French presidency, but in some ways his iconoclastic style of politics and scorn for convention prefigured the rise of other European nationalists and the successful campaigns of Donald Trump in the US in 2016 and 2024.

The high point of Jean-Marie Le Pen's six-decade career in politics was on 21 April 2002, when he stunned France by beating the Socialist prime minister Lionel Jospin in the first round of the presidential election, thereby eliminating Jospin and qualifying for the runoff against the incumbent centre-right president Jacques Chirac. It is hard to overstate the impact of this political earthquake in a nation grown accustomed to the left–right cycle of politics in the Fifth Republic. The French establishment had always seen Le Pen as an extremist and his party as a fringe movement, but his triumph showed that 4.8 million voters, 16.9 per cent of the total, had chosen him over the other candidates. (Chirac won 19.9 per cent in the first round, and Jospin— who promptly retired from politics—16.2 per cent.) I was lucky enough to have a reporter's front-row seat for this drama. I was at the Socialist Party headquarters on that fateful Sunday night waiting for the first results, which are released at 8 p.m., when a Socialist Party contact whispered in my ear that Jospin had lost to Le Pen; it was the first and only time I have ever called my news desk and uttered the words every print journalist wants to be able to tell his editors: "Hold the front page."

IN THE BEGINNING WAS THE FATHER

Le Pen, who had not prepared a government team and never seems to have envisaged actually taking power, was as surprised as anyone by the result. But, with an eye on the second-round run-off two weeks later, he quickly drafted a speech that characteristically appealed over the heads of establishment politicians to voters worried about crime, violence, bureaucracy and tax and regretful about the decline of French influence in the world. "Don't be afraid to dream, you, the ordinary people, the little people, the rank-and-file, the excluded. Don't let yourselves be shut in by the old divisions of right and left, you who have put up with all the mistakes and corruption of politicians for the past 20 years." He appealed to "miners, steelworkers, labourers of all those industries ruined by the Euroglobalism of Maastricht [the EU treaty], farmers with miserable pensions driven to ruin and disappearance, and you who are the first victims of crime in suburbs, towns and villages" to seize the chance for national recovery. A populist long before Trump, Le Pen emphasised the far-right insistence that national identity transcended the old politics of left and right. "Socially I'm on the left, economically I'm on the right and more than ever I am nationally of France."[9]

As with the Brexit referendum in the UK and Trump's first victory in 2016, I and many of my fellow-journalists had failed to read the signs of public discontent that should have led us to expect a strong Le Pen performance in the 2002 presidential election. My myopia on this was particularly striking given that my boss at the time gave me the specific job of covering Le Pen and the FN during the campaign because he did not think they were important enough to merit his own attention. A month before Le Pen's first-round triumph, I even wrote a piece from Toulouse in south-west France headlined "Le Pen's star on the wane as rivals step in". I noted that Le Pen was already seventy-three and that most of the supporters at his campaign rally were elderly whites, in a university town that was and is notably youthful and multiracial and had been a refuge for fugitives from Franco's Spain in the 1930s. Although the giant artificial torches on the stage and Le Pen's fulminations about an "invasion" of immigrants and "catastrophic" crime figures gave the meeting a neo-fascist air, the mood was more nostalgic than menacing. "Our young people are directionless, and our leaders don't keep their promises," I was told by Antoine Morin, a seventy-eight-year-old former soldier who had served with Le Pen in Vietnam in 1954.

Le Pen's programme for government was also somewhat eccentric. As well as his usual rejection of immigration and the EU—the euro was "the currency of occupation", he said, and a federal Europe would mean future French presidents having less power than the governor of Nebraska—Le Pen suggested suspending income tax (another Trumpian touch) and creating a ministry for animals, an idea apparently aimed at appealing simultaneously to pet-lovers, hunters and meat-eaters. The opinion polls at the time suggested Le Pen would only win about 10 per cent of the vote, below the 15 per cent he had already reached in 1998 and 1995.[10] In the end, the polls did record a last-minute surge of support but still under-predicted his actual performance, a problem that was to become a common feature of populist victories around the world.

After his initial triumph, the traumatised establishment—and the mass of French voters—quickly rallied to ensure that Le Pen had no chance of winning the Élysée palace in 2002. On 1 May, between the two rounds of the election, more than a million people took to the streets of France and turned May Day marches into a nationwide protest against Le Pen, who was condemned as a fascist and a racist. The demonstrations were the biggest seen in many cities since the upheavals of 1968 and in some places since the celebrations following France's liberation towards the end of the second world war. French business leaders, after a week of embarrassed silence, finally rounded on Le Pen, with

IN THE BEGINNING WAS THE FATHER

Ernest-Antoine Seillière, the aristocratic head of Medef, saying that his protectionist, anti-EU election programme "would cause a steep economic decline, a sharp rise in unemployment, an unprecedented financial crisis, an increase in inflation, the impoverishment of all and explosive social tensions".[11] Left and right, Communists and conservatives, joined forces to ensure that Chirac—even though he was detested by many left-wingers—was comfortably re-elected in the runoff on 5 May, with 82.2 per cent of the vote, against just 17.8 per cent for Le Pen, barely higher than his first-round score. The result was an early triumph for the *front républicain*, the system of temporary alliances between political enemies that would continue to exclude the far right from national political power into the 2020s; only now is it beginning to falter in the face of the increasing popularity of Marine Le Pen, Jordan Bardella and their renamed party.

Attention then turned to the legislative elections in the summer, in which Jean-Marie Le Pen hoped to build on his sudden rise to prominence to win seats in the National Assembly after years in the political wilderness. (The FN had won a respectable thirty-five seats out of 577 in 1986 but only because President François Mitterrand had briefly introduced proportional representation in a bid to split the right.) For those elections in 2002, I went to the northern French rustbelt in the Pas-de-Calais to watch Marine Le Pen, then a regional councillor, campaigning in the old coal-mining and industrial district where the FN was starting to win votes in communities that had previously been staunchly Socialist or Communist; in the presidential contest, Jean-Marie Le Pen had gained more support from the voters in the area than the two left-wing candidates combined. "There are enormous problems of drugs and unemployment here," she said while canvassing for votes in the market at Harnes near Hénin-Beaumont. "There could be a fair number of Front National deputies in the National Assembly. If we continue with the rising trend in our share of the vote, we will be in a position at some point in the future to lead this country." But it was not to be—or not yet, anyway. The FN won not a single seat in the National Assembly that year, and it took another fifteen years before she finally became the member of parliament for Hénin-Beaumont.

As if to underline the far right's relegation to the fringes of French politics, Maxime Brunerie, a twenty-five-year-old neo-Nazi militant, tried to assassinate President Chirac with a .22 rifle during that year's Bastille Day military parade as it was being watched by myself and thousands of others lining the Champs-Élysées in Paris. Brunerie missed his target and was arrested and jailed. Luckily for Jean-Marie Le Pen, Brunerie turned out to have been a municipal election candidate not for the FN but for the Mouvement National Républicain, a splinter movement led by Le Pen's former colleague Bruno Mégret. Brunerie had, however, flitted in and out of militant neo-fascist factions also frequented by extreme FN supporters, including a Paris Saint-Germain football supporters' gang and the now-banned student organisation Groupe Union Défense, which had a black rat and a Celtic cross as its symbols.[12]

After the round of elections in 2002, Jean-Marie Le Pen disappeared from political view. When I interviewed him later that year in the hilltop gated community of Montretout in Saint-Cloud—at his mansion bequeathed by a reclusive right-wing millionaire—he was bitter that his evident popularity had not been transformed into political power, even in the relatively ineffectual National Assembly. "The French parliament has no power any more," he said, surrounded by military mementoes and Joan of Arc statuettes, "but at least there's a show. We're not even allowed into this virtual-reality show, even though I got millions of votes." He called France a totalitarian democracy in which established politicians were plotting to reserve the arena for the two mainstream groups of right and left and pointed at a boomerang on the wall of his study: "It will come back in their face."

IN THE BEGINNING WAS THE FATHER

Immigration, Le Pen maintained, was the problem that would kill the West. "We are witnessing the beginning of formidable migration that will bring billions of men and women from the third world to demographically aged populations like ours." This fear of migrants from abroad and this resentment at being excluded from power at home were emotions that would reappear in ever more virulent forms among populists around the world in the years ahead, but at the time it seemed as though Le Pen's brief moment of glory in the spring of 2002 had been a French flash in the pan, or perhaps even the last gasp of a dying colonialist generation. In my article about Le Pen, I quoted a political analyst as saying that the FN would continue to be an important force but faced so much resistance that it could not achieve anything. "They are a vector of the fears and anxieties of the French, but they can't turn it into anything positive," he said. Although he continued for years afterwards to resist being pushed into retirement, Le Pen himself acknowledged that he would eventually have to hand over to his daughter. "I'm not the Pope," he said. "I don't think I have to stay until death."[13]

Marine Le Pen owes much of her subsequent success to the strong foundations laid by her father, and like him, she showed herself to be a forceful party leader: she finally expelled him in 2015 from the party he founded because his latest antisemitic comments were undermining her attempts to "detoxify" the FN and make it electable. By this time, however, he had established what was arguably the most successful far-right party among the democracies of post-war western Europe. Who was he, and how did he do it?

* * *

Jean-Marie Le Pen, the son of a fisherman, was born in La Trinité-sur-Mer in Brittany in 1928; he died in Paris at the age of ninety-six in January 2025. In his two-volume, 1,000-page memoir, he comes across as charismatic, provocative and patriotic, scornful of authority and the establishment and always ready—like his daughter Marine—to burst out laughing. He loved to sing, especially military songs that recalled his time as a paratrooper, and when he was trying to make a living in between the stages of his political career he established a media company called Serp that specialised in recording martial tunes and controversial historical reportage in the days before digital media made such material easily available. Notoriously, the tunes in question included Nazi favourites such as the Horst Wessel song—but also the anthems of the revolutionary left. Le Pen describes how he was once accosted by a group of angry leftist students who started singing the Internationale at him but did not know all the words—so he sang it for them in full.

Known because of his size and endurance as "the menhir", after the prehistoric standing stones of Brittany, Le Pen's unpredictability, mendacity and overbearing presence made him a forerunner of later, more successful populists such as Trump (though Le Pen, unlike Trump, was well read in history and literature). After meeting Le Pen for the first time in his office at the European Parliament in Brussels while studying for her PhD, the political scientist Catherine Fieschi described the contrast between "the hulking presence and booming voice" filling the room and his "average" appearance: "He could easily have been one of the guys hollering and heckling behind a market stall." Le Pen talked almost non-stop, asking and answering his own questions. "Over the course of the next few hours, this mountain of a man ... would sing, dance, laugh, flirt. And lie," she wrote. Facts and dates were repeatedly contradicted. People referred to as friends at one moment would be dismissed as traitors the next:

> Part of the discomfort was the contrast between physical heft and immovable solidity—and an approach to narrative that was the very

IN THE BEGINNING WAS THE FATHER

opposite: uncontrolled, manic, almost demented. Over time, I realized that this was, in fact, an incredibly effective control mechanism: it scrambled the wires and kept you permanently off balance, confused and guessing.[14]

This was in 1996, twenty years before Trump first won the White House.

As a politician, he played on his relatively humble origins and the deprivations under German occupation in the second world war. When he was a child, the floors of the family home were of beaten earth, and there was no electricity or running water. His father Jean was prosperous enough to own his own boat but was killed in 1942 when he pulled up a mine in his trawl net, and his only son became a *pupille de la nation* or ward of the nation because the father was deemed to have "died for France". Jean-Marie Le Pen, who had a lifelong love of the sea and of sailing, described himself as a native Breton and Frenchman (the phrase *français de souche* has long been used by some French whites to distinguish themselves from immigrants), and he was proud that the "little Breton" he was had made it so big in politics. Unlike some of his fellow politicians on the right, however, he had little love for the Catholic Church, in part because the priests at one of the schools he attended during the war one day got rid of their undisciplined sixteen-year-old pupil by telling him his widowed mother had died: he wrote in his autobiography that he rushed home in tears to find her alive and well.[15]

Le Pen moved to Paris to study law and began his political career by presiding as a virulent anti-Communist over La Corpo, the law students' association. He volunteered as a soldier (despite being exempted from military service as a *pupille de la nation*) and served as a Foreign Legion paratrooper in three conflicts: France's failed colonial war to keep Indochina (although he arrived just after the decisive defeat of French forces at Điện Biên Phủ in Vietnam); the abortive Anglo-French–Israeli campaign to take control of the Suez Canal; and the battle of Algiers that preceded France's ignominious exit from a north African country it considered an integral part of France. As a teenager towards the end of the second world war, he had toyed with the idea of helping the resistance and said he followed a German soldier in the street but could not bring himself to shoot him in the back of the head with his father's pistol. He admitted he had a less-than-glorious start in military life (at one point, his mother stopped him joining an amateur resistance raid with his friends by hiding his trousers).

Throughout his adult life, Le Pen bitterly resented de Gaulle for what he saw as his betrayal of French Algeria in ceding its independence (though he had reached out to shake his hand when de Gaulle visited Auray on a tour to celebrate the liberation of France at the end of the second world war) and criticised the post-war punishments meted out to Pétain and his Vichy colleagues and to other collaborators with the Nazi occupation. Pétainistes, Nazi sympathisers and soldiers who had fought in Algeria were at the core of the FN and its predecessor parties.

An early indication of Le Pen's political genius was his association with Pierre Poujade, the right-wing, anti-establishment stationery shop owner who launched a short-lived but spectacular revolt by small traders against the state's burdensome tax audits with his Union de défense des commerçants et artisans; to this day, the word *poujadiste* is used to describe a reactionary small business owner. In 1956, Poujade's party won fifty-two seats in the National Assembly elections, and Le Pen at twenty-eight became one of the youngest *députés* in the chamber after proving himself as an effective orator and campaigner.

Poujadist demonstrations would have been recognisable to the *gilets jaunes* protesters who took to the streets of France more than sixty years later, for Poujadism was an early example of the kind of movement that can transcend left–right politics and is seen as championing ordinary people against the supposed met-

IN THE BEGINNING WAS THE FATHER

ropolitan elite. Poujade's supporters in the north and west were often extreme-right antisemites and fervently supportive of French rule in Algeria, but the movement also won the backing of Communists in the south and centre of France. "Provincial suspicion and dislike of the capital were as important Poujadist themes as the popular suspicion and dislike of the well-off, the well-educated and the well-placed," wrote the political scientist Philip Williams:

> Poujadism—like American Populism—was a protest against metropolitan sophistication, wealth and success in which a deep but confused sense of grievance found expression (often with highly reactionary overtones) in the popular accents of the underprivileged provincial cut off from the seats of power and unable to understand, let alone influence, the forces which were undermining his way of life.[16]

Le Pen's verdict on Poujade was that he was a great man and a "precursor". Poujade, Le Pen wrote, "for a moment gave people real hope. He was half a liberator."[17]

A decade later, Le Pen became campaign manager for the anti-Gaullist 1965 presidential bid of Jean-Louis Tixier-Vignancour, the former Vichyist who was the lawyer of the antisemitic, pro-Nazi writer Céline and of Raoul Salan, one of the four generals who attempted a putsch against de Gaulle to stop France abandoning Algeria. But Tixier-Vignancour lost, and Le Pen described the campaign as "the one big regret of my political life" and 1965 as his *annus horribilis*.[18] As with Poujade, Le Pen bridled under the leadership of another and felt he was a better orator and politician than the man he was supporting. So he ended up co-founding and leading his own party.

In the late 1950s and early 1960s, Le Pen had already set up two Fronts Nationals, the Front National des Combattants (later simply the Front National Combattant) and the Front National pour l'Algérie Française, both banned by the government, and it was not until 1972 that the FN itself—its full name was the Front National pour l'Unité Française—was created to prepare for the following year's municipal elections. At the time, the Ordre Nouveau (New Order), an extreme-right faction, was looking for a way into politics, so Le Pen got together with like-minded militants to found the new party.[19] They included party treasurer Pierre Bousquet, who had been a corporal in the Waffen SS in its Charlemagne division and defended Hitler's chancery in Berlin in 1945; Léon Gaultier, another SS officer and collaborator; Holocaust-denier François Duprat, who was later killed by a car bomb; and Roger Holeindre, who had been in the banned Organisation de l'armée secrète (OAS), the group co-founded by General Salan that had fought in vain for France to keep Algeria and whose assassination attempts on de Gaulle were fictionalised in the book and film *The Day of the Jackal*.

Le Pen soon took control of the party—he had warned the others when they asked him to be the figurehead, "If I commit myself, I won't let go"—and always denied being a fascist or a racist himself but was never able to shake off the stain of the FN's neo-Nazi origins. Its founding document, although drafted by the Ordre Nouveau, was neither a call to violence nor solely focused on race, instead decrying France's "intellectual, moral and physical decadence", stressing the importance of family, education, hard work and the nation and rejecting communism and footloose international capitalism. "The nation is the community of language, interests, race and memories in which man blossoms. It relies on its roots, on its dead, on the past, and on heredity and heritage," it said. In protecting the community, "the immigration and assimilation of foreigners are major concerns. There is no point in guarding our frontiers if a peaceful, legal invasion changes the nature and the characteristics of the French people."[20]

Le Pen was to put hostility to immigration at the heart of the FN's proposition to voters. He initially argued that his desire to include millions of Algerian Muslims as French citizens was proof of his lack of racism, although he later admitted that demographic trends meant there were too many of them for that to happen and that Algerian independence was therefore inevitable. Le Pen also spoke about his respect for other races and religions, and during the Suez campaign was praised by his commanders for burying the enemy dead—Egyptian Muslims—in accordance with custom with their heads towards Mecca. In founding the FN, he said, he wanted to succeed where de Gaulle had failed in reconciling the French. "I was proud to bring together Communists, Christian democrats, monarchists and Nazi sympathisers, as well as gathering together Jews, Christians, Muslims, pagans, blacks, Arabs, yellow people and native French people. I wanted to attract French people of all origins, provided they were patriotic."[21]

Although it grossly misrepresents the racially and religiously intolerant nature of the early FN, this statement does underline how Le Pen succeeded in federating both the splintered factions of the far right and anyone else who was "anti-system" or estranged from de Gaulle, including second world war resistance fighters and Vichyist collaborators. Camus and Lebourg suggest the party thrives on an "us" against "them" mentality because "all the subfamilies of the French far right have a sense that they belong to the same camp, that of the losing side in all the major breaks that have marked the history of France: the Revolution of 1789, the Dreyfus Affair, the Liberation, the loss of the colonial empire".[22]

Le Pen repeatedly denied he was a racist or a xenophobe and said he believed in equality of opportunity but also declared it was obvious that races were unequal and that French civilisation was superior, even if it had not perhaps reached the Himalayas and had only achieved the height of Mont Blanc in terms of quality. "People have gone so far as to talk of the absurd notion of the equality of races, but if now we're also going to talk about the equality of civilisations, I don't know how low we can go," he once told a radio interviewer.[23] At another time, he said: "At the Olympic Games, there is an obvious inequality between the black race and the white race. It's a fact. I conclude that the races are unequal."[24] Le Pen subscribed to the conspiracy theory that immigrants from Africa and the Middle East were engaged in a "great replacement" of native Europeans by foreigners of other cultures and religions, particularly Islam, and insisted there was a desire to change European society and make it multicultural and multiethnic by welcoming in millions of immigrants. "The white world is in the process of dying," he wrote.[25]

For all Le Pen's denials of racism, the mask of bonhomie began to slip by the time he was in his nineties and ranting in the final chapters of his autobiography about the "invasion" of immigrants and Islamists. "Let's look at a map. Paris was once surrounded by a belt of [Communist] red, but it's green today. The capital is surrounded and penetrated by Islamist rabble." It was time, wrote Le Pen, to prepare for the end of France and close the borders. "If the countries of the South continue to dump their 'peaceful migrants' here, what will we do? When they arrive, will we sink their boats? If we don't sink them, it's all over."[26]

Yet it was usually not generalised racism that got Le Pen into trouble with the courts or with public opinion. It was antisemitism and Holocaust-denial. Although he insisted he had Jewish friends and supporters, including one of his girlfriends, he had a habit of playing down the murder of six million Jews, the gravity of Nazi war crimes and the French collaboration under Vichy that contributed to them—and then repeating years later the same statements that had already led to him being convicted and fined. Most notoriously, he described the gas chambers as "a detail of the history of the second world war". Even though he knew he had blundered, instead of backing down or apologising, he later tried to justify the comment by saying that the gas chambers typically took up ten to fifteen lines of a 1,000-page history of the war, "which is what you call a detail". On another occasion, he made an antisemitic pun about a government minister called Michel Durafour, referring to him as "Durafour-*crématoire*" (a four *crématoire* being the oven of a crematorium). Then he said "the German occupation [of France] wasn't as inhumane as all that, even if there were screw-ups, unavoidable in a country of 550,000 square kilometres". Le Pen's doubling down on his "detail of history" remark in 2015 was the last straw for his daughter Marine as she tried to lead the party towards respectability. He was expelled from the party the same year and finally convicted again by the courts in 2018 over the comment, for denying a crime against humanity, after exhausting the appeals process.[27]

Another issue that dogged him for most of his political career was the set of allegations that he and his comrades had tortured prisoners during the 1956–7 battle of Algiers between the French and the Algerian National Liberation Front (FLN). At first, he made no attempt to deny it. "If you have to use violence to find a collection of bombs, if you have to torture one man to save a hundred, torture is inevitable and therefore, in the abnormal conditions in which one is asked to act, it is just," he said in 1957. Three years later, he implicated himself in an interview—"I have nothing to hide. I tortured because it had to be done"—before publishing a denial in the same newspaper. On at least two occasions, he let slip when confronted by the testimony of a witness that he should have done worse to them than he did, even killed them. He nevertheless sued those who accused him personally of torture—even when he could not be prosecuted for torture because French troops benefitted from an amnesty and because the events happened too long ago to be prosecuted—and he eventually won all his Algeria cases until the year 2000. But he lost his libel case against *Le Monde* for a further round of accusations published in 2002, despite his repeated appeals.[28] Le Pen returned to the subject in his memoirs, suggesting that forcing someone's head into a bucket of water, hitting them, subjecting them to electric shocks or threatening them with execution could hardly be called torture. When he had previously admitted to torture, he wrote, he merely meant those sorts of "special interrogations".[29]

It is tempting to speculate on what kind of president Jean-Marie Le Pen would have been had he ever been elected to France's highest office. He was clearly not a fan of human rights or of liberal democracy, although he generally tried to operate within its constraints. To the contrary, he admired dictators and right-wing white politicians, including Rhodesia's Ian Smith, Senator Jesse Helms of the US, Chile's Augusto Pinochet, Ferdinand Marcos of the Philippines, Syria's Bashar al-Assad and Iraq's Saddam Hussein, whom he met during the 1990–1 Gulf war as a poke in the eye for the French government, because France under Mitterrand had joined the US-led coalition to reverse the Iraqi occupation of Kuwait. Rather like the naive George W. Bush when he met Vladimir Putin and "was able to get a sense of his soul", Le Pen said that "a current flowed" between him and Saddam in Baghdad, where he said he was received like a head of state. "There was something. A natural sympathy between two pariahs who refuse to bow down before unjust power but search for human solutions to human conflicts."[30]

* * *

Le Pen had an exceptionally long political career of more than sixty years spanning the Fourth and Fifth Republics, and by his own account the FN he founded in 1972 had held sixteen party congresses and competed in sixty-one rounds of elections by the time he wrote his memoirs in 2019.[31] He had enough of a popular touch combined with a sense of history to shine as an orator and as a ferocious critic of the governments and leaders of his day, but—unlike his daughter Marine—he was never close enough to power to consider seriously what he would do with it if he had it. Instead, he remained an eternal provocateur and champion of lost causes, prompting Laurent Fabius, a French prime minister, to remark that "Le Pen sometimes asks good questions, even if he has bad answers to them."[32] After ceding leadership of the FN to Marine in 2011, and even after his expulsion from the party four years later, he grumbled on the sidelines about her lack of aggression and her continuing attempts to detoxify the party. After the 2022 presidential election, he would not even tell an interviewer whether he had voted for his daughter in the first round or for Éric Zemmour, the far-right rival who had looked like a threat to her dominance early in the campaign, saying the two candidates were pretty much the same.[33]

Jean-Marie Le Pen was such a totemic hate figure for the French left that when he died at the age of ninety-six in January 2025 hundreds of people took to the streets of cities such as Paris and Lyon to celebrate with champagne and fireworks. His grave in La Trinité-sur-Mer was desecrated by vandals who smashed the stone cross above it. Bruno Retailleau, interior minister at the time, issued a stern rebuke to those celebrating his death. "The death of a man, even a political adversary, should inspire only restraint and dignity. These scenes of jubilation are simply shameful," he said. "Nothing, absolutely nothing justifies dancing over a corpse."[34] Even so, the Macron administration itself was notably terse in its statement about the death of one of the country's longest-serving politicians and party leaders, calling him "a historic figure of the extreme right" and saying he had played a role in public life for nearly seventy years, a record for which "history will henceforth be the judge".[35]

It was left to his own party, now the RN of his daughter, to call him a "visionary" and point to his political achievements, which were to bring into the public eye the big topics that were now shaping political life: immigration, globalisation, the decline of France and the risk of having national sovereignty diluted by the EU.[36] As French political commentators had noticed years before, Jean-Marie Le Pen may have been "all talk" and have lacked a detailed political programme, but he had reframed the political debate.[37] This was part of the legacy he bequeathed to Marine Le Pen and the RN as they came ever closer to their goal of ruling France.

4

POLITICAL PATRICIDE

"I'm so excited," said Julie Niel as she glimpsed Marine Le Pen emerging from the Hôtel Normandy in Vernon. "She's the one who will save us from all this, from everything: the cost of living, the state of the economy, all the things that Macron has done, petrol at €2 a litre, food prices." Niel, a thirty-five-year-old worker at a Leclerc supermarket, was gripping her daughter's hand while trying to take a picture of Le Pen on the 2022 presidential campaign trail through a jostling crowd of supporters and journalists.[1]

After decades in the political wilderness in the shadow of her father Jean-Marie, Marine Le Pen transformed the extreme-right, anti-immigration movement he founded. In 2022, the RN multiplied by ten the number of seats it held in the French National Assembly to eighty-nine to become the biggest opposition party. By late 2024, it was the largest single party in the assembly and also the largest in the European Parliament, having trounced Macron's centrist alliance in that year's EU elections.

Marine Le Pen, who turned fifty-seven in the summer of 2025, has been in politics longer than most of her rivals. Her blonde hair and husky voice make her an instantly recognisable political star in France. Unlike her father and again unlike her rivals, she is known to almost everyone by her first name, Marine—an obvious advantage for a populist. Her supporters and associates are called simply *marinistes*. She is not a great orator nor a woman of ideas, but she is a formidable politician on the streets in an election campaign. Le Pen has made mistakes and frequently been defeated at the polls but has always come back fighting. The presidential race that took her to Vernon was her third.

When she visited Vernon, a town on the banks of the Seine about an hour's drive from Paris and just inside Normandy, in the later stages of her 2022 race against the incumbent President Emmanuel Macron, it was the forty-sixth French town or village she had visited in a few months in a gruelling "go local" campaign. Against the wishes of some of her advisers, she had decided not to emphasise the RN's core topic of fighting against immigration, which had become less of a concern to French voters during the Covid-19 pandemic. (Restrictions, including on travel, were imposed in France with varying degrees of severity between March 2020 and the spring of 2022.) Le Pen focused instead on the cost of living. The idea was to contrast herself as a smiling mother of three who understood the concerns of ordinary people about rising prices and crime with a supposedly aloof, hyper-intellectual "president of the elite" ensconced in the Élysée palace in the middle of Paris.

It seemed to work. "When she speaks, she's frank. She says what she thinks," said Niel, predicting that Le Pen would take decisive action to make life better, whereas Macron "doesn't like French people, he just denigrates them". It was the same story down south. "She is the candidate who loves the people," gushed Florelle Bonnet, a thirty-two-year-old carer for the elderly who had come to see Le Pen visit the Good Friday market in the Provençal town of Pertuis, where the stalls overflowed with fresh produce from asparagus and artichokes to mussels and sea urchins. "She is beautiful, she's radiant and one feels that she really is up to the top job."

Le Pen went into the 2022 election with several advantages. The first was that Macron was much less popular as he came to the end of his first term than he was at the start, his presidency tarnished by the popular *gilets jaunes* uprising.[2] Most French presidents quickly lose popularity when in office and tend to regain it once they have stepped down, and the perception that the incumbent Macron was aloof and arrogant, a "president for the rich" who was trying to save public money by raising the retirement age and who went about quoting philosophers rather than talking about the price of petrol, made him particularly vulnerable.

Le Pen's second advantage was the weakened state of the economy after the Covid pandemic, as well as the full-scale Russian invasion of Ukraine in the final weeks of the 2022 campaign, which pushed up food and fuel prices, something that could be blamed on Macron (even though Le Pen had been sympathetic to Putin and the party had previously been financed by a Russian bank loan after Moscow's annexation of the Ukrainian region of Crimea in 2014).[3]

The third advantage was that the old left-versus-right structure of politics no longer seemed relevant, even in France. The internationalist Macron had already stolen the old far-right slogan "neither right nor left" for his own use as a ground-breaking centrist, but the European political climate was shifting in favour of populist, nationalist movements such as Le Pen's. "We no longer have a left–right split but one between nationalists and globalists," she once told me in an interview in Paris. "In this confrontation we have every chance of coming to power at a time when across the world the idea that we promote—control of immigration, economic patriotism, rational and reasonable protectionism—is increasingly powerful."[4] The number of French voters willing to switch from the far left to the far right is proof that this trend is having a real impact. When politicians are focusing on the cost of living and the economy rather than immigration or crime, supporters of Mélenchon and his far-left, pro-migrant LFI party readily transfer their loyalties to Le Pen, because immigration and race, and sometimes the environment, are the only crucial matters on which the two have significant differences.

Lastly, in 2022 Le Pen ended up profiting from the unexpected irruption into the race of Éric Zemmour, an eloquent television talk-show polemicist who briefly challenged her for leadership of the far-right movement in France with provocatively anti-Muslim, anti-immigration rhetoric that had more in common with the Jean-Marie Le Pen of old than with his daughter's lower-key style of campaigning. "In this campaign, we saw hardly any *antifa*," one of Le Pen's advisers told me. The anti-fascist left-wing demonstrators who would in the past have shouted angrily at the Le Pens chose the even more controversial Zemmour as their target instead; he, for example, had been convicted and fined for hate speech when he said unaccompanied child migrants were "thieves", "killers" and "rapists".[5] In the first round of voting, Macron won 28 per cent and Marine Le Pen 23 per cent (slightly more than Mélenchon's 22 per cent), securing them places in the run-off. Zemmour won a respectable 7 per cent, and nine out of ten of his voters said they would switch to Marine Le Pen for the final vote. With large numbers of far-left and centre-right voters also adding to her tally, she was in with a chance.

In the end, on 24 April 2022, she again lost to Macron, but not by much. Although Macron was re-elected for a second term, it was Le Pen's best result of her three presidential campaigns. On her first attempt in 2012, she polled a solid 18 per cent in the first round but did not make it into the second, which was won by the Socialist François Hollande. In the second, against the newcomer Macron in 2017, she lost by 66 to 34 per cent. In 2022, she scored 41.5 per cent against his 58.5. The establishment had succeeded yet again in keeping the far right at bay, but by a narrower margin than ever. Before the election, French commentators had suggested that if she lost it would be her final attempt. Marine Le Pen, however, did not give up. She wanted to win the Élysée in 2027—or before if Macron tired of his inability to control the fragmented National Assembly and decided to resign. If her 2025 disqualification from standing for elections over the embezzlement of EU funds is upheld, her young and equally popular party president Jordan Bardella is ready to step in. Le Pen, Bardella and the RN have political momentum in France.

* * *

Le Pen's policy of *dédiabolisation* and moderation was contested by many in her own party, including her own father, and it took a decade to bear fruit and bring her and the RN to the brink of power in France. She took over from Jean-Marie Le Pen as president of the FN in January 2011, whereupon he became honorary chairman until she ejected him in 2015.[6] She later said the expulsion of her own father was "the most difficult moment of life other than giving birth" but said he had left the party with no choice.[7] When I interviewed her five years later and asked about the party's racist reputation, she said politics was about personalities: with Jean-Marie Le Pen as the face of the party,

> with the over-the-top positions we know about, of course that gave a certain kind of image of the movement, which was moreover at the time more of a protest movement than a government-in-waiting. I have struggled a lot to display the movement as it actually is, and not as it might be caricatured because of the behaviour of Jean-Marie Le Pen, and I think I've done that with some success. [She always called

him Le Pen when dealing with him as a politician, reserving *Papa* for their personal relations, which at the time she described as "tense".][8]

Marine Le Pen took another bold step in 2018, changing the name from FN, with its neo-fascist connotations—think of the National Front in the UK—to the more inclusive and less confrontational RN, often translated as National Rally. "It's not a cosmetic change," she said:

> It's a change of philosophy, a cultural revolution. A "Front" is to confront something, to be against it. By moving from Front to Rassemblement ... it's really a complete transformation of our philosophy. And the party has gathered people together, including people like Thierry Mariani, who was a minister under Nicolas Sarkozy, and Jean-Paul Garraud [another politician who defected from the Gaullist right]. The aim is to bring people together, to be present locally on the ground. The party is increasingly clear-eyed and capable of dealing with the challenges of our era and our country.

Instead of adopting the deliberately provocative, belligerent approach of her father or someone like Trump, Marine Le Pen has taken pains to portray the RN as a party of reason that has left behind its reputation for outbreaks of crude antisemitism and racism, brings together people of different opinions and can be entrusted with national power by middle-class voters:

> You will see that these [RN politicians] are profoundly reasonable and pragmatic people. We are not trying to stage any kind of revolution but to return to common sense—economic patriotism, lower taxes, saving money and putting a stop to the massive immigration which is undermining our security and our social security system.[9]

Unlike the late Jean-Marie Le Pen or some of the more unsavoury characters who have represented the RN over the years, Marine Le Pen has not been accused personally of blatant racism or antisemitism, even if her policies have been criticised as racist or Islamophobic by her critics. In her early career as a lawyer, she

POLITICAL PATRICIDE

sometimes defended undocumented migrants, and she was by all accounts an effective advocate. "[They] are human beings and they have rights, and they can't be blamed for immigration policies," she told Karine Le Marchand in a television interview when asked about this before the 2017 election. Le Marchand, who is partly of Rwandan origin, went on to ask ("as a person of mixed race, I'm sensitive to this") how Le Pen would feel if one of her daughters fell in love with a Senegalese. Le Pen said it would be up to the daughter concerned, although she would want to know whether he was smart or dumb, faithful or unfaithful and how he would treat the daughter. The answer to the next question—"What if he were Muslim?"—was more complicated and political and came in the form of more questions:

> Does he put his faith before the laws of the land, does he see himself as French first or Muslim first, will he try to influence her or impose his point of view, his values, will he treat my daughter as an equal as our culture demands, or will he try to impose his own?[10]

Still, her attitude to black and Muslim French people seemed a long way from that of her father, who notoriously complained on several occasions that the national football team was insufficiently French because it had too many players of colour. Her adoption of more moderate rhetoric on racial matters was not pre-ordained.

* * *

What was perhaps inevitable was that Marine Le Pen, like her father, would eventually become a politician. Her independent legal career never really took off, burdened as she was with the Le Pen name made notorious by her father, and in 1998 she became the FN's full-time legal adviser—there were always plenty of legal battles to be fought for a controversial party on the fringes of French politics—before pursuing her political career and taking over the party from Jean-Marie Le Pen in 2011.

The youngest of three Le Pen daughters, she was the closest to her father in childhood, and when she considered her career choices, she found that the Le Pen name that would give her instant recognition in politics had blocked other professional opportunities and recalled that in her youth it had set her apart from other children. Among her bitterest childhood memories are of the teachers, pupils and parents of pupils who singled out her and her sisters at school because of their father's politics. She recalls that one school assistant named Fatima, who was horrified by this treatment and helped protect the Le Pen girls, found the words "fascist father" written in pencil on one of her sister Marie-Caroline's schoolbooks.[11] Marine first helped her father in a Paris municipal election when she was fifteen and said of the experience that she had decided to go into his world because he would not come into hers (he took little interest in her troubles with bullying at school). "I think politics is a virus that you have inside you," an infection that can lie dormant but will someday return, she said later.[12]

Born near Paris in 1968, she had an unconventional childhood. Her father Jean-Marie was a larger-than-life figure, and friends would drop round for bouts of political argument, drinking and singing into the early hours of the morning. Her father and Pierrette,[13] her mother, sometimes went away for weeks at a time—he was a keen ocean sailor—and frequently left the children with friends, sometimes even at Christmas. Marine, who was nicknamed "Miss Happy" or "Miss Daredevil" by her mother because of her cheerfulness and recklessness on a bicycle, on a moped or on skis, said her parents had more time for each other than for their children. "They were a Bohemian couple, very in love with one another, but very much a couple—perhaps they were a couple more than they were parents," she recalled. "Our father was strong, our mother was beautiful, and when you're a child, it's kind of the ideal image."[14]

POLITICAL PATRICIDE

Marine was eight years old when a bomb attack targeting her father destroyed their Paris apartment building, an act of extreme violence that she recalls in vivid detail to this day. It was just before 4 a.m. on 2 November 1976 when the blast ripped out the staircase of 9 Villa Poirier in the 15th arrondissement and shattered twelve flats. The Le Pens suffered no serious injuries, but a neighbour's baby was flung from the fifth floor, miraculously escaping with only a broken arm after landing in a tree with the cot mattress to which he was attached. "I was eight and realised with a jolt that my father was someone well known and that people had it in for him," she wrote in her autobiography's opening chapter, "Welcome to a World without Pity". She went on: "I also realised that my father might die, that he was at risk of dying, and what was worse, at risk of dying because people wanted to kill him." She complained that her father never received any message of support after the attack from the president at the time—Valéry Giscard d'Estaing—or other government officials, and the establishment soon forgot about the attempt to assassinate one of France's political leaders.

"Since that time, I have really lived with the awareness of danger," Marine Le Pen wrote. "I know that we are confronted by people who do not hesitate and in this attack did not hesitate to endanger the lives of ten families to kill a single person."[15] The crime was never solved, and it is not known whether the bomb was indeed a political assassination attempt or perpetrated by someone jealous of Jean-Marie Le Pen's contested inheritance of a fortune from Hubert Lambert, a reclusive right-wing millionaire. Among the assets was a mansion in the hilltop gated private community of Montretout in Saint-Cloud in the well-to-do western suburbs of Paris, which the Le Pen family made their home.

In 1984, at the age of sixteen, Marine Le Pen suffered an even more traumatic emotional blow when her mother left without warning after embarking on an affair with a journalist who was writing a biography of Jean-Marie. Marine was devastated not merely by the sudden departure but by the fact that her mother never saw her or called her. It was fifteen years before they spoke. Pierrette's friend Dany Debuchy explained that Marine's mother had been married to her father for twenty-five years and then met someone who wrote her poems and told her she was beautiful. "The house was overrun with politics and Pierrette is not a political woman. For the European elections of 1984, all the campaign staff ended up at Montretout. She had no space for herself, and as for Jean-Marie, he was campaigning all across France."[16]

It got worse. Two years later, Pierrette posed in *Playboy* magazine, naked except for a maid's apron, under the headline: "Madame Le Pen does the house work, and does Monsieur's bidding".[17] The exhibition, and the accompanying interview, shocked her family (although Jean-Marie Le Pen himself initially burst out laughing when he was shown the magazine and said "She actually dared to do it!"). Pierrette's appearance in *Playboy* came in the midst of a savage, public post-separation battle between the two. He refused to return her mother's ashes. She would not give back his spare glass eye that she kept in her handbag, accusing him of cruelty and depriving her of the money she was due. The three daughters took his side and accused her of lying. Her peculiar form of revenge in *Playboy* was a response to an earlier interview he had given to the magazine in which he had said she was well provided for, but if she wanted money she could be supported by her lover or go to work, "including doing housework, there's no shame in it".[18] Marine was unable to face going to school for two weeks and later said she bitterly resented her mother for the "unbelievable psychological violence she inflicted on us". She noted angrily that an opinion poll published in the press showed that 87 per cent of the French found the whole thing funny.[19]

Marine was intensely loyal to her father but never seems to have shared his taste for antisemitism or racial provocation.

POLITICAL PATRICIDE

Sandrine Seigneure, a school friend with whom Le Pen smoked her first cigarette, told Marine's biographer Christiane Chombeau how her father's politics had made her a celebrity even for left-wing students. On one occasion, she met a north African friend of Sandrine's, and, as her father would have done, they sang the Internationale together, "and he realised that she wasn't the way people said she was". Sandrine said:

> She's an open, honest girl who does not reject her family. She is crazy about her father. She adores him. She understands what he is or isn't and if he does something stupid she tells him, but she admires him still ... As for Marine, I never heard her say "filthy Arab" or "filthy Jew" or make racist comments.[20]

As a teenager and young woman, Marine was quick to laugh and liked to party, although she once said that her reputation as *la nightclubeuse* was overdone and probably arose from encounters where partygoers would say they had seen "the daughter of Jean-Marie Le Pen" the night before and assumed it was her when it was probably one of her older sisters.[21] But when she qualified for the bar as an *avocat* in 1992, she faced discrimination and hostility because of her father's far-right politics, just as she had at school. On one occasion, she said, a delegation of young lawyers unsuccessfully petitioned the *bâtonnier*, the president of the bar, to stop her working as a public defender on the grounds that it was "shameful that the Le Pen daughter should defend immigrants". Even some FN activists were shocked by her breach of party "orthodoxy" in defending undocumented migrants. She rejected criticism from left and right and maintains that her defence of individual clients was unaffected by her political views on the "idiotic" and liberal immigration policies of the day. One extraordinary incident during her first case underlines how her father's notoriety could unexpectedly affect her professional life. In place of the senior lawyer who had taken her on in his chambers, she was representing an airline stewardess who had been raped when the judge at the hearing asked the victim a question about the alleged rapist "Mr Le Pen". The judge quickly said sorry, but people in the court, including the victim, burst out laughing at the mistake. The judge was mortified and later summoned her to his office to apologise. "I wasn't thinking of your client, I was saying to myself, 'Isn't that the daughter of Jean-Marie Le Pen?'" She later won the case, and the rapist was jailed for seven years.[22]

After only two years of legal work, during which she also helped to represent the haemophiliac victims of blood transfusions infected with HIV, Le Pen decided she wanted to be her own boss, but she could find no partner willing to work with her. In any case, the truth was that much of her work was for her father's FN, or for its members with their personal cases, so she abandoned her own ambitions as a lawyer and from 1998 became a full-time FN employee with a mandate to establish a proper legal service for the party. In the same year, she gave birth to her first child, Jehanne. Like her parents, and her sisters Yann and Marie-Caroline, Marine has not had a particularly tranquil family life, and her role as a single mother has given her a feminist outlook sometimes at odds with the patriarchal, traditional and Roman Catholic currents in the FN/RN. Her first husband from 1997 to 1999—and father of Jehanne and the twins Louis and Mathilde—was Franck Chauffroy, who ran a small company renting tables and chairs for receptions and shows. The second was Éric Iorio, an FN official and regional councillor in northern France where she too launched her career as an elected representative; they married in 2003 and divorced three years later. After that, her partner for a decade was Louis Aliot, another FN leader who went on to be elected mayor of the southern city of Perpignan. More recently, she has shared a home with her childhood friend Ingrid, and several Bengal cats, in a house near Paris where she gardens and Ingrid cooks. It has become a centre for Le Pen family reunions, including for her now reconciled mother Pierrette.

Marine Le Pen had her three children in the space of less than a year (she once took a bet with the audience at an election campaign speech in Reims that she was the only person there who could make such a claim),[23] which she says explains her sympathy for single mothers and the need for the social security system to support them and allow them to work. She has also supported the right to abortion under the 1975 Loi Veil, although she decries the social and economic pressures that push women into making that choice. Politics, she argues, is a much harder profession than people realise, especially for women. "Those who have never given a live interview with France Inter while locked in the toilet because Jehanne is screaming 'Mummy, Louis has ripped the head off my Barbie!' have no idea what it's like to be a political leader with three young children."[24]

Le Pen worked her way up the party—inevitably always accused of benefitting from parental favouritism—winning an elected post for the first time as regional councillor for the FN in what was then the Nord-Pas-de-Calais region in 1998. Four years later, when Jean-Marie Le Pen shocked France in the 2002 presidential election by qualifying for the run-off, Marine Le Pen was among those FN leaders invited on to TV news discussions to discuss the final result. At the time, there was no doubt that the right-wing Chirac would win comfortably, and he indeed triumphed with 82 per cent of the vote against Jean-Marie Le Pen's 18. The legally trained Marine Le Pen, however, made her mark in the aftermath as a forceful and colourful debater well suited to television. She said she was content with the election result, given what she saw as the two weeks of hateful unanimity in opposition to her father between the two rounds. "France has been transformed into a psychological re-education camp," she said. "The French were afraid because people made them afraid. It was said that if Jean-Marie Le Pen were elected, the rivers would stop flowing, the sun would no longer rise and it would be the start of a new ice age."[25]

From the start, she worked to detoxify not only the party's image but also the party itself, with the aim of eliminating the fear and hatred it provoked under her father and bringing the movement closer to the mainstream. The continuing clean-up campaign has become the hallmark of her leadership, but it has not been a linear process given the ideological confusion and range of views always embraced by the FN—including "fundamentalist Catholic and pagan" identities, "anti-Jewish and anti-Arab" sentiments and ideas in favour of workers and business bosses[26]—since it was founded more than fifty years ago. And as the French philosopher and writer Michel Eltchaninoff pointed out in his book *Inside the Mind of Marine Le Pen*, hers was hardly the first attempt to detoxify the party. "Even its creation in 1972 was a response to the desire to give a respectable face to the anti-Semitic, violent and neo-fascist far right of the period," he wrote. "The group Ordre nouveau (New Order) asked Jean-Marie Le Pen to act as its 'shop window' in the hope of winning votes and seats."[27]

Marine Le Pen, however, relaunched detoxification after her father's 2002 election performance and the mass protests against the far right that helped ensure his final defeat. Pushed by Louis Aliot and others, she wanted an electable party, a party of government rather than one consigned forever to the role of angry opposition.[28] She wanted a party considered "republican" and respectful of national institutions, not a chaotic mix that included skinhead thugs, disaffected Communists and antisemitic and Islamophobic aristocrats. If the FN was routinely considered simply as racist, it was little more than a useful punchbag for the left and even for centre-right politicians portraying themselves on election day—as both Chirac and Macron did—as bulwarks against right-wing extremism.

Marine has been particularly keen to turn her back on her father's antisemitism, not least because the RN has been gaining increasing support from right-wing French Jews who appreciate its outspoken opposition to Islamism and to mass Muslim immigration from north and west Africa. Jean-Marie Le Pen always maintained that his provocative comments kept the party in the public eye. After a row with Marine over an interview in the far-right weekly *Rivarol* in January 2005 in which he said the Nazi occupation of France had not been "particularly inhumane" even if there had been a few mistakes, he made a trenchant criticism of her attempt to normalise the FN. "Marine is really nice but her *dédiabolisation* strategy has brought us nothing. The media ignore us. A nice Front National is of no interest to anyone! I wasn't looking for a scandal to break the code of silence. But you've got to agree that it works!"[29] Marine Le Pen, however, rejected her father's antisemitism and his provocative tactics, and by the 2020s the party had won over many Jewish voters. After Hamas's attack on southern Israel on 7 October 2023, she joined a Paris march against antisemitism. The following year, she declared that the roundup of Jews in 1942 at the Vel d'Hiv, a Paris velodrome, for deportation and extermination was ordered by "the French authorities", something she had previously blamed on the Nazis to exonerate France.[30] Serge Klarsfeld, a well-known Nazi-hunter whose father died at Auschwitz, met her at his son's home and declared that the RN had shed its old attitudes and now supported Jews, whereas he saw the far-left LFI as "resolutely anti-Jewish". He said he would vote for the RN in the 2024 legislative elections if it was competing against LFI.[31]

Marine Le Pen has also attempted to moderate the party's longstanding Islamophobic image, but it has been much less vigorous and harder to discern than the very obvious effort to root out antisemitism. She and her colleagues seek to distinguish between those they see as ordinary Muslims and extremist Islamists and say Muslims have the right to practise their religion as long as they do not impose it on others or put Islam before the secular laws of the republic. Back in 1997, she was among the FN leaders who supported the idea of courting black French people, including those in the overseas departments and territories where the RN now performs strongly, and the millions of immigrants from north Africa who have been naturalised and need, in the party's eyes, to become "real citizens" who are "wholly French".[32]

Eltchaninoff's view is that the FN, now the RN, is "a movement that needs enemies" because its discourse presents France as "enslaved, invaded, threatened by various aggressors" and that the party has targeted first Jews and now Muslims as those convenient enemies. After toning down its antisemitism, he writes, "the FN's new, much more clearly delineated target for hostility is Islam—a line imposed by Marine Le Pen, who sees nothing but profit in it". Even the anti-Muslim rhetoric is disguised, however, and rather than condemning Islam outright she might mention such issues as school canteens or public swimming pools, "semantic signals" to remind her listeners of controversies over halal meals or gender segregation in government buildings. "With each passing year," Eltchaninoff writes, "Marine Le Pen has shown herself to be increasingly prudent in her declarations concerning Islam."[33]

In socially liberal France, neither Marine Le Pen nor the majority of the party's supporters are strongly conservative in the social sense—unlike some populist parties of the radical right abroad. That helps her detoxification campaign and allows her to claim that the party is modern and electable, including by Jewish voters. "Marine Le Pen has been able to incorporate the neo-populist shift and the defense of women, gays, and Jews, by pointing a finger at phallocratic, homophobic, and anti-Semitic Islam," wrote political analysts Camus and Lebourg. "That has served to frame the FN almost as a gay-friendly party, though not without internal tensions, and the proportion of women in the party has grown tremendously (about four militants in ten are female, and the FN respects gender parity in choosing its candidates)." Marine Le Pen's opposition to ultra-conservative Catholics in word and deed—including her moderate stance on abortion, the fact that she has lived with men outside marriage and the reality that neither she nor Bardella are practising Christians even if they adhere to what they call "Judeo-Christian" culture—was part of the process of normalisation. She even told extreme Catholics to leave the FN in 2004. "Opposition to the Catholic nationals is an easy way for the FN to differentiate itself within the far right by appearing more progressive," wrote Camus and Lebourg.[34] It helps, of course, that Marine Le Pen is a woman and would be the first female president of France if she were elected.

* * *

Following the 2002 election in which Jean-Marie Le Pen shook France by showing that the far right could one day put a president in the Élysée palace, it took nine years for Marine Le Pen to wrest leadership of the FN from her father. It was appropriate that the contest at the party's national congress in Tours in January 2011 was between the relatively moderate Marine on one side and Bruno Gollnisch on the other. He is a right-wing Catholic and close associate of her father who managed the 2002 campaign and has also become embroiled in controversy: in the 2000s, he was accused, convicted and ultimately exonerated over alleged Holocaust denial following his public comments about the gas chambers and the number of Jewish victims.[35] Gollnisch, a rare intellectual in the FN and professor of Japanese language and civilisation, bowed out with good grace after he lost the party vote with 32 per cent against Marine Le Pen's 68 per cent.[36] Marine Le Pen had already noticed that he was among those hard-line FN activists unenthusiastic about *dédiabolisation*, quoting him as saying he was unsure if the party was doing well despite the strategy she championed or because of it.[37]

In 2015, Marine Le Pen finally expelled her father from the party he had founded, led and bequeathed to her. Eliminating his disruptive influence, she believed, was the only way to make the movement acceptable to French voters and ensure its success, even if it called into question the significance of the instantly recognisable Le Pen brand. Jean-Marie Le Pen was characteristically curmudgeonly, saying "I handed over the FN in a perfect state of repair, and bang!, she shows me the door." He said he had forgiven her as his daughter but could not unreservedly support her as president of the RN. She had pluck and dynamism and was good at repartee but lacked self-confidence and was therefore dictatorial and bad at choosing political allies, he said. She needed to reflect on the history of France. "To be able to grasp the extraordinary movement that is shaking Europe and the world, she needs to feel it, to understand it, and understand her own mistakes which have made it hard for her to do that better until now." He was particularly annoyed by the detoxification strategy and the "childish error" of changing the party's name after her failure to beat Macron in the 2017 election. He even said it was perhaps lucky that she did not win, given the lack of a good team of people around her ready to take the reins of power and run the French administration, a criticism that others have also made about the RN.[38]

Emotionally, Marine Le Pen remained close to her father, although she had finally abandoned the family's Montretout mansion in 2014 after one of his Dobermanns had eviscerated her beloved Bengal cat Artémis. (A self-confessed cat-lady, she told an interviewer the young cat's death was the last time she had cried, and she had moved out to save the other cats.)[39] Politically, she was ruthless in dealing with her father and remained so until the day he died. "We broke off ties precisely because of the ambiguity of Jean-Marie Le Pen, which I saw as a political mistake that prevented us from making common cause," she said in an interview published on the day of the Paris march against antisemitism in which she participated in 2023. "It was a difficult decision and I suffered emotionally [but] when it comes to antisemitism there is no room for ambiguity."[40]

The 2017 election—in which Marine Le Pen confronted the new-kid-on-the-block Emmanuel Macron after emulating her father in knocking out the left-wing candidates and qualifying for the runoff—nearly ended her career. Although on that occasion she was always unlikely to win the presidency, she comprehensively buried any prospect of success with a dismal performance in the televised debate with Macron between the two rounds of the election. It was a prime-time train wreck for the RN, in which an agile, fluent Macron who had completely mastered the topics under discussion left Le Pen looking ill-informed and unprepared as she fumbled through her notes. She started solidly, comparing the ex-finance minister and Rothschild banker Macron, "the candidate of rampant globalisation", with herself as the "candidate of the people", while Macron retorted that she was the inheritor of a party that prospered on anger. Then it began to go off the rails for Le Pen.

First she tried unsuccessfully to satirise a previous warning from Macron about insidious rightists infiltrating society and the internet. She rolled her eyes, gestured dramatically with her arm, said in a horror-movie voice "Ooh, they're here, in the countryside, in the cities, on social media—the invaders are coming", and laughed maniacally; it was so bad it became a meme. Second, she mixed up her notes on the companies SFR and Alstom while trying to attack Macron for privatising French state assets, which gave Macron the chance to say smugly: "You are reading some notes on a matter different from the one you're talking about. It's sad for you because it shows our fellow citizens that you are badly prepared ... One of them does telephony, and the other makes turbines and other industrial products." Lastly, she was clearly confused about how currencies work even though one of her core policies at the time—later dropped—was to leave the euro and return to the French franc. Like US president Joe Biden in his disastrous television debate against Trump in 2024, which prompted his replacement by Kamala Harris as the Democratic candidate, Le Pen did not come across as someone who could be trusted to run the country.[41]

Unlike for Biden, the issue for Le Pen was not age or infirmity, even if she was older than the upstart Macron, who went on to become president the following Sunday. For her, the problem was that the debate had exposed her greatest weakness—her ignorance about the French economy and how it was intimately connected to the rest of Europe and the world. It was a severe political blow, and although in 2017 she nearly doubled her father's 2002 score in the runoff, it took a year before she recovered her confidence. Yet she persevered and learned from her mistakes. Electoral defeats were not new to Le Pen, and she had developed a thick skin to deal with the disappointments.

Le Pen was therefore much better prepared for her election debate with Macron five years later, in 2022. Now the incumbent president, Macron was unable to land the killer blows that had sealed her defeat in 2017, and he was burdened with a mixed economic record despite his promises of bold reform. He was also hampered by the memory of the recent *gilets jaunes* demonstrations and by some of the popular grievances—the high cost of living, the lack of rural infrastructure and poor services—

being emphasised at the time by Le Pen and the RN. She accused the liberal Macron of having a "very bad economic record" and "an even worse social record" as president and profited from her rival's reputation as an arrogant know-it-all. During nearly three hours of sometimes tetchy confrontation, Macron repeatedly interrupted Le Pen, questioning her facts and then sitting back looking sceptical with his arms folded. One of the journalist moderators had to tell the president: "Emmanuel Macron, let her speak!"

Le Pen, on the other hand, still looked uncomfortable when addressing economic topics, and Macron was able to exploit French fears about Russia's full-scale invasion of Ukraine two months earlier to corner her over her links to Russia—including the 2014 Russian bank loan to the RN, still being repaid at the time of the debate—and her earlier fraternisation with Vladimir Putin. Le Pen, on the defensive, accepted the need to help Ukraine in its war against the Russian invasion, but she stood by her rejection of sanctions on Russian oil and gas on which much of Europe then depended. "We can't commit hara-kiri in the hope of doing financial damage to Russia, which will no doubt sell its oil and gas to other countries anyway," she said. Subsequent events showed there was some merit to that argument, but Macron had reminded viewers of the RN's Russian connections, and Le Pen had no answer to the facts.[42] French media reports of the debate suggested that Macron had done better than Le Pen, but she had held her own and scored some points against him as well. The right-wing newspaper *Le Figaro*'s headline was "Macron dominated, but Le Pen stood firm".[43] In short, it was nothing like her debate disaster of 2017 and probably made little difference to the outcome of the election run-off, which Macron won by 58.5 per cent to her 41.5 to start his second and final term at the Élysée. The RN was closer to power than it had ever been before, and French eyes were already turning to the next presidential contest scheduled for 2027.

PART II

RISE OF THE RASSEMBLEMENT NATIONAL

5

THE ROAD TO POWER

Before 2022, it had been a foregone conclusion that Jean-Marie and Marine Le Pen would fail in their campaigns for the French presidency. In 2022, however, Marine Le Pen came tantalisingly close; opinion polls had suggested the race would be even tighter than the final outcome. In the legislative elections that followed the presidential vote, the anti-RN front prevailed again but was weaker than it had ever been. Macron lost control of the National Assembly, and the RN won a record number of seats, eighty-nine, to become the single largest opposition party. The once-great parties of left and right seemed to be on their knees. In the first round of the presidential vote, the Socialist candidate and Paris mayor Anne Hidalgo won just 1.75 per cent, and Valérie Pécresse of the Gaullist Les Républicains only 4.63 per cent. Scoring less than 5 per cent in France is the equivalent of a UK parliamentary candidate losing their deposit, because the state does not refund the campaign spending of the weakest candidates. Three of the four top candidates in the first round—Le Pen, Éric Zemmour and Jean-Luc Mélenchon—were extreme right or extreme left, with only Macron representing the republican centre.

The RN is now an entrenched political party in France. It has long performed well in the south and has taken over former Communist and Socialist strongholds in the industrial north, where Le Pen has been a regional or departmental councillor since 2004 and an elected MP in Hénin-Beaumont in the Pas-de-Calais since 2017. In the 2020s, the party has been making inroads in big cities and even in parts of western France where it was barely present in the past. Among its advantages are longevity, the consistency of its messaging and the recognisability of the name Le Pen. Macron's Renaissance party—previously La République en Marche! and simply En Marche! when it was founded in 2016 to back his first presidential campaign—seems to be fading. The centrists, Socialists and moderate Republicans who joined its effort to break the left–right mould of French politics are now drifting back to the traditional parties. And although politicians from the two established parties of left and right hope for a comeback in the final, lame-duck years of Macron's rule, the reality is that many of the French are starting to see the RN as a viable, and even an inevitable, government-in-waiting. This raises the question: what sort of government is it offering to voters?

After replacing her father, Marine Le Pen laid out her policy stall in 2012 in a book that amounted to a campaign manifesto for her first presidential bid in the elections that year. The front cover of *Pour que vive la France* (So that France may live) shows her walking on a beach, smiling, her arms outstretched, her blonde hair blowing in the breeze, with waves breaking behind her. French presidential elections are about personalities as much as politics, and most readers would have known that the Le Pens were fishermen and mariners from Brittany. But this book, unlike her early autobiography *À contre flots* (Against the tide), has little about her personal life. It is a sustained if disorganised polemic against ideological enemies and enemy ideologies—

"hypercapitalism", "ultraliberalism", "elites", "Euroglobalist thought", "giant oligopolies", the "international globalised dominant class", the euro, banks, the International Monetary Fund (IMF), the Lisbon Treaty and the incumbent president of the time Nicolas Sarkozy, "the champion of immigration". A recurring theme is that the right-wing Sarkozy and the Socialist François Hollande—who went on to win the 2012 election and become president—are simply two sides of the same globalist coin, part of an elite conspiracy to impoverish the French and undermine France. She says she wants to analyse

> the globalist project, the role played in its realisation by our political, media and financial elites, the war they are waging against the people, the Republic and the Nation, and the violence against democracy to which they are committed so they can remain in power ... Then I hope you will understand why these elites are battling for extreme economic liberalism, financialisation, free trade, a supranational Europe, and immigration—in a word for the fulfilment of the globalist project.[1]

Like all good French politicians, she wants another "revolution" (Macron's campaign book for his 2017 victory was titled simply "Revolution"), albeit a peaceful one, to help the victims of this conspiracy. "The forgotten ones for whom I'm fighting are low-wage workers, employees, civil servants, labourers, the middle class, the retired, the unemployed young and old—the France that has been scornfully dismissed as 'the France beneath' or sometimes 'the decaying France of the past'."[2]

Immigration, always the underlying issue for the French far right, is attacked not only for its economic impacts on workers and taxpayers but for its supposed deployment by the globalists as a secret weapon in their efforts to weaken French identity:

> By imposing multiculturalism, the fruit of mass immigration, on the French, they have progressively cut them off from their culture,

seeking to weaken the national consciousness that is a rampart against the construction of the "global village". The arrival of millions of immigrants in a few decades, a first in our history, of course shakes people to the core and triggers a natural unease. It weakens old solidarities and makes society more accepting of the globalist discourse. Immigration has helped the work of uprooting the French, who are supposed to rejoice in this new Benetton-style society. Racial mixing, which should be the result of an entirely private personal choice, has become institutionalised.[3]

The palpable resentment of Benetton is telling—the multiracial fashion advertisements of United Colors of Benetton in the 1990s and 2000s were so popular that people would refer to a mixed group of friends as being "like a Benetton ad"—and is a European example of the kind of anger against immigration and "political correctness" that in the US would propel Donald Trump into the White House in 2016. Like Trump, the RN portrays ordinary people as victims of an overbearing, complacent elite, but in 2012 Le Pen did not offer much in the way of clear policy solutions to their problems, other than referendums, moves to roll back "positive discrimination" in favour of minorities and cost savings from reducing immigration, eliminating regional authorities and cutting France's net contribution to the EU.

European policy is the area in which Marine Le Pen has made her biggest U-turn since taking over the party. After the Europeanist Macron defeated her the first time in 2017, she abandoned the idea, unpopular in France, of leaving the European Union and the euro, the common currency for twenty of the twenty-seven EU countries. Even so, she remained hostile to Brussels and found herself encouraged in the years that followed by the surge in nationalism and anti-EU sentiment in countries such as Hungary, Poland and Austria. The powers of Brussels have always been a fruitful campaign issue for the far right, whose opposition to the EU's capture of some sovereign powers from its member nations was vindicated in 2005 when the French voted No in a referendum on a consolidated European constitution. The result—55 per cent against, in one of the key founding countries of the union—stunned the pro-European establishment and was in retrospect a precursor of the Brexit vote in the UK eleven years later. The Netherlands also voted No in 2005, but in the end most of the provisions of the proposed constitution were adopted anyway by national parliaments in the form of the Lisbon Treaty, a process condemned to this day as a perversion of democracy by the European far right; Le Pen quoted a satirical political poem by Bertolt Brecht in which he asks if it would not be simpler "if the government simply dissolved the people and elected another".[4]

* * *

To try to understand this revolt against the centre that has pushed Le Pen into the vanguard of French politics, I went during the 2022 election campaign to an industrial region in south-central France where the extremes win large shares of the vote. First I met Cyrille Bonnefoy, the Communist mayor of La Ricamarie, a town in the industrial valley of the Ondaine river that joins the Loire near Saint-Étienne, who recalled the good old days of coal mining, heavy industry, strong trade unions and thousands of jobs that drew in waves of migrants, initially from southern and eastern Europe and later from France's former north African colonies. Since the 1980s, new migrants have come from rural Turkey and, as refugees, from the former Yugoslavia. La Ricamarie has suffered from a middle-class exodus; unemployment at over 20 per cent is more than double the national rate,[5] and most of the town's homes are either in government housing or in a poor state of repair. Bonnefoy, who works as a nurse at a local hospital, remarked wryly on the way Le Pen's supporters could now campaign easily in a town that was once a leftist stronghold. "That would not have been possible thirty years ago," he said.

When he asked me who else I wanted to meet in the town, I suggested someone with views diametrically opposed to his own, and he generously pointed me in the direction of a nearby café. There I met the owner Gilles Lermet, a right-wing nationalist who said he had had enough of forty-five years of work, enough of the apparently endless left–right cycle of French politics, enough of cars being set alight by hooligans on the street (a French urban tradition), enough of the shortage of doctors, of declining public services—and of immigration. "There's too many migrants," he said from behind the counter. "It's not that they take our jobs, because there aren't any. But we have to pay for them." (That is, workers have to pay for benefit claimants, his assumption being that French-born people contribute and immigrants receive.) When I met him, he had been running the Bar Roulette in the town's main square for the past thirty-six years, and it is here that white, working-class men in their sixties come to find solace with a glass of pastis or cheap wine. The mood is un-Parisian: in other words, it is small-town friendly, and each man when he enters typically shakes hands with the half-dozen already inside. They are nostalgic for *les trentes glorieuses*, the three decades of industrial and economic growth after the second world war. "There was work, there were the old miners, there was camaraderie," said Lermet. "It was marvellous ... 20,000 people used to go to Firminy every day to work at Creusot-Loire [the steelworks] and the other companies down the road. Now there's unemployment."[6]

But it is not only the far right that benefits from popular anger at the government's failings. The far left profits as well. Naella Amman, a third-year law student in nearby Saint-Étienne, was just as fed up as Lermet with the state of the nation when I met her in the city centre. Far from blaming migrants, however, she is a Frenchwoman of Algerian origin who was fervently supporting Mélenchon and his far-left LFI party. She was worried by the rise of Le Pen and the RN, and furious about what she saw as Macron's dictatorial decisions to deprive the French of their liberties during the Covid-19 pandemic, including the "absurd" health pass that gave access to public transport and entertainment venues for the vaccinated. She accused Macron of destroying public services, including health and education, and she supported Mélenchon's radical policies, including guaranteed jobs for all, increased taxes on the rich, the legalisation of cannabis and withdrawal from Nato.

With the important exception of immigration and the environment, it is remarkable how similar are the grievances of far-left and far-right voters in France and how similar the policy solutions proposed by their parties. Both sides are suspicious of liberal capitalism, big companies and international institutions and are relatively sympathetic to Russia. Both sides vow to protect the French from the depredations of foreign trade and to restore public services with the help of higher taxes on the rich. These similarities present a significant political opportunity for the RN, which appears to be in better shape under Le Pen and Bardella than the LFI under the ageing, cantankerous Mélenchon, who is a generation older than Le Pen and more than forty years the senior of Bardella. "We are not a little bit better than the right, or on the right of the right, we're somewhere else altogether," Le Pen told the party faithful at the RN's eighteenth congress after the 2022 elections:

> We are the defenders of the people and the defenders of all peoples. For all the peoples of the world, we call for identities to be respected. Identity is about two realities. First, identity at the deepest level is what makes us the individuals we are. But, second, identity is also what makes us identical, in a culture that has been received, adopted and transmitted, close to one another, and which makes us see all

our compatriots, whoever they are and wherever they're from, as members of the same big family.⁷

Le Pen's views on immigration and French cultural identity, however offensive they might be to leftists, liberals or Muslims of immigrant origin, are shared by millions of voters and are unlikely to lose her an election. Where she is vulnerable is on the economy: she knows that her poor grasp of the subject and the lack of qualified potential ministers around her makes investors nervous and puts off middle-class voters who might otherwise be tempted to switch their support from the parties that occupy the centre ground. Her solution is to say that she is open to the idea of forming a government of national unity rather than one composed purely of RN loyalists, given that she is likely to have drawn support from both left and right to get elected. When I asked her at a press meeting about her likely choice of finance minister for 2022, she said she had yet to choose "because I want to put in place a government of national unity and therefore the ministers in my cabinet would not necessarily all come from the Rassemblement National".⁸

She likened herself to Boris Johnson, the former British prime minister, who had succeeded as Conservative party leader in winning seats from Labour in the so-called "red wall" of northern England in a landslide election victory in 2019. "A whole section of the left voted for Mr Johnson when before they could never have voted for a candidate like him. Why? Again because these left-wing voters saw Johnson as the candidate capable of controlling globalisation who would stop them becoming the systematic losers from globalisation."⁹ Although some political commentators assume she would turn to the centre right if she needed someone from outside the RN to run the economy, she might equally be tempted by a candidate from the left who would be less inclined towards economic liberalism. "I could very well have people, for example, from the Chevènement left, in other words a sovereigntist left, a left which supports re-industrialisation, the defence of our great industries," she said in another interview, referring to Jean-Pierre Chevènement, a left-wing republican who was interior minister in the late 1990s under Socialist prime minister Lionel Jospin.[10]

The far right still looks to be on track to govern France in the years ahead. In the summer of 2024, the RN under Bardella triumphed in the European elections. In the previous election of 2019, Bardella, then still in his early twenties, had narrowly beaten Macron's centrists, but this time the RN crushed Macron's team, winning more than twice as many votes and twice as many seats in the European Parliament, where it became the largest single national party. On the night of the results, an infuriated Macron announced the dissolution of the French National Assembly and called a snap general election, apparently believing that French voters would see the error of their ways, abandon the extremes and reinforce his centrist, republican mandate to govern France. "For me, as someone who always considers that a united, strong, independent Europe is good for France, this is a situation which I cannot countenance," he said in a televised address to the nation. "I have decided to give you back the choice of our parliamentary future with a vote."

It turned out to be a disastrous miscalculation for which many of his supporters have yet to forgive him. In the first round of voting three weeks later, the far right took the largest share of the vote, followed by a hastily assembled left-wing coalition called the Nouveau Front Populaire (the New Popular Front). Only by means of the awkward construction for the election's second round of yet another "republican front"—in which rival parties of left and right withdraw their own candidates as needed and support the one most likely to defeat the RN—was the RN relegated to the third biggest group in the assembly, behind the Nouveau Front Populaire and Macron's centrists. Bardella, who had been convinced that he would be prime minister, was bitterly disappointed by the success of the political manoeuvres against him, but the RN still emerged with a record number of seats as the largest single political party in the assembly. "The tide is rising. This time it did not rise high enough, but it continues to rise," Marine Le Pen said afterwards on TF1. "Our victory is only delayed."[11]

The snap legislative elections returned the National Assembly to the centre stage of French politics, which had been dominated for decades by near-monarchical presidents, from Charles de Gaulle to François Mitterrand to Emmanuel Macron. Because the election had produced a hung parliament, by 2025 Macron was a lame duck in domestic politics who could neither impose his own programme nor even "cohabit" with a strong government under a prime minister of a different political persuasion; he focused inevitably on foreign policy and international crises such as the war in Ukraine, the catastrophe in Gaza and the global turmoil triggered by Trump's second term in the White House.

When the 577 elected deputies gathered on the red benches of the chamber under the motto *Liberté, Egalité, Fraternité* to elect the president of the assembly in the summer of 2024, it by chance fell to the RN to provide both the day's acting assembly president (eighty-one-year-old José Gonzalez, as the oldest deputy) and the monitor of the voting urn (twenty-two-year-old Flavien Termet, as the youngest). Gonzalez irritated the left in his opening speech by alluding to his nationalist loyalties and tearily recalling his origins in what was then French Algeria, and many leftists in turn snubbed Termet by refusing to join other deputies in shaking his hand after casting their votes. By the end of the day, Macron's supporters had engineered the re-election of his centrist candidate Yaël Braun-Pivet as assembly president. The ostracising of Le Pen's party was completed the next day when it failed to win any parliamentary posts—a flagrant breach,

Le Pen said, of rules and customs given that the RN is the largest single party in the assembly.[12]

She soon had her revenge. Michel Barnier, the centre-right political veteran and the EU's former Brexit negotiator chosen by Macron as prime minister, was toppled in December 2024 after only three months in the job, making him the shortest-lived premier of the Fifth Republic. Le Pen joined forces with the left in the assembly to oust him in a no-confidence vote over the budget. "Mr Prime Minister," she scolded him in the chamber,

> you chose to prolong the technocratic winter into which France has been plunged since the election of Emmanuel Macron in 2017: detachment from democratic expectations, top-down decisions, a refusal to consult or compromise or respect the will of the French people on migration, crime, tax and the EU—despite the unambiguous election results of June and July.[13]

A few days later, a combative Le Pen described the ostracising of the RN by the mainstream parties—the *cordon sanitaire* and *diabolisation*—as a poison for democracy designed to stifle the views of the largest number of French voters, but said the strategy was no longer effective now that the RN held the balance of power in the National Assembly. "That is the big lesson of the past few weeks," she told the right-wing magazine *Valeurs Actuelles*. "Nothing can be done without us." The advantage of the *cordon sanitaire*, she went on, was that "[w]e owe nothing to anyone. Nothing to the banks, nothing to the big retailers, nothing to this or that corporation or consultancy. Nothing. We are free."[14]

6

WHO IS JORDAN BARDELLA?

Who is Jordan Bardella? For someone who cares so much about identity—specifically, French identity—the president of the RN had an awkward start to life. One problem was his first name, Jordan. Unlike the typical French Christian names derived from the long list of Catholic saints—Christophe, say, or Jean-Marie—being called Jordan is like "being branded, it's the identity card of my social class, tells the story of my origins and indicates to which decade I belong," he writes in his best-selling political autobiography *Ce que je cherche* (What I'm looking for).

In a book remarkable for how little it tells us about his personal life, Bardella dedicates a page and a half to the vexed question of his name and lower middle-class origins. He recalls with a hint of bitterness that his far-right rival Éric Zemmour, during the 2022 presidential election campaign, had labelled the names Jordan and Kévin as symptoms of the *défrancisation* (deFrenchification) of the French working class and had said they should not be permitted. Bardella went on to note that the most common names given in his home *département* of Seine-Saint-Denis in 2022 were Mohamed, Adam and Ibrahim, but these were more like religious markers, while Jordan and Kévin were social markers:

> Sure, giving a first name from the calendar of saints shows respect for the fatherland, but it would be simplistic to make it a barometer of Frenchness. To spell it out, the first name Jordan is of Hebrew origin, inspired by the River Jordan which crosses Israel and the country of Jordan and where Jesus was baptised. It appears in France in the Middle Ages with the crusades, then disappears into oblivion to reappear at the start of the 1990s.[1]

In politics, however, his name seems to do him no harm at all. On the contrary, being sneered at by the French establishment and Paris intellectuals such as Zemmour helps him identify with ordinary French citizens who feel similarly despised. RN rallies are routinely punctuated by enthusiastic shouts of "Marine!" and "Jordan!", but I have never heard anyone cry "Emmanuel!" at one of Macron's meetings. (They shout "Macron!" instead.)

A more serious issue for Bardella's identity as a politician who rails against immigration is that he is, as his Italian surname suggests, of immigrant origin. His mother Luisa Bertelli's parents emigrated from the working-class Turin suburb of Nichelino to Saint-Denis north of Paris in 1963, as France's fast-growing post-war economy sucked in labourers first from southern Europe and then from north Africa. His father is Olivier Bardella, whose own Italian father Guerino did construction work for the French company Bouygues in Egypt and Iraq, helped build the Hassan II mosque in Casablanca and loved Morocco so much that he retired there; Olivier's mother—Jordan's paternal grandmother Réjane—was of mixed north African Berber and Alsatian origins.

Jordan Bardella himself was born in 1995, by which time the migrants coming to Saint-Denis were largely from north and west Africa, and his parents divorced only two years after he was

WHO IS JORDAN BARDELLA?

born. An only child, he lived most of the week with his mother in a housing estate in Saint-Denis, spending weekends and Wednesday evenings (Wednesdays are typically a half-day at primary schools in France) with his father Olivier. He also had annual holidays in Morocco with his father, who went into business with his best friend and ran a drinks vending machine company there. To justify the apparent contradiction between his opposition to migration and his own foreign roots, Bardella seeks to distinguish between those he says assimilated into French society, particularly the Europeans, to the extent of adopting French names and habits, and the more recent arrivals, particularly Muslims, who he says did not. He recalls his mother reminiscing fondly about Saint-Denis in the 1960s and 1970s when everyone muddled along together, exchanged meals and favours and did not care much about religion. "At the heart of the housing estates, we are all the sons and daughters of immigrants," he writes. "The 'born and bred' French person is rare, and there are plenty of other Europeans from Italy, Spain, Poland or Serbia." However,

> the big surge of populations from elsewhere, the cowardice of the state when it comes to law and order, the rejection of authority and national pride, and of course the establishment of an aggressive Islam are the ingredients for an explosive cocktail and a situation that is out of control. Many new arrivals have come to the estates and turned their backs on assimilation. Drug-dealing is rife and has overwhelmed the good relations of old between families.[2]

Since the start of his political career at the age of sixteen, Bardella has played on his upbringing as a white boy in one of the toughest suburbs of France. He makes no secret of the fact that he was scarred by the frequent violence and shootings around the Gabriel-Péri estate where he lived during the week with his mother, and by successive Islamist terror attacks that culminated in the November 2015 killings of 130 people at the

Bataclan theatre, the Stade de France in his home neighbourhood of Saint-Denis and cafés and restaurants in the city. But when journalists investigated his background as he rose to prominence in the RN, they discovered his youth was not quite as tough as he makes out.[3] He was privately educated, and his father gave him a Smart car and regular holidays abroad. But his experiences in Saint-Denis, his white and partly working-class profile and his energy and confidence on the campaign trail suited him perfectly to the RN and Marine Le Pen, who quickly identified him as a rising star and as her likely successor.

When Le Pen named him to lead the party's European Parliament election campaign of 2019, he was only twenty-three, and the result suggested she had made the right decision: as we have seen, the RN came out ahead of every other French party, narrowly beating Macron's centrists despite an enormous effort by the president and his supporters to avert an RN triumph. It was during this campaign that Bardella really came to be noticed nationally and even abroad. With a colleague, I met him for the first time and interviewed him for the *Financial Times* in a café on the edge of Paris and found him to be confident and coherent despite his lack of political experience. He talked about the RN's plan to team up with other "sovereigntist"—that is, nationalist and Eurosceptic—parties from Brexit Britain, Italy and eastern Europe to challenge the EU's powers over national frontiers, migration and international trade. The 2016 Brexit referendum and the rise of nationalist politicians in remaining EU member states such as Italy, he said, showed a possible path to power in France for the RN. "I think we will come to power in the years ahead," Bardella said. "There is this last step to reach—that of credibility—and we're doing it." He went on: "When people want to emancipate themselves from an elite, an oligarchy ... they can. It is possible. I think there's a wind of hope, of expectation, that's blowing everywhere through Europe."[4] He was right. The

WHO IS JORDAN BARDELLA?

RN won that election, and five years later it triumphed again over its French rivals in the 2024 European elections, edging out Germany's centre-right Christian Democratic Union/Christian Social Union as the largest single party in the European Parliament. It was this victory that prompted Macron's politically disastrous decision to call an immediate legislative election in France three weeks later.

Under Jean-Marie Le Pen and even under his daughter Marine, the FN and its renamed successor the RN struggled for years to shake off a reputation as a redoubt for elderly, white, working-class racists. Especially in Paris and among students and the young, the party was definitely not cool. Bardella helped to change that. He is young, and he is handsome. The left-wing French magazine *Le Nouvel Obs* warned in mid-2024 that he was a worrying phenomenon because he appeared to many to be "a new man, clean and smooth". It continued:

> Although he's been a member of the party since the age of seventeen and is a pure RN apparatchik, he has the ability to knock down the last barriers against *lepénisme*. Thanks to his talents as a communicator—attacks and criticisms just slide off him—he represents the ultimate normalisation of the extreme right. And he excites a collective passion which, in a democracy, can lead to the highest offices of state.[5]

Bardella, in short, is charismatic. The man who used to spend hours blasting away at imagined enemies in the video game Call of Duty is now exceptionally big on the social media platforms popular with the young—at the time of writing, he has 2 million followers on TikTok and more than 800,000 on Instagram. He boasts of being impeccably dressed. He takes selfies with supporters ("Jordan Bardella is just Mr Selfie," grumbled Éric Dupond-Moretti, who was justice minister at the time, "because he's devoid of content"). When Bardella appears at rallies, there are usually a few enthusiastic fans shouting "I love you, Jordan!" or calling drunkenly for him to take his shirt off. Young men admire his physique and wonder how often he goes to the gym. Yet he also manages to appeal to the elderly and the middle-aged.

It is too early to say how he might use this charisma if he becomes prime minister or even president in the future—the RN has so far run only a few towns and villages and has been excluded from national government—but he has laid down some markers on his likely policy priorities. He has professed undying loyalty and admiration for his mentor Marine Le Pen and faithfully follows the party lines on curbing mass migration, constraining Brussels and protecting domestic industries and farmers. Yet he is more emphatic than she about the benefits of opening the RN's door to the traditional republic right—which, like the old left, has been in drastic decline in recent years—in order to take the lead of a broad, right-wing alliance to govern France. "My battle is to normalise the RN," he said in one of his interviews in *Le Journal du Dimanche*, which changed hands in 2021 and has since become a standard-bearer for the far right under the new ownership of Vincent Bolloré:

> I want all the French who share our ideas, or at least share our love for the fatherland, to be able to express it openly, without fearing they will be caricatured or suffer from preconceptions. My aim is to make it unremarkable to support a political party which believes in France's destiny and the genius of its people.[6]

One reason for this approach is purely tactical. In the French system of elections over two rounds, voters typically make a positive choice in the first round (voting for their favoured candidate) and a negative choice in the second round (eliminating the candidate they hate or fear the most by voting for the other). This is the basis of the *cordon sanitaire* or *front républicain* of unlikely political bedfellows in the second and final rounds of French elections, and it is why Jean-Marie Le Pen (once) and his daughter Marine (twice) were beaten each time they made it through to the second round of a presidential vote. "In France, to win a presidential election, you have to convince not only those who support us but also those who disagree with us and did not vote for us in the first round," Bardella said in the same 2024 Sunday newspaper interview. "France values reason: in a two-round election, the most extreme candidate is always eliminated. That's why I believe firmly in this strategy [of normalisation] and reject any form of backtracking or provocation. Normalisation is a step towards maturity for a political movement."[7]

There is also a strategic logic behind the idea of co-opting the weakened centre-right in the current political climate. Valérie Pécresse, the 2022 presidential candidate for Les Républicains (the latest incarnation of the movement dating back to Charles de Gaulle), did so badly in that election that she failed to make the 5 per cent threshold that would have qualified her for state financing of her campaign; she had to beg her supporters for money afterwards to repay the debt. And Éric Ciotti, who led the party for the following two years, was already so far to the right that he threw in his lot with Marine Le Pen in an alliance for the snap general election called by Macron in 2024 and ended up providing sixteen of the 142 MPs in her far-right bloc in the National Assembly. He was deposed by Pécresse and other Les Républicains leaders as a traitor amid farcical scenes at party headquarters in Paris.[8] Future victories for the RN, wrote Bardella in his 2024 book, "will come as a result of unity in the patriotic camp, and from an ability to bring together the orphans of a more Orleanist [constitutionalist-republican] right wing. I want to go further in this direction and hold out my hand. France can't wait!"[9]

Bardella's attempt to seem less scary to voters at the same time as continuing to champion hard-line policies—to organise a revolution without disturbing people—inevitably leads to some confusion. "To change everything without destroying anything, that's our project," he sometimes says (as he did in Budapest in 2024). Or, as he put it rather awkwardly in another interview:

> My vision rests on the "three Rs"—a Reasonable and Reassuring Rupture. France is at a turning point on matters of the economy, migration, security and industry. The choices made today will determine if France remains a power capable of meeting the challenges of the twenty-first century or if it plunges further into decline.[10]

There are signs that Bardella's co-opting of former centre-right voters and politicians is working, building as it does on Marine Le Pen's detoxification project. Plenty of French people who once supported Nicolas Sarkozy (the former president whose hard-line law-and-order policies prompted accusations from the left that he was flirting with right-wing extremism) now say they back the RN because Sarkozy failed to deliver on his promises. At one of Bardella's book-signing events in Sète on the Mediterranean coast, one of these ex-Sarkozyites, an entrepreneur called Cédric who has a Turkish partner and some Moroccan employees, told a reporter from *Le Monde* that the days of the outrageous positions of Jean-Marie Le Pen were over. "Today, the RN *is* the right," he said.[11]

Victory is never certain, however, even when you think it is—as Bardella discovered to his cost in the second round of the snap National Assembly elections in 2024. One challenge for Bardella and Le Pen when they advertise the RN as a responsible party of a government—a party that no longer explicitly promotes racism or panders to extremists—is that the outspoken and sometimes outrageous positions it took in the past are exactly what attracts it to many of its original supporters. But the party's strong performance in the first round suggested that was not the immediate cause of the first major setback of Bardella's short but spec-

WHO IS JORDAN BARDELLA?

tacular political career; his undoing was the traditional French *front républicain* against the RN. He and the party were so confident of victory that their manifesto, headlined simply "Bardella—prime minister" and scattered with photos of him looking prime ministerial, quoted him as saying: "As soon as I am named prime minister, I will bring concrete solutions to the concerns of our fellow citizens about the quality of life, law and order and immigration."

By his own account, he was shocked by the success of the barrage against him, which he called "an unnatural coalition of divergent beliefs and contradictory programmes, the monstrous alliance between Mr Mélenchon and Mr Macron!"[12] The Nouveau Front Populaire, the left-wing alliance whose largest component was Mélenchon's far-left LFI, won the most seats, followed by Macron's diminished group of centrist MPs. The concluding round of the election, in which millions of French citizens of left, right and centre voted tactically for whichever candidate in their constituency had the best chance of beating the RN, had relegated Bardella's party to third place. Afterwards, there was a round of soul-searching in the RN about the failure, while the media criticised the party's inadequate vetting of its candidates for the 577 seats and its failure to weed out some inexperienced or unsavoury characters in the few days available following Macron's dissolution of the assembly; one of them tried to explain that she was not racist because "my ophthalmologist is Jewish, and my dentist is a Muslim".[13] Bardella was contrite about the defeat, although he insisted that the poor candidates were just "four or five black sheep".[14]

Although the RN did not do as well as it hoped, the party had dominated in many constituencies, and RN leaders hoped the 2024 vote would prove to be one of the last hurrahs for a successful anti-extremist *front républicain*—a strategy that had also been applied against the far right in Austria and Germany but is looking increasingly fragile in those countries too. That was certainly Bardella's view when he voiced his disappointment at not winning an absolute majority in the National Assembly that year. "Emptied of all ideological substance and all sincerity, reduced to a tired alliance of opposites, the 'republican front' is weakened but has still done its job," he wrote. "But I bet that this is its last success."[15]

* * *

Another reason for Bardella and Le Pen not to be too downcast by the election result was that they could remain firmly in opposition to the government of the day—untainted by the awkward compromises of power—until the next presidential election. While Macron has cycled through prime ministers who were given the unpleasant job of trying to appease voters and politicians of left and right without further undermining France's already parlous public finances, RN leaders could stand above the fray, mocking Macron's inability to govern and criticising inevitable but unpopular decisions to raise taxes and cut spending. If the RN had won outright, the inexperienced Bardella would instead have had nearly three years at the prime minister's official residence in the Hôtel Matignon during which he might have messed up and would certainly have discovered that his uncosted manifesto was big on ideas but short on the specifics of how to pay for them; among other goodies, it offered to abolish income tax for anyone under thirty, to reduce VAT on all energy and raise guaranteed prices for farmers.

Bardella's failure to become prime minister in the summer of 2024 does not mean he has forfeited that position in the future, and he is still assumed to be the person that Marine Le Pen would appoint to Matignon if she were elected president in 2027 or sooner. And if Marine Le Pen is definitively excluded from elected office by her disqualification after the European Parliament

WHO IS JORDAN BARDELLA?

embezzlement conviction, he is likely to be the party's candidate for president—the so-called "Plan B" for the RN. He is certainly ambitious and increasingly confident. When I asked him in May 2025 whether he was not too young to be president or prime minister (he would be just thirty-one at the time of the scheduled 2027 elections), Bardella replied:

> No, no, I do not feel too young. I am doing at twenty-nine, nearly thirty, what people normally do in their lives when they are fifty. So I have grown up very fast on the political battlefield, and at the age I am now I am president of a party with 130,000 members, which has dozens of employees and 170 MPs and MEPs—so unfortunately I don't feel young in my mind and I am crushed by responsibilities. And in politics, age is not necessarily a measure of effectiveness.[16]

Bardella's declarations of loyalty and respect for his mentor—it was she, after all, who gave him his chance in politics soon after she met him and identified his talent—have been frequent, effusive and sometimes treacly. "Of course, I myself have spared no effort," he wrote in his autobiography, "and our duo has enabled us to convince more French people. But the record of success is primarily hers, the result of her choices, of her determination, of her pugnacity, of her instinct, and her desire to leave the opposition benches for the levers of power." Marine, he says, "arouses interest and passion. She's a rock star." Irritated by media speculation about their relationship—he quotes one journalist as asking whether his use of the polite *vous* form rather than *tu* when addressing her is a sign of respect or of distance—Bardella insists that their mutual trust is "absolute". He goes on: "She knows my doubts and my fears, and I share with her all of my hesitations. Nothing and nobody will succeed in sowing the slightest discord. I know the extent of my debt to her. The rest is just chatter."[17]

A few cracks have nevertheless appeared in the façade of unity between Bardella and his mentor (who at first called him a "lion cub" and then upgraded him to "lion"), mainly over personnel but also over policy. Bardella has pushed vigorously for a moderate political line to court voters from the centre right and on the economic front is considered slightly more open than Le Pen to free-market policies, including lower taxes and more reward for work—a shift of emphasis away from the protective welfare-statism entrenched in the party's thinking since Le Pen took over from her father. Bardella told me he rejected the simplistic notion of "the people versus the elite" for this reason.[18] Some analysts therefore distinguish between the northern—more statist, more Le Pen—and southern—more liberal, more Bardella—tendencies in the party and point to Bardella's removal of the northern RN barons Steeve Briois and Bruno Bilde from the party's executive in 2022 as a sign of such ideological tensions. Personal animosity was probably a bigger factor (Briois had once called Bardella *un petit con*—a little wanker—to his face), and their removal was also a sign that Bardella wanted to flex his muscles as nominal party leader given that they were both long-time confidants of Marine Le Pen. In 2014, Briois was elected mayor of Hénin-Beaumont in Pas-de-Calais where Le Pen was subsequently elected as an MP, while his personal partner Bilde has served as MP in a neighbouring constituency.

Bardella, in common with other right-wing leaders, bitterly resents what Trump would call the "mainstream media", particularly their attempts to unearth details of his private life (including his not-so-grim childhood in the suburbs and his distant Berber immigrant origins), their portrayal of him as robotic and ambitious, and their suggestions that he plotted to overthrow Marine Le Pen as the RN's boss. One of the few personal details to appear in his own book—perhaps because it was already public knowledge—was his three-year relationship with Le Pen's niece Nolwenn.[19] When a television interviewer asked Marion Maréchal, another niece and also a right-wing politician, in 2023 about her

WHO IS JORDAN BARDELLA?

views on Bardella and compared him and her to Ken and Barbie, she retorted jokingly: "Well, he's already going out with my cousin, so it would be a bit weird if I start to go there." Another girlfriend, back in 2017, was said to be Kerridwen Chatillon, daughter of far-right figure and financier Frédéric Chatillon.[20]

Bardella has sometimes been prickly even with friendly media, not least Fayard, the publisher of his book. When new chief executive Lise Boëll—a publisher who had previously handled successful books by right-wing politicians Éric Zemmour and Philippe de Villiers and brought Bardella's project with her to the company—tried to persuade Bardella to put in more details about his girlfriends to scotch the rumours that he was gay, Bardella objected and ended up being edited by Catholic writer Nicolas Diat, a confidant of right-wing media mogul and Fayard owner Vincent Bolloré. Jean-François Achilli, a journalist for state-owned broadcaster Radio France, was meanwhile fired for having agreed to help Bardella with the text of the book; Bardella said no formal agreement was reached and questioned whether Achilli would have been punished if he had been discussing a book with Gabriel Attal, a young, charismatic centrist who was one of Macron's prime ministers.[21]

Bardella does not say much about his personal feelings, except to say that he is a solitary sort of person, but he does reveal his early excitement with politics and his astonishment at finding himself a prominent public figure so early in his career. The boy who enjoyed evenings at home playing video games is now hobnobbing with presidents and prime ministers in palaces and parliaments. He is defensive about his lack of "real life" experience—he quit his geography studies at Sciences Po university to work full time for the RN—but insists he is "profoundly ordinary" and points out that his peer Gabriel Attal and the much older Michel Barnier have also dedicated their lives to politics.[22] "I confess that politics engulfs my whole existence, buries it, makes me dizzy and drunk, crushes me like a massive wave," he writes. "Politics is a gift, a priesthood, and you adopt it as you would a religion."[23]

Bardella's lack of experience and his apparent lack of political vision—his economic and foreign policy positions seem to lack substance and depth despite his repeated references to de Gaulle—might make it absurd for him to be considered a possible prime minister of France, let alone the president of a nation at the heart of the EU that is also a nuclear power and permanent member of the UN Security Council. To which the obvious response is: that is what many Americans used to think about Donald Trump. On reading Bardella's book and hearing him speak, Raphaël Llorca, an expert on the far right at the Jean Jaurès Foundation thinktank, concluded that behind the scenes there was "no trace of what really matters in politics, no vision, no value system, no project". Unlike Trump, however, Bardella eschewed outrageous comments and espoused "insignificance" as part of the RN's strategy of appearing "inoffensive" and disarming critics who regard it as dangerous, wrote Llorca.[24] Several of his former party colleagues also see him as someone devoid of political vision who gets away with saying what people want to hear. "He is a very good politician, but that doesn't make you a statesman," said Florian Philippot, a senior FN figure who left to launch his own fringe party on the far right.[25]

For the left, for liberals and for the entire French establishment, the fear is not that Bardella is going to be insignificant but that the man who as a child worshipped superheroes and wanted to be "Superman, James Bond and in the front line with the GIGN [an elite unit of the Gendarmerie]" might eventually have ambitions to be a French strongman.[26] In the past, he has had friends and associates from the "identitarian", extremist fringes of the French far right, and he is so obsessed by cleanliness and tidiness that even Marine Le Pen called him "manic" on the subject.[27] His rhetoric is still a long way from Trump's messianic claims, but then Trump has been around for nearly fifty years longer, and even Bardella has started likening the "violent" experiences of his youth to the endless labours of Sisyphus.[28]

Perhaps the most worrying moments are when he suggests the primacy of personality over policy, which comes perilously close to a modern-day philosophy of "L'État, c'est moi." In one 2024 interview, he stated that he wanted to correct falsehoods and misunderstandings and said:

> I also think the French nowadays are looking more for strong personalities than for fixed ideas. It is essential to bring together the working classes, the middle classes and even part of the elites around common sense values: work, the reward of merit, defence of identity and the reestablishment of authority. I'm convinced that these principles could unite a majority of the French.[29]

There can be no doubt that he is one of the "strong personalities" he has in mind.

7

NORTH AND SOUTH

Southern stronghold

He sounds almost like a French Donald Trump. "I am counting on you for the battles to come because the most beautiful battles and the most beautiful victories are ahead of us," Bardella tells a crowd of admirers in the main square of the southern French town of Beaucaire. At the age of just twenty-nine, he is Marine Le Pen's *dauphin* and the head of her RN. He has already won two European elections for the party, the first when he was only twenty-three years old. The RN, once on the fringe of French politics, is now the biggest single national political party in both the French National Assembly and the European Parliament.[1]

But this flying visit to Beaucaire between Avignon and Nîmes on a freezing winter Saturday in late 2024 is not so much a campaign stop as a victory lap. Bardella is here on friendly turf— Beaucaire's inhabitants, many of them resentful about migrant workers arriving from north Africa and Latin America, have elected an FN/RN mayor for the past decade—to open a political office next to the town hall for his number two Julien Sanchez, and to hawk his own best-selling autobiography to eager fans.

Hundreds of them have come from across the region and will soon be queuing in the cold for as long as four hours outside a tapas bar-turned-bookstall to buy a copy, have him sign it and take a selfie with the man they call "a star".

"Two years ago, there were six of us at the National Assembly, but now we are 143 with our friends from Éric Ciotti [the former centre-right leader who defected to the RN]," Bardella says from a makeshift platform in the square. "The situation of the country, whether we're talking about the economy, crime or immigration, demands a complete break, a change of government, an alternative that we represent," he says. "The moments we will live through in the coming months will be vital for our country. I'm counting on you. Marine Le Pen is counting on you." The crowd chants "Marine! Marine!" and, for the second time that morning, lustily sings the Marseillaise, the French national anthem.

A dozen left-wing protesters have been trying to interrupt the speeches from the back of the square. "No more fork-tongued fascists!" they chant. "Le Pen and Bardella are evil incarnate." But the group is so forlorn that Bardella mocks them when they stop singing and draws guffaws from his supporters. It is hard to overemphasise how much of a shift this represents in the balance of power in French politics since a decade earlier. Even a few years ago, the party's candidates struggled to campaign in the streets because they were pursued by crowds of protesters who hurled abuse and called them fascists and racists. When it came to the biggest protests—such as the marches in 2002 by hundreds of thousands across the country against Jean-Marie Le Pen when he shocked France by qualifying for the second round of the presidential election—the left would be joined by the traditional republican right.

Now the boot is on the other foot, as some of the Beaucaire protesters ruefully accept. "We are in the process of losing," says fifty-one-year-old Benoît, a commercial diver by profession, who supports Mélenchon's far-left LFI party and has come from Arles, a half-hour drive away, to join the protest against Bardella and the RN. "They want a society based on hate, on lies," says Benoît, explaining that he and his fellow demonstrators want to present an alternative to the "fascist discourse". The FN, he recalls, was founded in 1972 by Jean-Marie Le Pen and a former member of the Waffen SS.² "Today is the anniversary of the liberation of Strasbourg [23 November 1944 during the second world war]. It's ironic." The problem for the left, Benoît acknowledges, is that while Bardella is "a little Nazi" and the party is founded on "racism and xenophobia", there is also a "real discourse of populism that works": it is true that the left and the right disagree profoundly on immigration, but the RN's nationalist, anti-globalisation economic policies "could come from a left-wing party".

At the same time, the French media, which has long been dominated by the liberal-left Paris establishment, especially in broadcasting, is increasingly falling under the sway of the right and the extreme right, Benoît observes; it was indeed the right-wing Roman Catholic billionaire Vincent Bolloré's Fayard publishing house, part of Hachette Books, that published Bardella's autobiography *Ce que je cherche*, complete with a striking and rather sinister black-and-white cover photograph that to liberals makes him look like a strongman-in-waiting. In another sign of the left's desperation, trade unionists persuaded the company responsible for advertising in French railway stations to ban publicity posters for the book on the grounds that it would breach a requirement for political neutrality, prompting a lawsuit from the publisher and mockery from Bardella.³ In Beaucaire, he generates more laughs by pointing out how odd it is for the left to try to ban a book. "We are fighting against all these attempts at censorship," he said. "But the more they try to forbid us from speaking, the more the French who might perhaps be interested in what we have to offer will try to read us, to listen to us and to join us."

Like Democrats in Trump's America, or Labour and Lib Dem supporters in Britain, French leftists and centrists are baffled by the appeal of the populism and nationalism voiced so emphatically by the far right. "People seem to be caught in the headlights,"[4] says Benoît in Beaucaire. "People are being persuaded to vote against their interests." That suggestion that far-right voters are dupes is exactly the kind of comment that irritated Trump supporters in the US and infuriates those who have queued up in their hundreds for Bardella's book. When asked about their political views, the common views that emerge from the crowd are that crime is worsening; immigration is out of control; and economic mismanagement and arrogance at the top have made life harder for workers and—these days—for the middle class as well. (Crime statistics are a contested area of study, but in France as in many other western countries, crime, including murder, has mostly declined from the start of this century, although there has been a rising number of burglaries and other crimes not involving violence since 2020.)[5]

Everyone who speaks out rejects the implication that they must be racist because they support Le Pen and Bardella. "Nowadays when you walk in the street, you're worried about being attacked with a knife," says a sixty-one-year-old woman, who works as a carer for the elderly. "We have no money and they keep taxing us. We've always voted for them [the FN/RN], except the time we voted for Sarko because he said he would use the Kärcher—and he didn't." (This is a reference to the controversial phrase used by right-wing republican Nicolas Sarkozy, who later became president, to describe how he would "clean up" the Paris suburbs where many immigrants live—Kärcher is the brand name of a high-pressure water machine for cleaning the streets.) "There are too many foreigners," she adds, and hints at the dangers of "Islamisation" by remarking that she has Muslim women friends who previously went unveiled but now cover themselves when they go out. Her beret-wearing husband is equally grumpy about the state of France. "We're not racists," he says, "we've always been a welcoming country," but "I'm a hunter and used to have a [Citroën] 2CV, and I would leave my rifle in there with the car unlocked", which would be impossible today.

The diversity of the Bardella fans on the streets of Beaucaire shows how the RN has widened its support, which used to be based on two pillars: the industrial working class in northern France and the nostalgic *pieds noirs*, the former colonists from Algeria, in the south. RN supporters now include middle-class professionals and civil servants, as well as voters from parts of central and western France that were once solidly left, liberal or centre-right republican, all of whom would previously have balked at the idea of voting for a Le Pen.

"I think it's our last chance to be saved given the situation that France is in," says Delphine Deville, a forty-year-old accountant, bemoaning the level of crime and the state of the country's hospitals and schools. "In the middle class we are too rich to be called poor, and too poor to be rich. Immigration is completely out of control." She says she is not particularly loyal to the RN as a party and approves of Bardella's idea of bringing other right-wing parties, including Les Républicains from which the southern French politician Éric Ciotti defected in 2024, into a broad governing alliance. "It hurts to constantly be called 'extreme-right'," says Michel Cecchinato, a nurse and long-time RN supporter. "We are not anti-system, we're not racist. The name of the RN still makes people afraid ... The image sticks for years." He is one of the many sympathisers who credits Marine Le Pen with distancing the party from the hard-line rhetoric of her father and thinks she and Bardella make a great political duo. "I've read the [Bardella] book. It's good to read someone who's honest," he says. "What's important is where he comes from—a working-class environment—and he hasn't done the *grandes écoles* [the elitist higher-education institutions where many French politicians and leading business figures were trained]." His wife Sylvie, an entrepreneur who runs a business providing carers for the elderly, says she has changed her views over the years and come around to the RN in part because of disillusionment with the way successive governments have treated small businesses—not least by burdening them with costly social security obligations towards their employees, which she calls "over-the-top social policy".

Yves Fages, a retired civil servant who also became a major among the volunteer firefighting and first aid force (the *sapeurs-pompiers*), is scathing about the French authorities' failure to control immigration. "I've saved more Moroccans than I've saved French people," he claims. "It's not about immigration or racism, it's about living together, and when that's not possible you have to take decisions: you mustn't give French nationality to all and sundry." Fages, now seventy-one, insists he is concerned about passports and not about people's colour, given that those from French overseas territories such as Tahiti, Martinique and Guadeloupe "are like us, they are French". He ticks all the boxes of RN policies, from economic nationalism (the Germans lost the second world war but went on to destroy French industry, and the Americans were on the winning side but have done the same), to contempt for the French left in general and the Socialist Party in particular (the *pompiers*, he says, are attacked by the left on the grounds that they wear uniforms). If anything, he is more radical than Bardella and Le Pen, who have been promoting their party as one of responsible, republican values. "We must start again from zero," says Fages, "and get rid of the [existing] laws."

Perhaps the biggest difference between the RN voters today and those of twenty years ago is the lack of embarrassment about being associated with a party the French establishment has long dismissed as fascist, racist and beyond the pale. At least in Beaucaire, it is the left that is on the defensive nowadays. "No one would admit to voting RN previously," says Fages. "Now it's the majority. France is going to have a radical change of direction."[6]

* * *

Beaucaire, a historic town of 16,000 inhabitants and the first in the Gard *département* to have an RN mayor, is a good place to measure the changing mood in France—and you get a taste for what is happening as soon as you cross the Rhône and enter the town from Tarascon on the other side. There is nothing unusual about the typically florid sign at the end of the bridge announcing Beaucaire's attractions for tourists: "Town of Art and History, Town of Water and Stone", it says. But the sign at the town limits just in front is blunter, declaring in dark blue capital letters: "Here We Defend: Our Identity; Our Flag; Our Traditions; Our Agriculture." That is a message from the RN, printed in the party colours.

For more than a century, waves of migrants have come to work in the fields, orchards and factories of the south of France, and many stayed. Spaniards and Italians have been coming since the nineteenth century. A childhood friend of Julien Sanchez—Sanchez is an RN vice-president who was mayor of Beaucaire from 2014 to 2024 before becoming an MEP—notes with amusement that both Sanchez (Spanish) and Bardella (Italian) have surnames that betray their immigrant origins from southern Europe. The same man, who disagrees strongly with Sanchez's politics ("Populism will never work in France," he says), also recalls that Sanchez's parents were Communists and that their son used to be seen with them in the town square hawking copies of *L'Humanité*, the Communist Party newspaper.

From the 1960s, it was the turn of the Moroccans, Algerians and Tunisians from France's former north African colonies. More recently, there has been a surge of immigrants from Latin American countries such as Peru and Ecuador, many of them with Spanish passports that give them the right to live and work in France, sent from Spain by employment agencies to provide local farmers with badly needed seasonal fruit-pickers for apricots, peaches and cherries. The families of north African origin wandering through the Christmas market of Tarascon and watching the seasonal parade—including donkeys, white horses from the Camargue and three camels for the magi—are chatting in Arabic, the women dressed in abayas and headscarves. It is common to hear both Spanish and Arabic on the streets of Beaucaire and Tarascon, and some of the older Latin Americans struggle in French.

Poverty, high unemployment and white working-class resentment of immigrants: Beaucaire has all the characteristics of a town that previously voted for radical leftists and Communists but now votes for the far right. The local economy could hardly be more different from that of Paris or Lyon. A glass of decent Rhône valley red wine in the Bar Le Saint Jean over the river in Tarascon, where the television screens on Friday night are showing France beating Argentina at rugby at the Stade de France, costs just €1.50. That is a third of the price it would cost in the capital. Nelson Chaudon, the new, thirty-two-year-old mayor of Beaucaire, who replaced Sanchez when he became an MEP, says outside Bardella's book launch that the RN in a decade has turned around a town that was abandoned and "seen as the dustbin of the *département*"; among recent or planned investments are a new potato-processing plant, a logistics centre for supermarket chain Lidl covering the south of France and a hotel from one of the big hotel groups. Immigrants, he says, are welcome if they integrate into the local way of life. "I want people to adapt to our customs." It is not a problem if they want to live in Beaucaire, "but they have to behave like *beaucairois*".

NORTH AND SOUTH

Sanchez, meanwhile, acknowledges his Communist parentage and says his mother and father are now proud of the political career he has pursued for the FN/RN since the age of sixteen, although his ambiguity suggests they might still be sympathetic to the left. "They voted for Chirac against [Jean-Marie] Le Pen in 2002," says Sanchez. "They wouldn't vote now for Macron against [Marine] Le Pen." He says he doubled the number of municipal policemen to twenty-six after he was elected, cracking down on rooftop burglaries and other crimes he says were linked to immigrants, and so gained the support of older, established former migrants of Moroccan origin who were happy to see the town made safe for their children. "Today lots of professions—medicine and so on—are moving towards us. Public services are collapsing, and people are attached to these services. Lots of people on the left are turning towards us." He agrees that parties like the RN are on the rise not just in France but across Europe. Why? "Because the problem of immigration is not being dealt with—so the populist movements are rising everywhere—even in Germany. Who would have thought that would happen?"

* * *

Northern breakthrough

It is not just in Jean-Marie Le Pen's old strongholds in the south of France—where white exiles from north Africa long resented de Gaulle and the French establishment for abandoning French Algeria in 1962—that support for the RN has been surging in recent years. In the industrial towns of northern France, *les trente glorieuses*—the three post-war decades of economic growth—once fuelled support for the French Communist Party as well as for de Gaulle, but that heady period of confidence and rising prosperity eventually gave way to stagnation and de-industrialisation in an era of globalised manufacturing dominated by China.

The second bastion of the FN and its successor the RN thus became the industrial north, where people whose parents had been staunch Communists often voted for the far right at the other end of the political spectrum, concluding that the Le Pens understood their fears about unemployment and immigrants taking their jobs better than the left, while at the same time the Le Pens echoed the comfortingly protectionist, anti-capitalist economic messages of the Communists and Socialists. Marine Le Pen made her political career in the Pas-de-Calais in the north and has repeatedly been re-elected member of parliament for the constituency that includes her base in Hénin-Beaumont near Lens, in a former coal-mining area stricken by high unemployment.

It took many years of political campaigning by Marine Le Pen and her colleagues, and the failures of successive centre-right, Socialist and centrist governments, for the RN to break out of these two political strongholds in the south and the north. But the elections in 2022 and 2024 showed that the far right is now a nationwide political force, winning votes even among former Socialists and Macron loyalists in western France and among former centre-right Republicans in the countryside.

This rightward lurch in France's fractious politics was visible in rural Normandy on a cold, drizzly day in December 2024 at an RN rally addressed by Marine Le Pen and Jordan Bardella at a rural estate near Étrépagny, south-east of Rouen.[7] "I voted for Mélenchon [the far-left leader] in 2022 in the first round, and in the second round I voted for Le Pen," said Jade, a twenty-nine-year-old teaching assistant from Bayeux, struggling to make herself heard above the music and the shouting of slogans in the conference hall. She was referring to the presidential election of that year in which Macron defeated Le Pen in the run-off. In some countries, it might seem strange for a voter to switch so easily between the far left and the far right, but populist, nationalist parties at the extreme ends of the spectrum have much in common with each other in Europe. In France, the main point of difference is on the place of immigrants in society: the RN wants them out, while Mélenchon's LFI wants them in, and indeed wins many of its votes from Muslims because it is seen as more supportive of immigrants and more sympathetic on the Palestinian question.[8]

What does unite the far left and the far right in France is their loathing of Macron and the Paris elite and a simmering anger about the state of the economy. "Now I would vote for Le Pen in the first round [of a presidential election]," says Jade, who stands out from the crowd with her flame-red hair and two studs in her lower lip. "I absolutely don't want to vote for Macron, and I no longer recognise myself in the left." She does not agree wholeheartedly with Le Pen's hostility to immigration, but she resents being insulted and accused of "fascism" by leftists for supporting the RN, whereas she does not recall being insulted by the far right when she was openly on the left. I ask her why so many French voters hate Macron so much. "He's dumped us in the shit for five years," she replies. "The rich keep getting richer and the poor are dumped." So will Marine Le Pen be elected in 2027 if she is allowed to stand? "I hope so," says Jade.

Her older sister Laetitia, a forty-two-year-old butcher in Bayeux, is with her and eager to see Le Pen in person and hear her speak for the first time. She too emphasises the economic problems that have pushed the French middle class into the arms of the RN. "Perhaps they will give a thought to those of us who work," says Laetitia, complaining about high electricity bills and the huge social security charges that French employees and the self-employed pay to maintain the country's generous welfare state. (Employers typically pay the equivalent of around 40 per cent of an employee's gross salary in such charges.) "There comes a moment when you can't cope."

One of the local RN MPs—who replaced a centre-right *député* in the snap election rashly called by Macron in the summer of

2024—is also in the crowd at Étrépagny waiting for Le Pen and Bardella. Asked why the RN is having so much success politically, Robert Le Bourgeois, who used to work in the region for the Société Générale bank, points to the rage against the establishment that is a feature of politics in so many countries today, not least in France. "There is anger," he says. "There's an extraordinary defiance against the political class, which has been the same for the past forty years. You see that with [Michel] Barnier and [François] Bayrou [appointed by Macron successively as prime ministers after the election]. They are representative of the problem." In places such as Étrépagny in rural France, there is the added obstacle of a lack of local services in remote areas. "The real problem is isolation, transport, mobility," says Le Bourgeois. He is not wrong: it was impossible for me to come to this meeting by public transport because even if I had made it by train from Paris to Gisors, there was only one bus a day on Sundays from Gisors to Étrépagny.

The hall where Le Pen is about to speak is packed with 1,500 noisy supporters, and a further 1,000 are in a spill-over room behind. Loudspeakers are blasting out an eclectic mix of Latin American and western music, including numbers from Boney M. and Mika. The crowd waves French flags, and every now and then there are chants of "Marine!" and "Jordan!" in front of the stage where the backdrop declares *Jusqu'à la Victoire!* (Forward to victory). But so many people have driven in from the surrounding countryside that hundreds will not get in at all. It's another show of strength from France's strongest political party. Cars are parked on the muddy edges of the sugar beet fields all the way from the venue into the town, and latecomers are having to walk the final kilometre to reach the rally. "Well, at least it's a big success," says one. "That bodes well for 2027."

The mood outside the elegant 1890 town hall in the middle of Étrépagny is much less upbeat. A few dozen trade unionists, feminists and other leftists have gathered over hot soup, coffee and reggae to protest against the far right. Frédéric Barreau, who works for an industrial company and is the sixty-two-year-old local secretary of the Communist-affiliated CGT union, says the aim is to "denounce the pretence" that the RN supports workers. "People are not necessarily racist, but they are angry with the government," he says. "The FN, the RN profits from that" while failing to acknowledge that immigrant workers are actually big taxpayers, says Barreau, who compares the success of Le Pen in France to the rise of Trump in the US, Jair Bolsonaro in Brazil and Giorgia Meloni in Italy.

Standing next to Barreau at the protest is Charles Caigneaux, a forty-four-year-old organic vegetable farmer who says he supports Mélenchon's far-left LFI party and Attac (the Association pour la Taxation des Transactions financières et pour l'Action Citoyenne), an anti-capitalist activist group named after its original aim of taxing foreign exchange transactions. Casually quoting Hegel and Gramsci—Britons such as myself are easily startled by the intellectualism of French voters—Caigneaux has experienced at first hand the recent surge in support for the RN, telling me how shocked he was to meet someone who complained about poverty and concluded that "we must vote for the RN" to find a solution.

At this point, some RN supporters drive past on their way to the rally, revving their engines mockingly at the handful of left-wing demonstrators gathered in the square. "We won't be tempted by the provocation," says Barreau mildly. "The CGT has been around for 130 years and for all that time we've fought against the ideas of the FN/RN."

* * *

Back at the rally, Marine Le Pen launches into her speech and says she has decided to focus on France's beleaguered farmers, particularly the sugar beet farmers threatened by imports from

Latin America following the conclusion in 2024 of a free trade deal between the EU and Mercosur. To visitors shocked by the bleakness of the northern French countryside here—huge beet fields unleavened by hedgerows or trees, and an occasional industrial processing plant to transform the piles of root vegetables into sugar, not to mention the farmers' relentless lobbying for the use of dangerous pesticides banned by the EU—her flowery praise for the bucolic merits of the country's mythical peasant farmers seems absurd. "They are the day-to-day and moment-to-moment creators and builders, the sculptors of our countryside, the leading artisans of the grandeur and beauty of France," she says of the farmers. But the speech goes down well enough. She quotes de Gaulle on the importance of self-sufficiency in food, condemns Brussels and its onerous regulations, and lambasts free trade.

There is not even a nod to two glaring contradictions in the rhetoric: first, the illogicality of supporting international trade protectionism and simultaneously demanding that France's already substantial agricultural exports to the rest of the world be further increased; and second, the non-sequitur of condemning the financial impact on French farmers of the EU's safety rules for food and agriculture, and then condemning the health impact on French consumers of the supposed *absence* of those same rules applying to imported food. (In any case, the EU is remarkably strict about the standards of the food it imports.)

Next it is the turn of Bardella, now officially the leader of Le Pen's party and its rising star. He's wearing a black polo-neck and remarks how hot it is in the crowded hall, prompting ribald cries from a couple of women admirers urging him to take his shirt off. He ploughs ahead regardless, paying tribute to the beauty of Normandy's "fertile plains", woodlands and village bell towers, condemning Mercosur, demanding that French schoolchildren should eat French food, defending the RN's decision to topple Barnier with a vote of no confidence and attacking the establishment media for failing to respect the RN. "For the first time in decades, they are facing a party that does what it says, and says what it does," he says. "Given the pretensions of a 'government of national interest' which in reality will just be an alliance of those who have sunk France, we are the real alternative." He ends with a characteristic condemnation of mass immigration from the Muslim world ("Since we're told that Syrian refugees here are rejoicing at the downfall of Bashar al-Assad and his dictatorship, then let's begin their return to Syria, and let Europe close the door after their departure"), a nod to France's Christian culture and an expression of delight at the reopening of the fire-damaged Notre-Dame cathedral in Paris.

All this is fairly routine. But I am struck by his explanation of the RN's tactics and how it has succeeded in reaching disaffected voters who feel abandoned by other political parties. He shows a Trump-like understanding of how much ordinary people resent the metropolitan elites they see as out-of-touch in our increasingly polarised societies. One reason for the meeting, Bardella says, is because the RN wants to run a "permanent campaign". Other parties, he says,

> call on the French people when they need them, that is to say at the time of elections, then they disappear. We want to be different, and we are the only party in France to maintain this closeness to the French, to explain what we are doing, and most important of all, to meet you and listen to you.

Such on-the-ground campaigning could be the aim of any sensible politician, but the bitterness about how the RN has been disdained over the years is palpable. Now that the RN is powerful, the establishment is suddenly taking an interest in the party's voters, says Bardella (much as Remainers in the UK or Democrats in the US have been forced to ask what has been driving support for Brexit and for Trump).

"All year, you count for nothing, you are just a mass of angry people who vote 'the wrong way'. You are 'extremists'," says Bardella:

> They barely think to ask about the real reasons for the RN vote. Oh, sure, they do it sometimes by calling for help from "sociologists", that is to say these great specialists, often from the left or the extreme left, who come to "observe" the areas where people vote RN, just as one observes insects or visits a zoo.

One such place observed very closely over the years by those interested in far-right voters is Hénin-Beaumont in the Pas-de-Calais, the electoral fiefdom of Marine Le Pen.

8

FAR-RIGHT FIEFDOM

The gritty post-industrial town of Hénin-Beaumont in the Pas-de-Calais in northern France is not the place where most people would expect to find a street named after Brigitte Bardot, the Saint-Tropez film star and global sex symbol of the 1950s and 1960s. In fact, despite her fame and perhaps because of her racial views, there were no such Bardot roads at all in France until 2023, when a right-wing mayor on the Côte d'Azur named a boulevard after her in Villeneuve-Loubet. And here, two years later and at the other end of France, was Marine Le Pen in a Hénin-Beaumont car park on a sunny International Women's Day in March 2025, unveiling the blue-and-white sign marking the new Avenue Brigitte Bardot before a few dozen curious onlookers.

The ceremony makes sense when you know that Bardot's friendship with the Le Pens goes back to the 1960s and that the star of *And God Created Woman* (and the first woman to become the official face of the French revolutionary icon Marianne) endeared herself to the family both with her love of animals and with her vociferously right-wing, anti-Muslim, anti-immigrant views. If there was anyone who clearly symbolised French womanhood, Marine Le Pen said, it was Brigitte Bardot. Asked by a French journalist whether that could still be true given Bardot's repeated court convictions for hate speech,[1] Le Pen said it was. "Yes, in spite of those convictions, she is a free woman who speaks freely … a symbol of femininity, of liberties, of freedom of speech. A woman of character and commitment. She abandoned her career, her beautiful career, to devote herself to the defence of animals." Marine Le Pen's father Jean-Marie had felt the same, recalling how Bardot had joined him in visiting hospitalised French soldiers wounded in Algeria, and how the American film star Marilyn Monroe was "a mere waitress" when compared to the inimitable "BB". "She likes animals, and is nostalgic for a clean France," wrote Jean-Marie Le Pen.[2] Bardot went sailing with the Le Pens in the 1990s, and it was through them that she met her fourth husband, an FN member and businessman called Bernard d'Ormale, who represented his eighty-eight-year-old wife at the ceremonies in Hénin-Beaumont that day.[3]

The town is badly in need of some film-star glamour. Its 28,000 inhabitants live in the heart of the old northern French coal belt, where mining and metalworking industries once provided tens of thousands of jobs and sucked in migrants from Poland, Morocco and elsewhere to help do the hard labour. Many locals will tell you their grandparents and parents worked in the factories and mines, whose giant slag heaps still dominate the otherwise unremarkable terrain, but the last shaft closed at Oignies to the north in 1990, and unemployment of nearly 20 per cent is more than double the national rate.[4] After the second world war, there were 220,000 miners in the region, falling to 20,000 in 1976 and none today.[5] Manufacturers shut down, moved out or cut their workforces, including the US luggage-maker Samsonite, whose ex-employees became local heroes for flying across the Atlantic to seek compensation from one-time owner Bain Capital, a private equity group, and to protest against its founder Mitt Romney, who was then a US presidential candidate.[6]

The collapse of the local economy, and popular disenchantment with entrenched and sometimes corrupt municipal councils dominated for decades by Socialists and Communists, turned out to be a political opportunity for the FN/RN. Pushed by northern RN leaders such as the local power couple Steeve Briois and Bruno Bilde, the party diligently exploited that opportunity as it extended its influence. Advised by Briois and Bilde, Marine Le Pen made Hénin-Beaumont her political base as an MP. She does not live there—her home is on the outskirts of Paris—but she has visited the town several times a year and at the time of writing has been MP since 2017. Her popularity in Hénin-Beaumont is unquestioned; in the snap legislative vote called by Macron in mid-2024, she was re-elected in a landslide victory in her constituency, winning outright in the first round with more than 58 per cent of the vote. Marine Le Pen is good at getting on with ordinary people.

Le Pen is at ease with the working-class voters of the Pas-de-Calais she says have been affected by poverty, unemployment, the exodus of big employers and the associated ills of alcoholism, obesity and pupils dropping out of school.[7] "So she applies herself to being seen regularly with the working-class poor, to mixing with them, not hesitating to embrace them, touch them, laugh, drink with them, in short to generate sympathy in a world where politicians are seen as distant from the concerns of 'ordinary' people," wrote the French political sociologist Sylvain Crépon in his analysis of her transformation of her father's party. "Despite being a Parisian apparatchik and daughter of a millionaire, she manages to appear as the spokesperson for the 'simple' people of the north. That's a serious snub to the left, Socialist or Communist, which has largely moulded the working-class identity of the region by defending low-paid labourers."[8] Crépon concluded back in 2012 that Le Pen in the Pas-de-Calais had won what he called "both social and political legitimacy from a population that had largely been on the side of the left". The evidence from the elections thereafter is incontrovertible. Despite the other parties of left, right and centre ganging up on Le Pen's RN in the second round of those snap National Assembly elections of 2024, she and her party's MPs ended up holding ten of the twelve constituencies in the Pas-de-Calais.[9]

One of the reasons for the RN's success in the region is Steeve Briois, the party veteran who has been mayor of Hénin-Beaumont since 2014. Burly and affable, he is credited even by political rivals with bringing order to the administration and finances of a town shaken by the corruption and mismanagement of one of his Socialist predecessors: Gérard Dalongeville was accused of embezzlement, cronyism and fraud, convicted in 2013 and sentenced to four years in prison and a €50,000 fine and declared ineligible to vote or stand for election for five years. Unlike some towns won in previous years by the FN/RN in southern France—and where FN/RN-led local councils were accused of adopting the same dubious practices as the right-wing administrations they had replaced—Hénin-Beaumont has become a showcase for the FN/RN and Le Pen. This is exactly what she predicted a few months before Briois was first elected mayor, when she foresaw victories for the party in the 2014 municipal elections, which meant "we will at last be able to show the French what we are capable of doing".[10] Elected mayors and municipal governments are important and visible in French daily life and French politics—much more so than in the UK, for example—and their influence has been enhanced in times of economic crisis by the decline of other, previously dominant institutions such as the Catholic church and the trade unions.

Marine Tondelier, national leader of the French Green party Les Écologistes and a resident and opposition municipal councillor of Hénin-Beaumont, has bitterly opposed Briois and the RN but accepts that he campaigned for twenty years for his victory and thinks the political barons of the left in the region were naive to think that a far-right administration in the town would be so bad that it would "vaccinate" voters against making the same mistake again. Tondelier has been the object of personal attacks from the far right on social media ("waterfalls of hate") and sidelined and shouted down at the municipal council—she says RN politicians are deliberately divisive and emulate Trump and Brexit supporters in caricaturing their enemies as bitter, hateful and bent on revenge—but she also says the left's contempt for the far right has been counterproductive. "The struggle against the Front National has too often moved from the field of politics into the realm of demonology," she wrote in her book on the rise of the FN in Hénin-Beaumont, a previously obscure town that is now frequently scrutinised by journalists and researchers for clues about the rise of the French far right and the decline of the left:

> Some try to fight this party as though they were organising a collective exorcism. The damage caused by this strategy, which is humiliating for voters and ineffective for those trying to convince them, is today well known. The phenomenon is international. But habits die hard, and it seems to me that the far right still has some good times ahead.[11]

Even residents who were once suspicious of the far right say they admire what Briois has done. "He's pretty good," says Denis, one of the amiable customers of the Café de la Paix in the town centre, a bearded ex-Communist who sports Led Zeppelin and Che Guevara patches on his faded jacket. "He organises the small things that need doing, fixing the drains, repairing the roads and the pavements in the housing estates—which the old people really appreciate." Other mayors, says Denis, would typically do nothing more than build a sports hall and have it named after themselves. The achievements of Le Pen, Briois and their colleagues in taking over hard-left towns and transforming them into bastions of the hard right should not be underestimated. In retrospect, such victories may look inevitable, but they were far from obvious at the start and took many years to achieve. Briois later recalled making a speech when he was just fifteen at his school in 1988. Hénin-Beaumont, he said, "was an impregnable citadel. It was as though the far left wanted to do something in [famously posh] Neuilly-sur-Seine! It was character-building."[12] Along with other voters in the town, Denis has now turned decisively to the right and appreciates Marine Le Pen and the RN's focus on the cost of living.

As a young man, Briois saw immigration as a fundamental problem for France and was shocked when he heard people of his own generation speaking Arabic between themselves at school and wearing T-shirts with an image of Algeria. "I was beside myself," he said, believing that such immigrants were guilty of anti-French racism and unwilling to assimilate in the same way that his family's and his friends' Spanish and Polish forebears had done.[13] Even before he became mayor, he tussled with a liberal Catholic abbot who used a new version of the Lord's prayer on the occasion of a local religious festival in honour of Saint Barbara, patron saint of miners. The prayer calls for solidarity, justice and the protection of the sick, the exploited and the persecuted, and Briois denounced what he called a "bolshie, third world, political" mass and continued the feud with the church after he became mayor, according to Tondelier.[14] As mayor, he also pushed through a "No migrants in my community" vote in the Hénin-Beaumont council, symbolically refusing to house any refugees even though there were no plans for the town to host any.[15] He removed European flags in keeping with the party's nationalistic, anti-EU policies. Yet he also heeded Bilde's advice that the FN should not talk only about immigration and crime but also about economic and social issues and has approvingly quoted the nineteenth- and early twentieth-century Socialist politician Jean Jaurès and moved his bust into his own office.

Briois also authorised the building of a big €1-million mosque that will be able to hold 1,000 men and 500 women worshippers from Hénin-Beaumont's large population of Muslims. I come across Boufeldja Lasri, the Ennasr mosque president, as I arrive at the site to look at the construction work next to the existing mosque. It is the holy month of Ramadan, and as we talk in his office, people wander in and out to drop off packets of dates, bottles of water and other food and drink for the breaking of the fast in the evening. Lasri, who emigrated from Algeria at the age of eight in 1958—his father worked as a foundryman—insists there has never been a problem with the FN/RN local council, although he and his colleagues regret the way the mood in France has turned against Muslims and immigrants as a result of Islamist extremist violence, including the 9/11 attacks in the US in 2001 and the Paris terror attacks of 2015:

> The FN since Marine Le Pen and her father split, the policy has changed, although at the base there are still people who are racist, there are good and there are bad, but in all political parties there are people who are racist, and there are good and bad. The interest of the FN [now the RN] is to defend France, and they don't want clandestine immigration.

Lasri, who is now in his seventies, says nostalgically that when he first lived here there was much less consciousness of a person's racial or religious identity. "In my youth there was love, friendship and mutual help. I never heard anyone say, 'This one is Polish, or Italian, or Muslim.'" Nor did Muslim women wear veils or head scarves, he says, until the arrival of new generations—"les barbus" (the bearded ones), supporters of the

Muslim Brotherhood. Meanwhile, the existing French population began to resent the newcomers as jobs were automated, disappeared or became less secure. "It changed because there was less work. The French began to bridle at immigration. [Yet now] we are not immigrants, we are French by origin," says Lasri, who dismisses as "shameful" the newer, undocumented migrants—he singles out black Africans—who come without work permits and camp in Calais before trying to cross the Channel to England. "I think as long as the immigration problem is not resolved there will always be difficulties between countries and between immigrants and the French. The problem is they no longer need foreign labour—except specialised labour ... In the old days we did the roads, the mines, the factories." Whether Briois and the RN like it or not, Hénin-Beaumont today is a town with an established Muslim minority, and intermarriage means an increasing number of people have mixed or dual identities. "At first there were only about 1 per cent Muslims," says Lasri. "Now in Hénin-Beaumont—I'm not talking about the surrounding area—it's 10 to 15 per cent of the 28,000 population." The list of twenty-five births in the latest municipal magazine tells the story: the names are a mixture of Arab Muslim, French Christian, Italian, Polish and Flemish.

Back on the streets of Hénin-Beaumont after the brief Bardot ceremony, Briois escorts the cat-loving Le Pen to the town's shelter and feeding point for stray cats, which proudly displays billboards with huge blow-ups of Bardot's handwritten letters of appreciation to the mayor. He is also telling her in public how Hénin-Beaumont can indeed be a fine example of how the RN can run a town and restore its previously "disastrous" finances. Everyone repairs to the town theatre for refreshments, followed by a play about Bardot, where Bardot's husband d'Ormale tells me about his wife's animal welfare work and how much the couple hate the uncaring attitude of the European Commission and its German president, "What's her name? I call her Madame von Papen." (Franz von Papen was the German politician blamed for bringing Hitler to power; the EU Commission president is Ursula von der Leyen. Neither Bardot nor d'Ormale could be described as politically correct.)

Hénin-Beaumont, previously an obscure, medium-sized town in northern France, has become almost a household name because of its associations with Marine Le Pen, but its very ordinariness makes it a good place to try to understand the woes of "peripheral" France outside the big cities. A woman in Lille told Haydée Sabéran, the local correspondent for the newspaper *Libération* and author of a book on Hénin-Beaumont, that she avoided e-commerce dealings in the town because she thought there was "a one-in-two chance that I would come across a fascist". So "stereotypes stick to the town's inhabitants," Sabéran wrote in 2014. "Hénin-Beaumont, however, is neither a ghetto, nor a place of cut-throats nor overrun with skinheads ... Hénin-Beaumont is a small town of 27,000, where people feel abandoned. A town of ordinary people."[16]

The residents confirm it. "There is absolutely nothing to do here," says a waitress in the O'Classico burger bar (French eateries frequently add this Irish-looking O' prefix to their names because it sounds like *au* or *aux* meaning "at"). "Everyone goes to the Auchan mall." The allure of this vast nearby hypermarket and retail park, among the largest in Europe, helps to explain why there are so few businesses open in the old town centre; even on weekdays, the mall is packed with shoppers. So Hénin-Beaumont, first deprived of its mines, foundries and factories and then of its shops, is a forlorn French example of a small town struggling to thrive in a globalised world—the perfect base, in other words, for the populist, nationalist right and local MP Marine Le Pen. It still has a railway station, but when I first arrived on a Saturday the place seemed empty. A slight, elderly man crossing the road saw me looking at the shuttered, red-brick Le Rail Route hotel. "It's been closed for years," he said kindly, and pointed at some other buildings I took to be former cafés. "That one's closed too, and that one." Serge, it turned out, was a seventy-year-old former railway controller who retired for health reasons fifteen years ago. I told him why I was in town and asked if he was interested in politics. Not really, he replied. So what do you do? I asked. "I'm interested in prophecies and the apocalypse. It's coming."

Given the events of the previous few days—the re-elected Donald Trump had just overtly sided with Russia in its war against Ukraine—I thought he might have a point even if he obviously spent too much of his retirement following conspiracy theories on the internet. That's worrying, I said. Not really, he said again. "It will probably start with global dictatorships and be powered by AI." He's still on the money, I thought, but took my leave after the conversation spiralled into a debate about the Torah, Revelations, Greek etymology and the Chinese surveillance state. I walked off down the Avenue Victor Hugo and the Rue Jean-Jacques Rousseau, heading towards the brand-new Avenue Brigitte Bardot.

PART III

THE NEW FRANCE

9

THE BIG ISSUES

IMMIGRATION AND THE ECONOMY

Submersion or assimilation?

"From the moment you feel that you are being submerged, that you no longer recognise your own country, no longer recognise the ways of life or culture—from that instant, there is a sense of rejection. And that's where we are today." It was a powerful anti-immigration argument long familiar to followers of extreme-right politicians, and the words were carefully chosen. Yet the politically loaded French word *submersion* used about migration did not on this occasion come from the mouth of Marine Le Pen or Jordan Bardella or any other far-right leader. It was used very deliberately by François Bayrou—the epitome of centrism in French politics—who was prime minister at the time. The French left was aghast at what it saw as his adoption of racist and xenophobic tropes about migrants. It was January 2025, and Bayrou had just visited the French Indian Ocean territory of Mayotte after a cyclone and seen the grim living conditions of thousands of migrants who have moved to the islands from the neighbouring Comoros and elsewhere in search of a better life.

Bayrou, however, was not thinking only about the slums of Mayotte. He was sending a very clear signal to the French far right and the country at large that he took the challenge of immigration seriously—and deserved at least the tacit support of the far right in the National Assembly to stay in power at the head of his fragile government. He wanted to avoid the fate of his predecessor Michel Barnier, toppled only the previous month by a vote of no confidence backed by the far right as well as the far left. He did not escape for long, however, and was himself ousted in September 2025 and replaced by Sébastien Lecornu, another Macron supporter, who himself resigned in October less than a month into the job because he was unable to find parliamentary support for his new government or its 2026 budget plans though he was immediately reappointed. In his "submersion" television interview, Bayrou said that foreigners made a positive contribution to French society "up to a certain point", in the sense that one foreign family moving to a village in the hills of the Pyrenees or the Cévennes prompted generosity and mutual assistance, but "if thirty families move in, the village feels under threat". Two days later, far from backing down when criticised by the left, Bayrou stood by what he had said and told the National Assembly that it was not his words that were shocking but "the realities". He called for help in repairing what he said was the broken system for integrating migrants into French society.[1]

Immigration and the fear of the "submersion" of the native population by waves of Arab, African, and often Muslim, foreigners have been the most prominent weapon in the armoury of the FN, now the RN, for decades. France, a former colonial power that once controlled large parts of north and west Africa, already has the largest population of Muslims in western Europe (and also the largest population of Jews, many also originally from Algeria, Tunisia and Morocco). Since the turn of the century, the far right has been the most full-throated of the political movements in France in its calls for harsh restrictions on immigration and for the withdrawal of welfare support for foreign nationals, although every Islamist terror attack and violent crime involving a killer of immigrant origin has prompted widespread soul-searching about the openness of France—which once prided itself as *la terre d'asile* (the land of asylum)—to refugees and migrants.

The attacks in Paris on 13 November 2015, the deadliest ever in peacetime France, were particularly traumatic. Armed men with explosive suicide vests killed 130 people and injured more than 400 in three rounds of attacks on a Friday evening. Most of the victims were music fans at an Eagles of Death Metal concert at the Bataclan theatre; the others were slain at restaurants and cafés in the 10th and 11th arrondissements in the north of the city, and just outside the Stade de France, where a football match was being played. The massacre was planned by the extremist jihadi group Islamic State based in Syria, but most of the perpetrators were radicalised French and Belgian nationals of Algerian or Moroccan descent (two were Iraqi), which fuelled resentment in western Europe against Arab Muslim migrants and their descendants. The nine directly involved in the attacks were all killed, but a tenth man, the French citizen Salah Abdeslam, who apparently failed to blow up his explosive vest, was caught four months later and sentenced in Paris in 2022 to life imprisonment without parole. The French government declared a three-month state of emergency after the attacks and said some of the attackers had exploited the chaos of the Syrian civil war and the large numbers of refugees arriving from the Mediterranean to slip into western Europe without the knowledge of the authorities. Islamist terror continues to afflict France to this day and has inevitably led to a further hardening of official and public attitudes to immigration and asylum. In a particularly gruesome attack five years after Bataclan, an eighteen-year-old Muslim Chechen refugee from Russia, who had just been granted a ten-year permit to stay in France, beheaded the forty-seven-year-old teacher Samuel Paty outside his school in Conflans-Sainte-Honorine near Paris. He had been inspired by social media posts complaining about the use of cartoons of the prophet Mohammed in a class on freedom of speech.[2]

Bayrou's use of the word submersion, although much commented on in France at the time, was simply the culmination of a long process of normalisation for the hard-line views and policies of the far right about immigration and crime. Nicolas Sarkozy, the right-wing interior minister who went on to serve as president from 2007 to 2012, was lauded by the right and vilified by the left for declaring back in 2005 that he would "Kärcher-clean" a housing estate (see Chapter 7). He was talking to the family of Sidi-Ahmed Hammache, an eleven-year-old boy killed by stray bullets in La Courneuve, then a notoriously violent district of Seine-Saint-Denis north of Paris, densely populated by immigrants.[3] In 2019, Édouard Philippe, then President Emmanuel Macron's prime minister, echoed the UK's Brexiters in declaring: "We want to take back control of our migration policy." The French government's announcement of a drive to crack down on undocumented migrants and set quotas for foreign workers was a transparent attempt to win back the initiative on migration from the far right. Macron himself had already said that France's humanitarian approach to immigration was "too lax".[4]

In 2021, I went with a colleague to interview Gérald Darmanin, Macron's interior minister, at his office in the Place Beauvau in central Paris. Darmanin, former mayor of the northern town of Tourcoing, had a reputation as a hardliner and protégé of Sarkozy and was seen as Macron's not-so-secret weapon against the RN. He did not disappoint. "There are between 60 and 70 per cent of French people who say there is too much immigration in France, that Islam is not compatible with the republic, that there could be civil war," he told us. "When 47 per cent of people are ready to vote for [Marine Le Pen], you have two solutions. Either you call them idiots—but if you insult people, it's rare they end up voting for you—or you try to understand what they're going through." Darmanin, remarkably, had previously suggested he was even tougher than Le Pen, telling her in a television debate that she was "softer than we could ever be". The danger for France, he said in our interview, was "to let Madame Le Pen become president of the republic because we've [the government] shown ourselves to be too naive, too soft".

Unlike Le Pen, Darmanin is of north African immigrant origin, so he can dismiss accusations of Islamophobia and be an advertisement for France's faltering attempts to assimilate migrants from its former colonies. His grandfather was a Harki—an Algerian who fought for France in the former French territory's 1954–62 war of independence—and his middle name is Moussa. His father ran a bar, and his mother was a cleaning lady. "I have an aunt called Fatima and an aunt called Saada, and there's not an ounce of racism in the things I say," he said.[5]

* * *

The drumbeat of government immigration crackdowns and assertions of toughness from politicians of all sides—including sometimes from the centre and even the left—has intensified across Europe in recent years. In France, would-be presidential candidates from Gabriel Attal, a former Socialist who had joined Macron to become the country's youngest prime minister, to Laurent Wauquiez, a former leader of the right-wing Les Républicains, to Bruno Retailleau, another right-winger who became prominent as a hard-line interior minister from 2024 under Bayrou, were constantly telling voters how tough they had been or how much tougher they would be in the future on "clandestine" immigration. Retailleau has even stoked controversy, as has Trump since his return to office in 2025, by echoing the RN and suggesting it was time to suppress the *droit du sol*, under which people born on French soil have the right to citizenship—a right already restricted in Mayotte.

So when the RN's Jordan Bardella used his 2025 new year's press conference held in late January in Paris to demand a stop to the *submersion migratoire* (submersion by immigrants, that phrase again) of Mayotte and complain about what he said was the estimated €10 billion annual cost to France of social welfare for migrants, he may have been slightly more vociferous than other politicians, but he was not alone.[6] "I don't think there is any European society which is still unaware of the dangers of a policy of crazy levels of immigration that has got completely out of control," he said, noting that Olaf Scholz, then the Social Democrat German chancellor, had recently re-imposed border controls at Germany's frontiers. "Perhaps we should be inspired by what President Trump did with Colombia," Bardella said, recalling Trump's insistence shortly after his second inauguration on sending planeloads of shackled migrants back to their home countries. "Here in France we've been struggling for thirty years to fix the issue of [migrants from] Algeria and in a few hours Trump fixed the problem of Colombia with a policy of diplomatic strength that ensured respect for US interests."[7]

Western governments and mainstream political parties are all reacting to rising voter anger about what people perceive to be an "uncontrolled" surge of migrants into their countries. In the same week that Bardella and Bayrou spoke, the sensitive topic of immigration—made more sensitive still by news of a fatal knife attack by an Afghan asylum seeker—persuaded Friedrich Merz, the leader of the CDU in neighbouring Germany, to break a taboo on collaborating with the far right; he gained the support of the AfD party for a parliamentary motion calling for permanent border controls (despite Germany's membership of the visa-free Schengen zone), an entry ban on undocumented asylum seekers and other immigrants, increased deportations to Afghanistan, Syria and other countries and the immediate detention of those ordered to leave the country. It was the first time since Adolf Hitler that anyone had won a vote in Germany's parliament with the support of the far right.[8] Merz was criticised by the left—Robert Habeck of the Greens likened the AfD to a viper poisoning the CDU[9]—but also by his party colleague and former chancellor Angela Merkel. It was she who famously declared "Wir schaffen das" (We can manage this) when she welcomed hundreds of thousands of migrants from Syria in 2015. Only ten years later, the mood had changed so much that Merz was able to declare exactly the opposite: "Das werden wir nicht schaffen"—"We won't be able to manage."[10] Merz became chancellor in May 2025.

Across the world, then, governments have been slowly catching up with public opinion about migration. Donald Trump was elected US president for the second time in 2024 after threatening to deport millions of migrants, promising (again) to build a great wall along the Mexican border and falsely accusing Haitian immigrants in Springfield, Ohio of eating the pet dogs and cats of the town's residents. Philippe Olivier, a hard-line member of the European Parliament for the RN who is married to Marine Le Pen's sister Marie-Caroline (and father of Bardella's one-time girlfriend Nolwenn), has boasted of how far ahead of its political rivals the RN has been in highlighting the issue of immigration. "When I started distributing leaflets about immigration, it was the end of the 1970s, and nobody was opposed to immigration. Everyone was in favour. In the European Union, everyone was in favour. But nowadays, people have turned against it."[11]

By the time Trump's vice-president J.D. Vance lectured Europeans on their failed migration policies at the Munich Security Conference in early 2025 ("And of all the pressing challenges that the nations represented here face, I believe there is nothing more urgent than mass migration"), the EU and most of its twenty-seven member states were already tightening entry requirements and frantically looking for ways to stop undocumented migrants from entering. Even Vance's earlier justification in a Fox News interview for focusing on Americans rather than strangers was nothing new in Europe. "You love your family, and then you love your neighbour, and then you love your community, and then you love your fellow citizens in your own country. And then after that, you can focus and prioritise the rest of the world," the Roman Catholic Vance had said. When criticised, he mentioned St Augustine's concept of *ordo amoris*, an order of preference for one's affections, and ended up being obliquely upbraided by Pope Francis for his ungenerous interpretation.[12] Vance may not have been aware that the far right in France had been saying much the same for decades: the late Jean-Marie Le Pen is known in France among other things for having said "I prefer my daughter to my friends, my friends to my neighbours, my neighbours to my compatriots and my compatriots to [other] Europeans."[13]

In Munich, though, Vance was triumphantly pointing out to his listeners—who had thought he would be talking about European security and Russia's invasion of Ukraine—the obvious truth that many of their voters did not like immigration. "No voter on this continent went to the ballot box to open the floodgates to millions of unvetted immigrants," he said. "But you know what they did vote for? In England, they voted for Brexit … And more and more all over Europe, they are voting for political leaders who promise to put an end to out-of-control migration."[14] In the UK, the populists who campaigned successfully in the 2016 referendum for Brexit—Britain's departure from the European Union—did indeed win support in part by issuing dire warnings about the supposed horrors of mass migration from eastern and central Europe, most of whose EU citizens enjoyed freedom of movement within the union. This popular sense of unease about migration—leaving aside for a moment the question of what migrants actually do, what essential jobs they are performing and whether their numbers are in fact increasing or declining—is what has counted in European and US elections and votes such as the Brexit referendum since the mid-2010s. Prime Minister Bayrou took pains to talk specifically about the "feeling" of submersion, rather than declaring that France actually was being submerged by migrants.

Given this widespread public hostility to mass immigration, and given that even middle-of-the-road European politicians have come round to the idea that immigration needs to be curbed and that the post-war systems and laws for handling migrants and asylum seekers need to be changed, it would be naive to deny that immigration is a political problem in need of a solution. But is immigration a real economic and social crisis as well as a political one? Are millions of migrants not in fact needed to work in healthcare, agriculture and services in rich economies with ageing populations? How different is this migration wave from previous surges of guest workers and foreigners into western Europe? And supposing it is a real crisis, are the solutions envisaged by governments in France, the UK or Italy or Germany likely to work? How long will the far right in Europe continue to benefit from the fears about migration and migrants that it has helped to arouse?

* * *

Global mass migration is not a new phenomenon. Between 1840 and 1940, in a period known as the "first globalisation", 180 million people are estimated to have moved from one country to another.[15] Migration to north-western Europe from eastern and southern Europe, from the Middle East, from Africa and from Latin America also has a long history. In 1893, the inhabitants of Aigues-Mortes in southern France went on the rampage, killing between seven and fifty Italian immigrants—historians are not sure of the exact death toll—in a dispute over jobs at the local saltworks.[16] When I went to the south of France to write about migration during the presidency of Jacques Chirac back in the early 2000s, Marseille's population of 800,000—by 2025, it had reached nearly 900,000—included 300,000 of Italian origin, 120,000 north African Arabs and large communities of Comorian islanders, Armenians and Vietnamese.[17]

Locals born in Algeria and Morocco told me then that migrants from the north African Maghreb would eventually be integrated into France as the Italians were before them, and that the new arrivals, as in the past, often did the hard jobs on farms and building sites that locals were reluctant to take on. "Today people say the *maghrébins*, because they are Muslims, will never be integrated, but people said the same of the Italians at the start of the century," said Salah Bariki, an Algerian-born consultant and community leader. "They were insulted in the streets, and I think they suffered more than us because it was a different era—there wasn't much talk of human rights in those days." José Allegrini, who was then a deputy mayor in the city, said: "What's changed in Marseille is the origin of the migratory flows, but the fact of migration has existed ever since the city was founded."[18]

According to Insee, the national statistics institute, 7.3 million immigrants lived in France in 2023, making up nearly 11 per cent of the population—double their share in 1946—although 2.5 million of these might not be counted as immigrants under another country's system because they have already become French citizens.[19] Of the migrants living in France, nearly half are from Africa, a third from Europe and the rest from Asia and the Americas. According to the political and social analyst Jérôme Fourquet, one in five babies in France today are born to parents of Arab-Muslim immigrant origin, the result of migratory flows since the 1960s. "This figure makes the point that French society has become a de facto multicultural society," he wrote in his latest national study, *Métamorphoses françaises*. "Even if the process does not happen to the same degree or at the same speeds in every region, it is without doubt a major tipping point."[20]

After 2006, net immigration into France rose from around 150,000 a year to around 200,000 in 2016–18, before falling back again to 152,000 in 2020 at the start of the Covid-19 pandemic and 159,000 in 2021. In 2022 and 2023 (the latest years for which official statistics were available at the time of writing), the gross number of immigrant arrivals rose sharply, but since the numbers who departed were not yet available, the net number of immigrants could not be immediately calculated.[21] France, of course, is merely one destination among many. Legal migration to rich, industrialised countries reached a record high in 2023, according to the Organisation for Economic Co-operation and Development (OECD), which reported that about 6.5 million people moved to its thirty-eight member states.[22] Whether all these numbers show that immigration has led to the "submersion" of existing populations is hotly contested. In France, the RN and many on the right insist that it has; most on the left say it is nonsense. Hervé Le Bras, a historian and demographer, is sceptical about the evidence for "submersion" and says that by using the word Bayrou has encouraged people to believe exaggerated assessments about migration. Foreigners, he says, made up 7.5 per cent of the French population in 2023, up slightly from 6.5 per cent in 1931 but far below the 26 per cent share of the Swiss population today.[23]

Marine Le Pen, Jordan Bardella and their far-right equivalents across Europe have homed in on various grievances expressed by their supporters to explain their support for the now-notorious "great replacement" theory of French writer Renaud Camus, which argues that Muslims and non-whites are seeking to overwhelm and replace white Europeans in their own lands. First, there is that feeling of "submersion" of the local population by migrants in particular districts of big cities—for example Saint-Denis north of Paris, where Bardella was brought up and where African and Arab migrants make up a large share of the population and where drug-dealing and crime are often a problem. One political scientist I know suggested that old ladies were anxious about the possibility that they might not be able to buy their (pork) *saucissons* from their local shopkeeper selling halal products (although, as in the UK, people are paradoxically more anti-migrant when they live in places with fewer migrants; one study in France found that in communities where less than 1 per cent of the population were foreigners, 76 per cent agreed that there were "too many Arabs", which fell to 45 per cent in communities where more than 10 per cent of residents were foreign).[24]

Linked to this is the fear of crime, including Islamist terrorism which is indeed usually the work of foreign Muslims or those of immigrant origin. (Islamophobe right-wing extremists also commit crimes: in May 2025, the anti-terror prosecutor launched an investigation into the alleged killer of a Tunisian in the south of France on the grounds that it was a far-right, terrorism-related murder.)[25] Nearly a quarter of prisoners in French jails are foreigners—three times what you would expect given their 7.5 per share of the population—and many of those are from north and west Africa, although rights groups say that is partly because migrants are on average poorer than the French and more likely to be discriminated against by the police and the justice system.[26]

Second, there is the belief—shared by Bardella—that many north African Muslims are failing to assimilate into French society. According to Fourquet, the share of Arab-Muslim first names such as Hassan or Jamel for boys born in France rose from zero in 1900 to 7 per cent in 1983 and to more than 21 per cent of the total in 2021. For a historical comparison, the share of Polish first names for babies born in the Pas-de-Calais in northern France, where Poles made up 40 per cent of the miners in the 1920s, peaked at 3.6 per cent in 1932 before falling back to 0.1 per cent in 1950.[27] Assimilation is notoriously hard to assess, and opponents of the populist, moralist, anti-immigration right have noted with puzzlement that both Trump and Vance are married to women of recent immigrant origin, to a Slovenian and an Indian respectively, while Alice Weidel of the far-right AfD is a lesbian who lives with a partner of Sri Lankan descent in Switzerland. In France, Bardella has Italian and north African origins, Sarkozy's roots are Hungarian and Gabriel Attal's ancestors include Tunisian Jews, Greeks and Russians.

The leaders of the RN concentrate their cultural firepower on trying to roll back what they see as an Islamist takeover of French society enabled by mass immigration of Arabs from north Africa—the theme of Michel Houellebecq's bestselling 2015 novel *Soumission* (Submission)—because this is where they see the most political payback from worried voters. In 2021, for example, Marine Le Pen introduced an anti-Islamism bill that would have banned "Islamist ideologies", forbidden the wearing of the Muslim veil in the streets and allowed civil servants to refuse housing or social security payments to suspected Islamists.[28] "Instead of saying that Islam is terrorism, she simply insists that France is a secular nation that will not stand for hundreds of thousands of Muslims practicing their religious traditions," Vladimir Zhirinovsky, the Russian nationalist and xenophobe who was a friend of her father Jean-Marie, once wrote in admiration. "With this argument, Marine has cleverly defended the French people's right to a secular nation."[29] Zhirinovsky was not entirely accurate, since Le Pen would ban religious practices and symbols mostly only in schools and other state institutions where they are already largely prohibited. But the result is that RN politicians, along with many others on the French right, spend an inordinate amount of their time both as opposition MPs and elected local officials trying to strengthen the laws enforcing *laïcité* (a strict secularism whose origins lie in the French Revolution and which forbids religious practices or symbols in state facilities such a schools), by tightening restrictions on the wearing of veils, headscarves and certain kinds of swimming costumes (the cover-all *burkini* is frowned upon as being excessively modest and un-French). "The danger is on the rise," said Roger Chudeau, an RN MP, at the launch of another bill in early 2025 seeking to extend the ban on "ostentatiously religious" clothing to universities and school outings beyond the premises of the *lycée*. For every incident of sharia being applied in the school yard or single-sex sessions at public swimming pools, a hundred went unreported, he said. I asked Julien Odoul, the RN MP who was the main sponsor of the bill, whether the obsession with clothing was worthwhile and whether it could even be enforced. "Well," he replied, "it was done with seatbelts, and look at Covid—everyone had to wear masks and was prevented from moving about freely."[30] The far right, committed as it is to defending western Europe's "Judeo-Christian" heritage, is less enthusiastic about enforcing *laïcité* when it comes to Christian nativity scenes on municipal property, on the grounds that such displays are traditional rather than religious.[31]

The RN's third line of attack on immigration is its emphasis on the failure of successive French governments to enforce the law by expelling the thousands of migrants who are illegally in France after losing their applications for asylum or residency, and the willingness of the authorities eventually to "regularise" such overstayers for want of an alternative (usually because the countries from which they come are reluctant to take them back). A French Senate committee report noted in 2023 that only about 7 per cent of the tens of thousands of orders annually to leave France—

known as OQTF for *obligation de quitter le territoire français*—had been carried out in France since 2020. The same report described the official struggle against "clandestine" immigration as "a long-term policy failure" and lamented that the number of people receiving *aide médicale d'État*—free healthcare for those without papers or illegally in the country—had exceeded 400,000 for the first time in 2022. Clandestine migrants' free healthcare and the inability to expel those under OQTF are frequently mentioned by Bardella, Le Pen and other RN politicians in their campaign speeches, and any crime committed by an OQTF is immediately highlighted by the right-wing press as an example of the horrors of the immigration crisis.[32]

That brings us to the fourth right-wing objection to immigration—its economic impact and the costs or benefits to French society. Back in the 1970s, Jean-Marie Le Pen and other extreme-right politicians in Europe blamed migrants for unemployment, and a popular complaint was that "they're taking our jobs". I have not heard anyone say that since the Sarkozy era, because most people can see, as in the UK and the rest of western Europe, that migrants are either doing jobs in France that others do not want to do, including farm labour, construction and street-cleaning, or taking higher-end jobs, for example as doctors or nurses, where there are shortages of qualified citizens. It is the same story across the Channel in the UK. In the apple orchards around my home in Kent, the pickers in the 1960s were mostly local villagers. More recently, Poles, Bulgarians and Romanians from the EU did the seasonal farm work. Now, post-Brexit, the workers have to be flown in from Kyrgyzstan in central Asia under a UK visa scheme for tens of thousands of seasonal fruit pickers.

French unemployment declined steadily from 10 per cent of the workforce after 2015, although there was a jump during the Covid-19 pandemic, and was running at about 7 per cent between 2022 and 2025. Unemployment of 7 per cent is relatively high by the standards of other industrialised countries, but even at that level of joblessness French businesses large and small have posted tens of thousands of vacancies and been unable to find enough employees, in part because of relatively generous unemployment benefits.[33] Even Donald Trump said in his election victory speech in November 2024 that he wanted migrants to come to the US "legally", and in France the RN talks of allowing in a small number of qualified migrants to perform specific jobs for limited periods.

The popular complaints today—in France, the UK and elsewhere—are not that migrants are taking jobs but that they are crowding out citizens seeking access to healthcare, housing and education. In France, there is a particular gripe about the cost to the taxpayer of the free medical care available for "illegal" migrants. Yet studies in France and across the developed economies of the OECD show that immigration over time has had remarkably little impact on public finances, broadly because immigrants overall contribute in tax and social security roughly what they cost, or at least perform no worse than citizens in this regard.[34]

European voters, and most western governments, have nevertheless concluded that the legal and policing systems for handling millions of asylum seekers and other migrants are broken and need to be fixed. In France, Marine Le Pen and Bardella scored political points by recruiting to the RN the hard-line Fabrice Leggeri, who had been head of the EU border agency Frontex between 2015 and 2022, at the height of the EU's migrant crisis. He was elected to the European Parliament in 2024 after condemning *submersion migratoire*—that emblematic RN phrase. As Amy Pope, director general of the UN International Organization for Migration, wrote in January 2025, irregular immigration—that is, entering a country without prior permission—has been at "historic levels", with 2.5 million people seeking to cross into the

THE BIG ISSUES

US from Mexico in 2023, and 380,000 entering Europe in the same year, the highest since 2016. Pope said: "[T]oday's unprecedented levels of migration make plain that a decrepit, outdated system, built in the wake of World War II, is incapable of contending with today's humanitarian needs, demographic trends, or labor-market demands." Pope also said legal migration had been an "underutilized tool" to make up for labour shortages in developed countries. Just as Brexit Britain has allowed in more immigrants than ever since leaving the EU, so Italy under the right-wing nationalist prime minister Giorgia Meloni has sought to curb clandestine migration but also accepted the need for 450,000 new workers over the next three years to meet demands from farmers, hospitals and other employers.[35]

In seeking to restrict immigration, nations are bound by international law in the form of the 1951 Geneva Convention on refugees (and its 1967 Protocol), which says that those at risk of persecution in their home countries cannot be penalised for illegal entry to another country and cannot be sent back (the famous "non-refoulement" requirement). While other great powers, including the US, China and Russia, now pay scant attention to treaties or international law, the EU and the UK are among the places that still generally conform and have struggled to harden their immigration rules—to keep out undocumented "economic" refugees who are not entitled to asylum—while claiming that they remain in compliance. After lengthy negotiations, in May 2024 the EU adopted an "asylum and migration pact" designed to curb clandestine migration, help the countries from which the migrants come to tackle the problem at its source and improve solidarity between EU member states, given that those such as Italy and Spain where migrants land in small boats after crossing the Mediterranean from Africa are the primary targets. The pact is due to come into force in 2026, but in the meantime various countries have tried to deter would-be migrants by setting up agreements with neighbours or governments far away to house the asylum seekers—as the UK tried and failed to do with Rwanda and Italy under Meloni is trying to do with Albania. By 2025, France had made no such arrangements, focusing instead on trying to return undocumented migrants directly to their countries of origin.

It is not clear how much impact such external "return hubs" or the EU's new pact will have on the flow of migrants into western Europe. The UN estimates that 43 million people worldwide currently qualify as refugees, while a record 26.4 million were displaced by climate-related disasters, especially in Africa.[36] The EU's own Agency for Fundamental Rights, the FRA, has said that even if such migrant camps or hubs are located outside the EU, they are not "rights-free" zones, and EU legal safeguards should apply.

This new consensus, in which voters and governments have mostly come round to the far right's insistence on the need to curb migration, raises an interesting question for the RN in France and its allies in Europe: will the far right benefit because it is seen to have been correct all along, or will it be sidelined because other political parties have started to adopt similar approaches to immigration and are trusted more to manage the economy and foreign relations? The question is all the more salient because some far-right politicians, including Meloni but not yet Le Pen or Bardella, are these days more inclined to accept the need for tens of thousands of legal migrants in their ageing societies. "The migration emergency initially fuelled popular support for the far right. But since the heated days of the 2015–16 crisis much has changed," wrote political analyst Ivan Krastev before the 2024 European elections, arguing that "migration is not a divisive issue in the way it was five or 10 years ago. Rather than migration policy, it may be the European Green Deal that is most affected by the growing strength of the far right."[37]

THE BIG ISSUES

In France, it is common to meet voters who have recently switched from the pro-migration, far-left LFI party of Jean-Luc Mélenchon to the far-right RN—strong evidence that they are less concerned by immigration than by the economy, foreign affairs or some other aspect of policy. So while hostility towards migration is likely to remain a crucial part of the RN's policy platform, its significance in elections will depend on the circumstances and could diminish over time as earlier waves of migrants are slowly integrated into French society. Much will depend on how the issue of migration is debated on social media and what politicians say. The hard-line Darmanin, justice minister and former interior minister, has insisted that uncompromising *laïcité*, or secularism, will bind Muslims into the French nation, even if it takes decades, as it did with Protestants and Jews in a republican and once predominantly Catholic country. "It will take fifty years or a century, but [Muslims], like the Catholics, like the Jews, like the Protestants, will assimilate, provided we don't lower our guard," he said.[38]

The French economy: Achilles' heel of the far right?

As a journalist for the *Financial Times* and Reuters, I have had to puzzle over a fair number of complicated financial documents during my long career, but few as baffling as the one I am looking at now: it is an ordinary monthly French payslip for a junior employee. There are no fewer than forty rows of figures in the document to detail the salary, the deductions and the totals, including sixteen for different social security systems such as health, unemployment and pensions and their sub-sections. On a gross salary of €2,856, the employee pays only €125 in income tax, which does not sound burdensome. But on top of that, for social security, she pays €646 and the employer more than double that amount, including various obscure deductions such as the equivalent of 0.1 per cent of the employee's salary—€2.86—to finance trade union and employers' training.

The notorious French payslip—a whole industry has grown up to explain how they work and what they mean—tells us something about the economy that any successful far-right candidate would inherit after a future election. France is very bureaucratic, and the state takes a large share of the national income to deliver its services: France has the highest government spending as a share of GDP (58.1 per cent in 2022) of all thirty-eight members of the OECD, as well as the highest tax-to-GDP ratio, taking 43.8 per cent in tax in 2023 compared to an OECD average of 33.9 per cent (the tax take includes social security payments).[39] About one in five working people in France are among the country's nearly 6 million government employees.[40] The French state is also heavily indebted, because it has not balanced its budget since the 1970s. By 2024, it was running a budget deficit of 5.8 per cent of GDP, nearly double the limit set by the EU, and had accumulated debt amounting to 113 per cent of GDP, or more than €3 trillion.[41]

All this government spending means the state looks after its citizens, providing everything from free healthcare to good rural roads, while statistics show that real living standards rose slightly on average in 2024.[42] But that does not mean people are happy. On the contrary, more than half of voters say they struggle to make ends meet, and 73 per cent agree with the statement that "things were better in the past", according to a December 2024 survey on the divisions in French society.[43] People also resent rising inequality and, like many of Trump's supporters in the US, are inclined to blame foreign countries and globalisation. When I asked Jean-Yves Camus, an expert on the European far right, why voters might think the RN would be better at running the economy than the traditional parties of the left or the centre-right that have governed since de Gaulle, he replied: "Because they believe that the extreme right will break the chains—the chains of globalism, the chains of the international monetary system, the chains from the EU, from the European Central Bank."[44] Among western economies marked by inequality and complaints about the cost of living, France is unique in having moved into the dark years of Covid and the Russia–Ukraine war straight out of more than a year of *gilets jaunes* demonstrations, themselves born of the smouldering discontent of French working people.

The combination of millions of dissatisfied voters and lumbering, expensive public services in need of reform should make a tempting target for a radical opposition party hungry for power. But Marine Le Pen, Bardella and the RN have three big problems. First, they have always spent their time protesting about immigration from the opposition benches and only recently tried to develop credible economic policies they could implement once in government. Second, their economic ideology such as it is—including support for a strong state and condemnation of free trade and big business—is remarkably similar to that of the far left, which makes them ill suited to slash the bureaucracy or make drastic public spending cuts. Third, even if they were minded to embark on some radical reform, they would have to consider the record of the incumbent Emmanuel Macron: like many would-be French reformers before him, the self-professed liberal revolutionary ran into a brick wall of bureaucratic and popular resistance that slowed his achievements to a trickle. Even his inevitable and financially essential reform to the costly state pension system, which will increase the official retirement age from sixty-two to sixty-four (it is already set to rise to sixty-seven in the UK between 2026 and 2028, with a further increase due in the future), continues to be challenged by legislators in the fractured French National Assembly.

French investors have long been concerned about the likely competence of a putative RN government, and even among ordinary voters the party's perceived lack of economic or business expertise is an electoral Achilles' heel. Of the twenty-two proposals in Le Pen's presidential manifesto for 2022, at least fourteen by my count would have involved increased spending, including a €20 billion emergency allocation to the health system over five years and the plan to lower VAT on fuel from 20 per cent to 5.5 per cent, a promise that was retained for Bardella's attempt to become prime minister after the 2024 National Assembly elections. The RN in 2022 said the additional spending would amount to €68.3 billion a year and sought to reassure investors by outlining exactly €68.3 billion in annual savings, including a vague and implausible €16 billion from immigration reform and €15 billion from eliminating tax and social security fraud. Economists were not convinced, and the Institut Montaigne thinktank calculated that the RN's policies would swell the budget deficit by a massive €101.8 billion.[45]

Le Pen responded combatively when asked about her economic credibility at a meeting with foreign journalists shortly before that election. She said she wanted to form a government of national unity, and that it would be easy to find a finance minister from among the many hopefuls who would call her once it seemed possible that she would win. She confirmed unapologetically that she was a protectionist who wanted to rebuild French industry and was scathing about the supposed competence of the incumbent government and the financial establishment that criticised her:

> It's great to talk about credibility, but who exactly has been credible over the last forty years? You're telling me that the credible ones are the people who were world champions for debt, world champions for budget deficits, world champions for foreign trade deficits, world champions for unemployment, world champions for poverty, all of which are still increasing in our country. The least one can say is that if all those people are credible, then I'm tempted to say it's comforting not to be one of them.[46]

THE BIG ISSUES

It was hard not to agree she had a point. For all the supposed fiscal orthodoxy of Macron and Bruno Le Maire, who was his finance minister for more than seven years, the French economy, admittedly damaged in part by the heavy emergency spending of the Covid years, is in a perilous state. Since 2024, the national auditor, the Cour des comptes, has repeatedly sounded the alarm about French budget deficits, and it said in July of that year that the country was "dangerously exposed" to any fresh economic shock. "This situation would be less of a problem if it was the same for European neighbours, but that's not the case," said Pierre Moscovici, chair of the Cour des comptes, who also criticised the government's deficit reduction targets as "less and less credible".[47]

The Macron administration's waning financial credibility, however, does not magically make the RN's own policies any more credible. The populism of political parties such as the RN tends to boost election performance because they offer people what they think they want, which is why Marine Le Pen abandoned the party's unpopular plans to take France out of the euro and the EU after her defeat by Macron in the 2017 elections. But populist programmes designed to attract voters in an election usually weaken the party once it gains power, because the policies typically lack coherence and do not achieve the desired results once implemented. In the UK, Brexiters won the referendum to leave the EU in 2016, but since then the disadvantages of leaving the tariff-free European internal market where the UK did half of its trade have been mercilessly exposed.[48]

Even the first step in the populist process—promising people what they want—is fraught with uncertainty. An Ifop opinion survey for the Hexagone data analytics group and published in the far-right *Le JDNews* produced one welcome result for the magazine. When people were asked in late 2024 how they would ideally allocate the €1.5 trillion of annual public spending, including social security, they opted to nearly quadruple the money allocated to law enforcement, spend nearly ten times as much on courts and prisons and double defence spending. But that was balanced by an apparent desire to slash spending on the country's cherished pension and healthcare systems, which if actually implemented would probably trigger a second French Revolution given that even minor tinkering with health and pensions sends demonstrators on to the streets of Paris. Less comfortable for the far right was the finding that people also wanted to quadruple the existing amount of foreign aid and more than triple spending on the environment.[49]

When Macron unexpectedly called the snap legislative elections in the summer of 2024, the RN, like every other party, including Macron's own, scrambled to produce a plausible manifesto. The economic programme of would-be prime minister Jordan Bardella was barely more convincing for nervous business leaders than Marine Le Pen's presidential election offering had been two years earlier. Among other proposals, he said he would abolish two of Macron's hard-won economic reforms to cut the deficit, one concerning the pension system and the other on unemployment benefits. Macron's supporters and some independent analysts warned that the RN's budget-busting spending plans could trigger a Liz Truss-style meltdown of the government debt market, a reference to the financial crisis triggered by the unfunded tax cuts of the short-lived UK Tory prime minister in 2022. Bardella hesitated, hinting that he might not go through with reversing Macron's pension reform after all and postponing plans for a €7 billion cut in VAT on household necessities. The damage, however, was done.

"The 'programme' of the RN is a pure opposition platform, an aggregation of gifts to those with legitimate or illegitimate complaints. It is not a programme," said former IMF chief economist Olivier Blanchard. "The money is not there ... In any programme, saying that financing will come largely from the elimination of fraud is a giveaway. So is the notion that anti-immigrant measures will yield considerable revenues." Some bankers and company executives did compare the RN's programme favourably to that of the left-wing alliance dominated by the far-left LFI, which promised big increases in government spending and the minimum wage, although it did at least outline it would finance the expenditure with tax increases targeting the rich.[50]

As Le Pen, Bardella and their RN colleagues have drawn closer to occupying the Élysée presidential palace and the prime minister's official residence in the Hôtel Matignon, French business leaders and entrepreneurs have tried frantically to curry favour with France's potential future rulers—and educate them on some financial and economic realities. For their part, the RN leaders are pleased they are no longer ostracised by business. They are keen to solicit advice but also wary, and do not want to commit themselves to policies that may be anathema to their working-class voters. Bardella even spoke to the freemasons—an organisation the FN once vowed to abolish—at an €85-per-head lunch in 2024 at the venerable Cercle de l'Union Interalliée on the rue du Faubourg Saint-Honoré.[51]

Among the tycoons seeking to steer the RN away from socialist economics and towards an appreciation of free enterprise and trade are two discreet but powerful billionaires, both of them right-wing Catholics: Vincent Bolloré, who controls a diversified industrial, financial and agricultural conglomerate and has worked relentlessly via his expanding media empire to boost the far right's political chances in France, and Pierre-Édouard Stérin, an ultra-conservative entrepreneur living as a tax exile in Belgium who made his fortune with Smartbox, which calls itself the European leader in "gift experiences". Stérin, who is dedicated to "continuing to make money to serve Christ and France"[52] as well as opposing mass immigration, "wokeness" and what the French call *islamo-gauchisme* or Islamo-leftism, has set up "Project

Périclès",[53] a kind of right-wing thinktank and lobby group aimed at promoting liberal-conservative ideas, getting people elected to put those ideas into practice and helping them to be effective once they are in power. François Durvye, who heads Stérin's investment fund Otium Capital, is an economic adviser to Marine Le Pen, and the party is set to benefit from its financial support in the French municipal elections of 2026.

The RN's attempt to formulate a credible strategy for reforming the EU's second largest economy is still a work in progress, and neither Le Pen nor Bardella have yet found a way to overcome the challenge that faces every modern French government: reconciling the demands of working-class voters with those of big business and the financial markets.

10

ENVIRONMENTAL BATTLES AND CULTURE WARS

The green dilemma

"Mother of God, where on earth are the wild animals of yesteryear?" asked Jean-Marie Le Pen in his autobiography:

> At my home in Brittany, chemical agriculture and the hedge-destroying consolidation of fields have done terrible harm. When I was a child, the birds were so plentiful and varied that our hunting and egg-collecting had an insignificant impact on their numbers. The countryside rang and rustled with their songs, their calls, the sound of their wings. Tits, chaffinches, goldfinches, robins (in Breton *rouzicoet*, the little red bird of the woods), wrens, sparrows, buntings, nightingales, the larks that sang all the time they were in the air, warblers, the wagtails that often nested on overwintering boats.[1]

In France as elsewhere, the far right has a complicated relationship with the natural world and environmental policy.

On the one hand, ultra-conservatives are often nostalgic about rural traditions and peasant farming and realise that modernisation and industrial agriculture have damaged the country and decimated wildlife. On the other, prompted by their rural voters, they rage against the scientists who identify the causes of that damage and the French, European and international regulators who try to limit the harm by, say, reducing carbon dioxide emissions to curb global warming or by banning dangerous pesticides and herbicides. Jean-Marie Le Pen was as incoherent as anyone. As well as bemoaning pollution, urbanisation, the loss of birds, bees and butterflies and complaining about how the left unjustly portrayed itself as the champion of the environment, he mocked international efforts to limit acid rain, control population growth, close the ozone hole and tackle climate change as fearmongering and examples of "millenarian terrorism".[2] Reluctance to accept the need for national and international green regulations is not confined to the party: the far-right entrepreneur and former politician Philippe de Villiers, for example, echoes Jean-Marie Le Pen in lamenting the loss of birds and pollinating bees and condemns "agro-chemical" industrial farming, but he simultaneously scorns those he calls the "Khmers verts" (a play on Cambodia's extremist Khmers rouges), the green campaigners who want to protect the planet by reducing methane emissions from cattle and introducing electric cars.[3]

The confusion on the far right over the environment and farming has continued under the RN's current leaders Marine Le Pen and Jordan Bardella. In one respect, the incoherence now is even more pronounced because—unlike Donald Trump or the late Jean-Marie Le Pen—they accept the scientific consensus that climate change is a harmful reality but still push back against measures to deal with it on the grounds that they are too burdensome for French voters. When Macron called the snap National Assembly elections in the summer of 2024, Bardella's manifesto rejected "punitive environmentalism" and promised to drop the ban on petrol and diesel cars due to come into force in 2035, to abandon low-emission zones and to abolish all restric-

ENVIRONMENTAL BATTLES AND CULTURE WARS

tions and obligations related to the energy efficiency of buildings. But he also promoted hydro-electric dams, hydrogen power and geothermal energy. For farmers, he promised guaranteed profitable prices, stricter controls on food imports and an "Eat French" campaign for school canteens.

Marine Le Pen's much more detailed manifesto for the previous presidential campaign in 2022 also promised a reduction in VAT on fuel, the abandonment of unpopular speed limits (80km/h on rural roads and 30km/h in many towns) and a radical plan to demolish wind farms and "return to households the €5 billion in subsidies largely given to windfarms".[4] Like Trump, Marine Le Pen is peculiarly hostile to wind turbines and solar panels, partly because France generates most of its electricity from zero-carbon nuclear power stations and so has less need of renewables than its neighbours. She may, however, turn out to have overestimated the political and economic benefits of her stand, given the increasing efficiency and profitability of wind and solar power and the desire for France to reduce its dependence on imported natural gas.

Bardella, who did not include these anti-windfarm measures in his brief manifesto, comes from a younger generation more exposed to the existential threat of climate change and has at times taken a more nuanced approach to the environment than his mentor. He even said it would be foolish for the French right to ignore the dangers of global warming, just as it had been foolish for the French left to ignore the issue of immigration highlighted by the RN. "I think it's essential that we in the nationalist camp don't behave as the left has over immigration for the past thirty years—that is, by closing our eyes."[5]

Green regulations, however urgent they may be, nevertheless remain an ideal political hunting ground for populists around the world. As David Djaïz, author of *La Révolution obligée* (The essential revolution), told *Le Monde* in January 2025, "Populists seize on all problems to target the elites. In this sense, the environment, explained by scientists and requiring new regulations decided by governments, is a magnificent land of opportunity for them, especially if workers and the middle class feel they are being wronged."[6] And they do feel wronged. Dutch farmers who object to being told to reduce the number of their pigs and cows to cut nitrogen pollution of waterways turn to the far-right politician Geert Wilders and his Party for Freedom; French motorists with old cars resent the threat of anti-pollution restrictions imposed by urban low-emission zones and appreciate the anti-regulation message they hear from the RN; and Germans resentful about being told to replace their gas-fired boilers with heat pumps switch their political support to the extreme-right, climate-denying AfD party.[7] Among the French organisations to be targeted by the French right and the country's farmers—the messengers to be shot, so to speak—are Anses, the food and environmental safety agency; Ademe, the ecological transition agency dealing with the shift to a low-carbon economy; and OFB, the biodiversity agency.[8]

The French far right has gleefully exploited genuine environmental concerns by making wildly exaggerated suggestions of what bureaucrats and greens might want to do to deprive French citizens of their liberties: banning couples from having too many children, outlawing Christmas trees, forbidding the eating of meat or travelling by car to watch the Tour de France cycle race—to name a few fringe ideas cited in one article in the far-right press.[9] Bardella himself, brought up in the city and with no obvious rural connections, criticised proposals to limit further building on greenfield sites in the countryside by saying it was already hard to rent somewhere to live. "Environmentalism is all very well," he said, "[b]ut if tomorrow you can't travel anywhere, you can't take a plane, you can't build anything because there is a little green plant that must be preserved, well, it's very lovely but we'll all be dead."[10]

ENVIRONMENTAL BATTLES AND CULTURE WARS

Nowhere are the RN's inconsistencies more glaring than in its attitudes to the EU. Bardella recognises the dangers of climate change but has called the EU's Green Deal, which seeks to eliminate net carbon emissions by 2050, "probably one of the greatest de-growth plans this continent has seen in fifty years" and has condemned EU leaders as "ayatollahs plotting to impose this harmful plan on society with almost religious fervour".[11] The RN, perhaps unconsciously harking back to the peasant fascist "greenshirts" of Henri Dorgères in the 1930s, romanticises small farmers and artisanal fishermen and sees wine and food as markers of France's civilisational identity—but in practice it supports EU policies and subsidies that benefit the largest, least romantic and most destructive farms and fishing operations (France is the biggest beneficiary of the multibillion euro subsidy system under the Common Agricultural Policy). Lastly, the party has repeatedly called on the EU to reinforce trade protectionism to help French farmers by limiting imports while extolling the export performance of French farms and vineyards that themselves benefit from international trade. Unfortunately, the best that can be said for the RN's aggressively confused policies on the environment and agriculture is that the same faults are shared by other political parties in France, Europe and the world.

* * *

"Wokisme" and the culture wars

The flamboyant opening ceremony of the summer Olympic Games in 2024, played out in a dozen historical, musical and theatrical acts along the Seine in central Paris despite the torrential rain, was a defining moment in France's culture wars. There was immediate outrage from many conservatives, including the far-right politician Marion Maréchal, Marine Le Pen's niece, who was watching with her children. "It's difficult to enjoy the few scenes that actually work in between a decapitated Marie-Antoinette, the drag queens, the humiliation of the Republican Guard forced to dance to [French-Malian singer-songwriter] Aya Nakamura, the general ugliness of the costumes and choreography," Maréchal posted on the social media site X. "One looks in vain for a celebration of sporting values and the beauty of France in the midst of such crude, woke propaganda."[12]

Éric Zemmour, another far-right commentator and politician, was equally grumpy. He complained of a political spectacle in bad taste overseen by President Emmanuel Macron, the Socialist Paris mayor Anne Hidalgo and historical consultant Patrick Boucheron, who wanted "to impose on us a vision of mankind that isn't ours, a vision of France that isn't ours and that we reject, one that has left even foreigners astounded or saddened".[13] The responses to such posts underlined the deep divisions in French society, with some sharing Maréchal's horror at the scenes of libertinage and transgression and others delighting in her discomfiture, telling her to go back to the seventeenth century or leave the country. Among the most controversial scenes—between the relatively conventional performances to open and close the ceremony by an accordion player performing an Édith Piaf tune from the Pont d'Austerlitz at the start and Céline Dion from the Eiffel Tower at the end—was one featuring a Bacchanalian feast interpreted by angry conservatives as a blasphemous representation of Christ's Last Supper.

My favourite moment of the ceremony was the one decried by Maréchal when the uniformed band members of the staid Republican Guard (the British equivalent would be the famous King's Guard at Buckingham Palace) did their unexpected and incongruous joint number with Nakamura; she and her gold-dressed dancers end the song with a salute. But the whole four-hour ceremony—directed by Thomas Jolly and championed by Macron—is still remembered with distaste by many conservatives and far-right commentators. De Villiers, who favours a nationalist, nostalgic version of history in the pageants at his Puy du Fou theme park in western France, even opened his latest book *Mémoricide* with an entire chapter condemning a ceremony that he said had "deeply hurt" him and was a deliberate attempt to trigger an overthrow of the established order. "Everything was ugly, everything was woke," he wrote, scorning the artistic directors' desire to be "inclusive" and regretting that they had achieved their aim of displaying the chaotic opposite of Puy du Fou's virile, heroic and providential style of history. The ceremony was not just a spectacle, de Villiers wrote portentously. It was a turning point. "It was developed, matured, considered. It was a matter thought through at the highest level. It traces a new wake in the waters of the Seine: we are changing our society, we are changing our culture, we are changing our civilisation. Nothing less."[14]

There were two prominent far-right leaders, however, who said nothing in public about the ceremony or the controversy in its aftermath: Marine Le Pen, who has never seen eye-to-eye with conservative Catholics and long ago decided that matters of sexuality and personal preference were best left out of politics; and Jordan Bardella, who had already promised not to change anything in the organisation of the Olympics if he were to become prime minister before the start of the games. It is not that RN leaders eschew the culture wars altogether; it is just that they choose their targets carefully. So whereas in Donald Trump's US or Viktor Orbán's Hungary there are signs of an "intersectionality of hate" carelessly grouping together sexism, racism, homophobia and xenophobia,[15] the RN's leaders direct their ire towards the matters that concern them the most, namely immigration and Islam, and have decided that taking a strong stand on sexuality would be either useless or counterproductive. "Whether we are men or women, heterosexual or homosexual, Christian, Jewish, Muslim or non-believers, we are above all French!" Marine Le Pen declared at the movement's Joan of Arc celebration on 1 May 2011 shortly after taking over from her father.[16] That came as a shock to Catholic ultra-conservatives and the party elders of her father's generation, who criticised what they saw as her dissolute lifestyle and in one case had called her a "hussy" surrounded by "notorious queers".[17] Several senior figures in the RN are indeed gay, and voters rarely seem to give a damn, any more than they do about gay MPs on the far left or gay cabinet ministers (and the country's first openly gay prime minister) in Macron's governments. The final chapter in Sylvain Crépon's 2012 book examining Marine Le Pen's takeover of the party was titled "Un Front national féministe et gay friendly?"

* * *

If a cultural matter has implications for the nation, then the RN as France's biggest nationalist party will nevertheless probably have something to say. In the 2022 presidential campaign, Marine Le Pen proposed a "big, urgent action plan" to save the French language from "Anglo-Saxon hegemony", including by banning the use of foreign languages in advertising or communications in France. Good luck with that, critics might say, in a land where right-wingers routinely complain about *le wokisme* and *le cancel culture*. A desire to preserve the French language is by no means confined to the far right—the Académie française is notorious in the Anglo-Saxon world for trying to protect the country's culture from infection by English words and phrases—but Le Pen, targeting French words and grammatical constructions such as the gender-neutral pronouns *iel* and *iels* instead of *il*, *elle*, *ils* and *elles* for he, she and they, has been a vigorous proponent of banning "inclusive" grammar in schools, universities and government departments.[18] Bardella, among the youngest politicians in France, tends to comment on the issue mainly

ENVIRONMENTAL BATTLES AND CULTURE WARS

in general terms, using it as a cudgel with which to beat his left-wing enemies and accuse them of trying to obliterate the traditional values of western civilisation.[19]

For much of the time, however, Le Pen and Bardella have been happy to stand aside and let the two sides in the global culture wars fight their battles through the media. In France, each side in this conflict likes to caricature the other, as they did during the controversy over the Olympic opening ceremony. The left likes to portray the right as irredeemably fascist and racist, with a crude appreciation of art and a simplistic sense of history in which France is always fighting off barbarian hordes (but it really is, retorts the right). The right tends to see the left as politically correct to an absurd degree, preferring quinoa to *foie gras*, immigrant minorities to the white majority and windfarms to nuclear power and obsessed by vaccinations and climate change (but they really are important, retorts the left).

At least since the second world war, the liberal left has held the cultural high ground in western liberal democracies, dominating academia, thinktanks, the traditional media and the worlds of arts and film, and it is only recently that that the far right—empowered by new forms of digital communication outside the control of the liberal establishment—has started to turn the tables in Hungary, the United States and elsewhere. Among Trump's first domestic targets at the start of his second administration were the Ivy League universities, the media, museums and the Kennedy Center for the Performing Arts in Washington, DC, where he promptly made himself chairman of the board and promised a "GOLDEN AGE of American Arts and Culture" and—something that would have pleased critics of the Paris Olympics opening ceremony—"NO MORE DRAG SHOWS, OR OTHER ANTI-AMERICAN PROPAGANDA."[20]

In western Europe, the resurgent right is taking a leaf out of the left's old playbook as articulated by Antonio Gramsci, the

Italian Communist martyred in one of Mussolini's jails who theorised on the importance of "cultural hegemony" for a ruling class. Thinkers on the French right, albeit less numerous than those on the left, have long been intrigued by Gramsci and irritated by the cultural dominance of their leftist rivals: Alain de Benoist, one of the leading lights of the nationalist thinktank GRECE (the Groupement de recherche et d'études pour la civilisation européenne, whose initials make the French word for Greece, the country seen by many as the fount of European civilisation) published a collection of discussions entitled *Pour un "gramscisme de droite"* (For a "Gramsci-ism of the right") back in 1982. Nor has Gramsci been forgotten in the Age of Trump. His image was displayed alongside that of the Italian fascist philosopher Giovanni Gentile at a conference in Rome in late 2024 organised by the Alleanza Nazionale, a foundation linked to the hard-right Brothers of Italy party of Giorgia Meloni, the prime minister (and at the time almost the only EU leader from western Europe right wing enough to be considered acceptable by Trump and his sidekick billionaire Elon Musk).[21] Europe's cultural hegemony is once again in play, and the next time an EU capital hosts the Olympics, we may see a very different kind of opening ceremony from the one along the Seine in Paris in 2024.

11

FRANCE'S FOX NEWS AND THE BATTLE FOR PUBLIC OPINION

The speech in Paris was little noticed at the time, but two weeks before J.D. Vance shocked European leaders at the February 2025 Munich Security Conference by shrugging off the dangers of Russian aggression and scolding Europe about the "threat within" from immigration and what he saw as woke censorship, the RN's Jordan Bardella was haranguing the French media for much the same reasons.

When the US vice-president told his audience in Germany that "there is no security if you are afraid of the voices, opinions, and conscience that guide your very own people", Bardella had already told his listeners in France in January that "the French don't want to be told what to think or who's right and who's wrong". When Vance condemned the "commissars" of Brussels because they "warned citizens that they intend to shut down social media during times of civil unrest the moment they spot what they've judged to be 'hateful content'", Bardella had already condemned the French establishment for "censoring digital media, forbidding the promotion of a book [his own], rejoicing in the death of a political rival, [and] calling for the closure of [right-wing] television channels after targeted harassment".[1]

Vance told the Europeans:

> To many of us on the other side of the Atlantic, it looks more and more like old, entrenched interests hiding behind ugly Soviet-era words like "misinformation" and "disinformation", simply because they don't like the idea that someone with an alternative viewpoint might express a different opinion, vote a different way, or even worse, win an election.

Bardella told the French press:

> If a large part of the French people and the media are angry, it's not because of their "bad instincts" or "abuses" of freedom of expression that are supposedly going too far on social media, it's mainly because too many of the French have the feeling that the press is trying to tell them what to think rather than to inform them.[2]

These complaints are framed as defending the principle of free speech in liberal democracies, but they are also self-serving party policies: both men reject the need to regulate the internet or social media now that the far right has in many countries largely captured these new sources of information and opinion. Trump was elected twice not only with the help of Fox News but also of divisive, conspiracy-loving podcasts and social media platforms such as Elon Musk's X. Viktor Orbán, pro-Russian and self-professed illiberal prime minister of EU member Hungary, has largely seized control of the country's media, both traditional and online.[3] In neighbouring Romania, by contrast, the authorities annulled the presidential election after the previously little-known far-right candidate Călin Georgescu came out ahead in the first round of voting on the back of a viral TikTok campaign (25,000 new accounts were suddenly opened weeks before the voting, according to intelligence reports).[4] Vance was outraged by the cancellation and mentioned it prominently in his Munich speech.

THE BATTLE FOR PUBLIC OPINION

France, too, is having its Fox News moment, and the far right is starting to avenge the decades during which it was either ignored or demonised by the established media. My own anecdotal observations during three spells as a journalist reporting on France since the 1980s tell me there is some truth to the complaints over the years by Jean-Marie and Marine Le Pen, Bardella and others that they were not given a fair say in the traditional French media until their popularity and presence in the National Assembly became so dominant that they could no longer be ignored.

In the early 1980s, Jean-Marie Le Pen complained to François Mitterrand, the Socialist president who had promoted pluralism and the "shock of ideas", that he and his FN party were being boycotted by state television. Mitterrand replied sympathetically, and Le Pen was invited to appear on TF1.[5] Jean-Marie Le Pen also had a brief moment of media glory after qualifying for the runoff against Jacques Chirac in the 2002 presidential election but was disappointed that he could not fully deploy his proven oratorical skills because Chirac refused the usual televised debate between the two final candidates.

Since then, FN/RN leaders have routinely protested against the attitude of traditional media they perceive to be dominated by the left. Media reporting and investigations into the French far right were indeed polemical and usually hostile. A 2011 biography of Marine Le Pen even concluded with a chapter of advice for readers, "How to resist the 'new' FN?", which included condescending suggestions of how to distinguish between different types of extremists and how to change the behaviour of misguided far-right voters:

> People who vote for the Front National do it because it's easy, but doing so makes the situation worse instead of resolving problems. Those who nevertheless choose to vote FN are a little bit infantile. You have to be a big baby to believe that you can have everything:

the security of a strong state as well as lower taxes, zero immigration as well as retirement at the age of sixty.[6]

That may be true of far-right voters, but it is equally true of voters for all the other political parties of left, right and centre that over-promise and under-deliver.

Today, however, the balance of power is shifting in favour of the right in the French media, for two main reasons. First, the billionaire conservative Catholic Vincent Bolloré, like Rupert Murdoch, has established an increasingly powerful media empire that encompasses television, radio, newspapers and magazines and book publishing and whose news outlets lean sharply to the right. Second, as in the rest of the world, the rise of the internet and social media has sapped the influence of the traditional media and rapidly transformed the way voters receive news and form their opinions. Despite government subsidies for distribution and investment, the circulation of national print newspapers has fallen to fewer than 640,000 copies a day, a quarter of the level at the turn of the century, as readers have moved online, switched to other sources of information or stopped reading the news altogether.[7]

The "Bollorisation" of French media means that more time and space is given to the leaders of the far right and to previously marginalised opinions about the supposed horrors of mass immigration, the dangers of *wokisme*, the merits of Vladimir Putin and Donald Trump, the uncertainties over global warming and the high cost to ordinary people of environmental rules designed to deal with climate change (if climate change is even real).[8] France's broadcast regulator issued thirty-six warnings and fines totalling €7.6 million on Bolloré's C8 entertainment channel—for promoting conspiracy theories and fake news and not respecting pluralism, among other faults—before finally refusing to renew its licence and thereby closing the channel in February 2025. Most of the fines were related to the popular infotainment

THE BATTLE FOR PUBLIC OPINION

show *Touche pas à mon poste!* (Don't touch my TV channel) hosted by comedian Cyril Hanouna, who triggered a €3.5 million fine for the channel when he called a far-left MP on the show a "jerk", a "loser" and a "buffoon" after he insulted Bolloré.[9]

Bolloré himself—whose media outlets such as the CNews TV channel and *Le Journal du Dimanche* favour far-right and right-wing politicians from Le Pen and Bardella to Éric Zemmour, his partner Sarah Knafo, Le Pen's niece Marion Maréchal, former Les Républicains leader Éric Ciotti and Bruno Retailleau, the interior minister appointed in 2024—is also credited with Murdoch-like politician machinations in promoting the 2024 electoral alliance between Ciotti and Le Pen and with pushing for a broader agreement on the right in the future to ensure a conservative administration in France when Macron's presidency ends in 2027.[10] The right-wing messages are reinforced by a rotating cast of broadcasters, columnists and authors including Pascal Praud and Philippe de Villiers, who all appear regularly on air and in print. *Le Journal du Dimanche*, the previously middle-of-the-road Sunday newspaper turned into a kind of rabid French version of the UK's *Daily Mail*, has been so eager to promote the RN that the satirical paper *Le Canard enchaîné* called it "Le Journal du RN du dimanche".[11]

The closure of C8 inevitably prompted outrage on the French far right but was seen elsewhere as a rare triumph of anti-fake news media regulation of a sort unthinkable in the US. The triumph, however, is likely to be short-lived. CNews, the Bolloré twenty-four-hour TV news channel that has been hailed (and condemned) as France's answer to Fox News, was the most popular such channel in France at the start of 2025, although they all trail the historic terrestrial broadcasters such as TF1. Europe 1, the Bolloré-controlled radio station that shares some broadcasts with CNews, has also seen its audience surge, although it too still trails the established leaders France Inter, RMC and franceinfo.[12]

There is no doubt that CNews is right wing, as Fox News is in the US, but the French channel is constrained by French broadcasting rules under the Arcom regulator in a way that its US counterpart is not: the Federal Communications Commission abolished its "fairness doctrine" in 1987. Like the now defunct C8, CNews has repeatedly been warned and fined by Arcom for such failings as stigmatising immigration and climate denial.[13]

None of this answers the question of whether CNews is influencing viewers and making them right wing or is influenced by a growing right-wing audience to give viewers what they want. The answer is probably both. Culture wars and divisive politics increase both the supply of and the demand for a polarised outlook on the world. In a comparison of CNews and Fox News, researcher Julien Labarre concluded that CNews had the "most ideologically radical news audience in the French media", and the audiences of both channels were "disproportionately receptive to far-right candidates compared to other news audiences and their respective national samples".[14]

Marine Le Pen, who used to excoriate media mogul families such as Bouygues (TF1), Dassault (*Le Figaro*) and Lagardère (Hachette, Europe 1, *Le Journal du Dimanche*, *Paris Match*) and demand they be more tightly regulated when they preferred the traditional right to the FN/RN, has found an ardent supporter for her movement in Vincent Bolloré, whose Vivendi group bought control of Lagardère's media assets.[15] On the other side of the political divide, establishment concern over the Bolloré media empire's influence can be measured by Macron's cold response to a story in *Le Journal du Dimanche* accusing the French president of fearmongering over the Russian threat in early 2025. In an unusual official retort, the Élysée palace emphasised the seriousness of the situation but denied saying or intending to make the French needlessly afraid of Moscow. "In this grave period, during which, faced with the Russian threat, almost

THE BATTLE FOR PUBLIC OPINION

all of Europe's heads of state and government are taking unprecedented measures to assure their defence, everybody should take care to have complete respect for the facts," Macron's office said. "The moment calls for clarity, patriotism and national unity."[16] One of the reasons for this public falling out between Bolloré and Macron was the increasingly pro-Russian line taken by the commentators in Bolloré's media outlets, including de Villiers and Xenia Fedorova, the former head of the French channel of Russian television group RT, which was shut down in the EU by sanctions after Putin's full-scale invasion of Ukraine. Fedorova's book *Bannie: Liberté d'expression sous condition* (Banned: Free speech, but with conditions) was also published by Bolloré publishing house Fayard.

* * *

However significant they may have been in the past, these apparently momentous political battles in print, on television and on the mainstream media's websites and apps are of fading importance in the era of social media, the expanding digital ecosystem in which the far right has been extraordinarily successful in the US and Europe.

In France, the FN/RN has long been more tech-savvy than most of its entrenched political rivals. It was the first party in the country to have a website, in 1994, and Jean-Marie Le Pen said three years later—that is, nearly three decades ago—that he realised it was about "building a new relationship with our voters" and boasted of the party's "huge" database.[17] At the last count, Marine Le Pen had 1.8 million followers on Facebook, and Jordan Bardella 2.1 million on TikTok. "Fringe factions, particularly the nationalistic and far-right, excel in mobilising the European population digitally," wrote Eske Vinther-Jensen and Thomas Albrechtsen in their 2024 Danish report that analysed Facebook posts by members of the European Parliament before that year's 2024 EU elections: of 572 million posts and responses analysed, nationalist Italian MEP Silvia Sardone was involved in a remarkable 55 million, and Bardella, who would indeed triumph in the vote, had more than 13 million, while the average post from an MEP in one of the far-right alliances generated five times as many responses as one from a Green MEP.[18]

From Hungary to Italy and across to Brexit Britain, political strategists such as the Americans Arthur Finkelstein and Steve Bannon have skilfully weaponised digital media for populists and nationalists since 2010 and in some cases propelled them into government—or helped keep them there. They and their willing clients quickly understood some important characteristics about how information and opinions are propagated and consumed in the high-speed digital era: supposed "authenticity" is prized, but factual truth and the experts who can explain it are not; "instinct" or "gut feelings" count for more than reason; negativity and anger are more effective than positivity; and it is essential not to be boring, to keep your audience's attention and convince them that they have instantly understood the point however complicated the underlying question.

"In the populist playbook, lying itself is glorified; it is an instrument of subversion, its purpose to demonstrate that the liar will stop at nothing to 'serve the people'," wrote Catherine Fieschi, author of *Populocracy*. "The lies are signals that these politicians are not bound by the usual norms of the liberal democratic elite. Liberals have virtue signalling—populists have outrage signalling. This is the politics of appealing to the gut over the brain."[19] Giuliano da Empoli, the Italian-Swiss writer who dissected the populist-nationalist dominance of social media in *Les ingénieurs du chaos* (The engineers of chaos),[20] says his conclusions can be summarised in the equation "anger + algorithms = chaos". The goal, he says, is to divide society for political advantage. "In creating contradictions and clashes, they give rise to new governments which are not born of a convergence towards the centre, as in classical politics, but of an attraction towards the extremes."[21]

The problem for beleaguered liberals in both Europe and America is that Russia, and to some extent China, have expertly exploited the social media dominance of the populists and the far right to deepen divides in the western democratic societies they seek to undermine, sometimes with outright fake news and sometimes by simply emphasising and repeatedly reposting an existing item of controversial news that outrages one group of people or another in the target country.[22] The whole ecosystem of short video clips, punchy headlines and outrageous comments is perfectly suited to abuse by unscrupulous populists and malign foreign powers and leaves the liberals and the traditional media—with their quaint attachment to balance, science and the verification of facts—languishing on the sidelines. Government officials and researchers say the French are as vulnerable as anyone to the conspiracy theories, fake news and provocations pumped out on barely regulated social media platforms and often amplified by Russian or Chinese bots or American internet users—and made more convincing with the help of Artificial Intelligence systems. Even genuine video clips or news stories, if they are sufficiently violent or controversial, are selectively exploited to enrage or excite viewers and readers, and they are often taken out of context and relentlessly repeated for maximum effect—which is what happened during the *gilets jaunes* crisis, when Russian French-language websites, some since banned in western Europe, gleefully relayed scenes of violence and confrontation to their French audiences. The underpinnings of modern western societies—science, democracy and the rule of law—are constantly challenged by what researchers call "cognitive warfare": according to one analysis from 2024, nearly half of the French are climate sceptics, and some are also flat-earthers or believers in astrology.

"With growing exposure to this type of content and reduced confidence in traditional media, the French make easy victims for 'fake news', given that attempts to curb the spread of false information are weak and sporadic," according to data platform Statista.[23] Social media platforms claim to be transparent windows on the world, says da Empoli, but they are actually fairground halls of distorting mirrors that use algorithms to adapt their offerings to the expectations and prejudices of each user. It is, he says, a simple three-stage process: identify hot subjects that divide public opinion; publicise the most provocative positions (a demand for gender-free toilets, say) and make them confront each other; and then distribute and display the confrontation to as many people as possible to stoke the resulting outrage.[24]

Da Empoli hopes that the European Union will do what the US has never seriously considered and forcefully impose transparency and responsibility on the tech giants. "We must fight against the ridiculous submission of politics to technology and make the functioning of the platforms compatible with a sustainable political debate," he says.[25] It is a worthy aim, but with the far right on the rise, and Russia already interfering repeatedly in European politics, it may already be far too late.

PART IV

EXIT MARINE?

12

TO RUSSIA WITH LOVE

Marine Le Pen is accustomed to abuse from left-wing demonstrators calling her a fascist and a racist because of her hostility to immigrants, but this was something different. The man shouting at her from the far side of a fishmonger's stall on market day in Pertuis in the south of France was outraged instead by her ties to Russia's Vladimir Putin. "You should be ashamed of yourself!" cried Rémy Barthomeuf, a thirty-seven-year-old IT worker who had just fled from Lviv with his Ukrainian partner Oksana Romanyk following Putin's full-scale invasion of Ukraine in February 2022. The Franco-Ukrainian couple, who had ended up at his parents' home in Pertuis, said they were shocked by Le Pen's attitude to the invasion and her defence of the Russian occupation and subsequent annexation of Crimea back in 2014. "She thinks she can negotiate with Putin and make Nato closer to Russia," said Barthomeuf. "That is to deny reality."[1]

Marine Le Pen's past relationship with Moscow is embarrassingly (for her) well documented, and in the eyes of her detractors it is no excuse that the rapprochement was often more opportunistic than strategic, nor that other French politicians including

Emmanuel Macron have also been bamboozled in the past by the former KGB officer in the Kremlin. In the end, the war in Ukraine was not a decisive factor in her defeat for the second time by Macron in that year's French presidential election, held just two months after the full-scale Russian invasion. Yet the Pertuis confrontation and Le Pen's drastic U-turn on Russia (no longer officially a friend) since Putin's attempt to overrun Ukraine show that Donald Trump's return to the White House is not the only geopolitical issue clouding the outlook for a far-right movement that has never given too much thought to foreign policy: her twenty-two-point manifesto for the 2022 election made scant mention of foreign affairs except its call for an "alliance" with Moscow on European security and a promise to pay more attention to France's overseas territories that are in any case regarded as French and not foreign.

Until mid-2025, Le Pen's affinities with Trump were more problematic for her at home than her previous closeness to Putin, but the unknowable extent of the Russia risk remained. After all, Trump had proved a danger to Europe and the world because he had done what he always said he would do (impose tariffs, try to impose a quick peace on Ukraine and Russia) as well as adding some extras such as his threats to seize Greenland, Canada and Panama. Putin, on the other hand, was a danger to Europe because he had done things he said he would not do, such as attack Kyiv and try to eliminate or re-colonise the internationally recognised nation of Ukraine. The Baltic states, France's fellow EU members, could scarcely be blamed for fearing they might be the next targets for re-absorption into Russia's post-Soviet empire.

For the French far right, the two main attractions of Russia were money and ideology. In 2014, the FN was loaned €9.4 million by the First Czech-Russian bank to finance its political activities, of which the outstanding €6 million was finally repaid in 2023. For her 2022 election campaign, Le Pen was granted a personal loan of €10.7 million by a Hungarian bank with ties to the pro-Russian Hungarian prime minister Viktor Orbán, also since repaid with funds from the French election finance system because her strong performance qualified her for reimbursement of expenses.[2] Le Pen has always said she did not have much choice but to turn to eastern Europe given the reluctance of French banks to lend to a party at that time ostracised by French business and the establishment. She has also denied as "outrageous and offensive" allegations that the first loan from Moscow was linked to her party's support for Russian policies, although she was herself notably sympathetic to the Russian occupation of Crimea and boasted of her meeting with Putin at the Kremlin in 2017.[3] Macron ruthlessly exploited these ties in their televised debate during the 2022 election campaign. He told her "you depend on Russian power and you depend on Putin", and so whenever she talked about Russia "you're talking to your banker".[4]

Apart from the money, Le Pen and her father Jean-Marie before her also had a genuine if not deeply considered appreciation for Russia's world view under Putin, which in many respects—anti-Americanism, nationalism, support for authoritarian rule, social conservatism—matched their own, especially during the brief US dominance of a unipolar world after the end of the Cold War. "[O]ur national interest is to renew the traditional alliance with Russia to counterbalance the extreme imperialism of America, which today has no counterweight, in order to entrench this resurgent power," she wrote in her 2012 book setting out her stall for that year's French presidential election:

> To rely on Russia today represents a conception of Europe that embraces its full extent from the Atlantic to the Urals, with a Europe of nations pursuing their national interests and linked together in a civilisational community, something very different from the ultra-

liberal, American communalist model towards which the European Union is leading us.⁵

Before the invasion of Crimea and the seizure of other parts of eastern Ukraine in 2014—whereupon Russia was expelled from the G8 group of powerful democracies it had joined in 1997—the FN/RN's leaders were not alone among western leaders and politicians in dealing with Putin and trying to engage him in strategic and economic partnerships. Even after 2014, Macron repeatedly courted Putin, inviting him to the palace of Versailles shortly after being elected French president in 2017 and playing the diplomatic role of Putin-whisperer right up to the full-scale invasion of Ukraine. But where the FN/RN did stand out from the western establishment during this period was in having a real affinity with Moscow, a closeness affirmed by both sides of the relationship. In their study of far-right politics in Europe, Camus and Lebourg said Marine Le Pen's pro-Russian feelings were inspired by her former adviser Emmanuel Leroy, who had links to Moscow and was a veteran of the extreme-right Ordre Nouveau that was behind the establishment of the FN party. The FN, they wrote, was more important for Moscow than other European far-right movements because France has a permanent seat on the UN Security Council and is, along with Germany, the mainstay of the EU. Part of the Russian government "has thus become massively involved in the French far right".⁶ When Marine Le Pen was convicted in 2025 by a French court of diverting funds meant for European parliamentary assistants to the party's operations in France—and disqualified for five years from standing in an election—the distinctly undemocratic Russian government protested that France had "killed democracy".⁷

Michel Eltchaninoff, the philosopher who has analysed the views and policies of both Putin and Le Pen, called the FN in 2017 "an open ally of Vladimir Putin's Russia in its struggle against the West". His book on Le Pen, published after Moscow's annexation of Crimea and seizure of parts of the Donbas in the industrial and largely Russian-speaking east of Ukraine, recalled how Le Pen had echoed Russia's lines on its historical claims over Ukraine. "She follows the path traced by Putin, both officially and very faithfully," he wrote.[8] In 2011, she was so closely aligned with Russia that when *Time* magazine named her as one of its 100 "most influential people in the world" (also chosen were US president Barack Obama and footballer Lionel Messi), the person picked to write an assessment of her was her father's Russian friend, the nationalist and xenophobe Vladimir Zhirinovsky.[9] Marine Le Pen repeatedly expressed support for Putin's legitimacy and rejected the western view that Russia's annexation of Crimea was illegal. "There was a referendum, and the inhabitants of Crimea wanted to rejoin Russia," she said in 2017.[10]

Putin's full-scale invasion of Ukraine on 24 February 2022 forced Le Pen to drastically change her tune. Reflecting majority public opinion in France that favoured a beleaguered Ukraine, she said Putin had crossed a "red line" with the invasion, she welcomed Ukrainian refugees on the grounds that they were war fugitives rather economic migrants and tried to stifle the stridently pro-Russian views of some of her party members, including Thierry Mariani, a senior RN member of the European Parliament. She even accepted that Russian soldiers had committed war crimes and admitted that her manifesto proposal for a French alliance with Moscow on European security and other matters would not be possible for the time being. Le Pen did, however, maintain her opposition to sanctions against Russia on the grounds that they were ineffective and damaged the French economy by increasing energy prices.[11]

As it entered its fourth year, it was clear that the war on the borders of the EU had brutally exposed the lack of foreign policy expertise in the upper ranks of the RN and also opened up what looked like a rift between Le Pen and her ambitious protégé and likely successor Jordan Bardella, who was more forthright than Le Pen in publicly criticising Russia and supporting Ukraine after becoming president of the party in 2022. "Russia is obviously a multi-faceted threat for France and the interests of Europe," he said in March 2025.[12] It was an uncomfortable subject for Le Pen, who the week before had made an awkward speech on Ukraine during a debate in the National Assembly, hypocritically attacking Macron for the "twists and turns" of his Ukraine policy and calling for some kind of peace conference of nation states that would exclude international organisations such as Nato and the EU. The problem for Le Pen was that in her quest for the French presidency she had long insisted on formulating the RN's foreign and defence policies, leaving other officials, including Bardella, to follow the party line.

Many other French and European populists and nationalists also struggled to respond convincingly to the challenge posed by Russia's renewed aggression, although the pro-Russian appeasers—they tend to portray themselves as realists—had no qualms about ignoring Ukraine's right to national sovereignty. The far-right polemicist, businessman and politician Philippe de Villiers, for example, claimed like Trump that the war was the fault of Ukrainian president Volodymyr Zelenskyy, not Putin. "He wanted war. He had it. And he lost," he said (even though the war was still raging) on his weekly, hour-long broadcast on the right-wing TV channel CNews after Trump and J.D. Vance tried to humiliate Zelenskyy at the White House in February 2025. "We are very close to a resolution of the conflict," de Villiers said. "In a conflict there are winners and losers, and the main winners of this war are the Americans" selling US natural gas to Europeans who had cut themselves off from Russian supplies and paid billions of euros to support Ukraine. "We have lost everything in this war, a war between two Slav peoples."[13] De Villiers was just one of the Putin apologists given a platform by the increasingly powerful and pro-Russian hard-right media empire of Vincent Bolloré (see Chapter 11).[14]

Le Pen was far from alone in her naivete about Russia—the war forced Matteo Salvini, Italian deputy prime minister and leader of the far-right League, to disavow an accord with the ruling United Russia party struck in 2017—although her public support for Putin before 2022 made her credulity embarrassingly visible. The Russian assault to weaken, destabilise and divide western societies through cyberattacks, misinformation, murder and sabotage has been going on for years. In 2015, Michael Carpenter, Russia adviser to then US vice-president Joe Biden, told Catherine Belton, British author of the book *Putin's People*, that Russia was funding the FN in France, the right-wing nationalist party Jobbik in Hungary, both the Northern League and the Five Star movement in Italy, Syriza in Greece and possibly Die Linke in Germany:

> They're going after all these anti-establishment parties on the left and right. They are totally promiscuous in that respect, and they use these slush funds to do it. Their goal is to target the European countries to weaken the EU and to break consensus on sanctions. It's very serious. They've spent a lot of time and money on this.[15]

In France, Russia was accused of having interfered in the French presidential election that brought Macron to power in 2017, by having hackers leak thousands of Macron campaign email exchanges (and some fake documents) just before the vote, although the hack did not seem to affect the result.[16] (There was no suggestion that the FN/RN was connected to the incident.) Disinformation and the promotion of news designed to deepen the divisions in western societies have since continued, although the flow was slowed at least temporarily by the shutdown of Sputnik and RT in western Europe. One example of how Russia is suspected of operating to sow anger and division was revealed in Paris when people complained about what seemed to be an inflammatory antisemitic graffiti campaign involving the painting of Stars of David on buildings in and around the capital in 2023. The French authorities, who arrested two Moldovans who appeared to be working on orders from abroad, suspected the operation to be the work of Russian intelligence. *Le Monde* linked it to a Russian propaganda network called Doppelgänger that used computer bots to swamp social media with fake news and said the graffiti painters had a photographer with them who immediately posted the images of the graffiti online.[17]

The following year, five coffins draped in French flags and marked "French soldiers from Ukraine" were left on display near the Eiffel Tower—a propaganda stunt to discourage the French from helping Kyiv defend itself against Moscow; the perpetrators were again reported to have been paid by Russia to carry out the task.[18] Even the scare over French bedbugs that made headlines around the world in the months before the Paris Olympics was massively amplified by social media accounts linked to the Kremlin, according to Jean-Noël Barrot, France's Europe minister. "They even created a false link between the arrival of Ukrainian refugees and the spread of bedbugs," he said.[19]

Elections in western democracies nevertheless remain the prime target for Russia as it tries to shift public opinion—and western government policies—away from support for Ukraine. In the run-up to the European Parliament elections of 2024, France's Direction générale de la Sécurité intérieure (DGSI, the domestic intelligence service) was investigating suspected Russian attempts to get Moscow's sympathisers on to party lists so they could be elected.[20] In late 2024, the Romanian authorities annulled the first round of a presidential election in which the pro-Putin, far-right candidate Călin Georgescu had come out ahead, after intelligence reports alleged he had benefitted from an influence campaign run by Moscow, and they then banned him from a re-run of the election in May; Georgescu said he spent no money on his campaign, and his spokesperson suggested the reports of Russian meddling were released to discredit him.[21] The governments of Hungary and Slovakia, which like Romania are EU members, and of Serbia, which is not, are already sympathetic to Moscow.

In Germany, the federal election in early 2025—in which the extreme-right AfD, a party that opposes arming Ukraine and wants to end sanctions against Russia, scored its best result with almost 21 per cent of the vote—was clearly and successfully manipulated by Russia, according to the head of the parliament's intelligence committee. Konstantin von Notz, a Green MP who chairs the committee in the Bundestag, said: "It's happening massively—and in almost all democracies in the world. The proximity of the vast majority of far-right parties in Europe and America to Russia should give us something to think about ... We simply have to recognise that our elections are already being manipulated—and successfully manipulated."[22]

By the spring of 2025, however, Marine Le Pen, Jordan Bardella and the RN were more focused on events in a courtroom at home than on the role of the Kremlin in European politics.

13

EMBEZZLEMENT

"UNBELIEVABLE"—BUT TRUE

When Marine Le Pen said "unbelievable!" and, in the middle of the reading of the judgment, walked out of the courtroom where she was declared guilty of embezzling European Parliament funds, she did not even know her full sentence: she only knew from the judge's long explanation about how the court would apply the law that she would be disqualified for years from standing in future elections and would therefore probably never become French president.

This was a political earthquake for France. Until this verdict on 31 March 2025, Le Pen was the early favourite to win the 2027 election at the end of Emmanuel Macron's second term in the Élysée palace. If she won, she would have been France's first far-right president, fulfilling the ambition she inherited from her father and FN founder Jean-Marie Le Pen, and she would have been the first woman to hold the office. The 2027 contest—or an earlier one, if Macron were to resign—would have been her fourth attempt at the presidency, and she enjoys so much support among voters that she was the only one of at least a dozen potential candidates from the left, right and centre of French politics who was virtually guaranteed a place in the run-off, the second round of the election in which the two best-performing candidates in the first round face each other in the final. "The system brought out its nuclear bomb," Le Pen told RN MPs the next day. The left-leaning newspaper *Le Monde* called the judgment "a thunderbolt in French political life".[1]

It was in fact a timebomb with a very slow fuse. The scandal of the EU funds dates to 2004, when Jean-Marie Le Pen launched a system, later inherited by his daughter, for diverting the money that was supposed to pay the assistants of members of the European Parliament to the FN's cash-starved domestic political operations in France. "So in 2014, when twenty-three MEPs of the Rassemblement National were elected to the European Parliament, the system was designed to be a veritable cash cow for the party," the judges concluded, because the annual salaries for the assistants amounted to €6.5 million, double the RN's whole wage bill at the time. The money tap was only turned off because of the start of the investigation that ultimately led to the trial.[2]

Jean-Marie Le Pen was not included in the trial because he was old and sick, and indeed he died in January 2025 three months after the trial began. Marine Le Pen was sentenced to four years in jail, of which two were suspended and two were to be served not in prison but under home surveillance with an ankle bracelet, fined €100,000 and disqualified from standing in an election for five years. Along with Le Pen and the party itself, twenty-three others from the party were also found guilty of *détournement de fonds publics* (embezzlement of public money), to the tune of €4.4 million in total between 2004 and 2016, or concealment or complicity in the crime.[3] As Le Pen and the other guilty RN members repeatedly emphasised later, they were not accused of pocketing any money themselves for personal enrichment but of financing their party at home with funds destined for work at the European Parliament.

She immediately launched an appeal, which meant most of the penalties were suspended until the outcome of that appeal is known, but the judges ruled that the disqualification from elections must remain in place regardless—a decision that outraged Le Pen and her supporters. It even troubled some rival politicians, who feared that the exclusion from elections of a popular candidate who had yet to be definitively convicted of a crime would look like a political decision by the justice system and the establishment to suppress the will of the people. Jordan Bardella said: "Today, it is not only Marine Le Pen who has been unjustly convicted: it is French democracy that has been executed. #JeSoutiensMarine [I support Marine]."[4] In what appeared to be an acknowledgement of the political sensitivities surrounding the trial, the Paris court of appeal took the unusual step of announcing that it would hear the case sooner than expected, in early 2026—which is more than a year before the next scheduled presidential election in 2027 and would allow the campaign to proceed unhindered if she was cleared or if the disqualification was suspended or shortened while she appealed again.

The verdict unleashed a torrent of by now fairly predictable condemnation from populist and far-right leaders around the world—a group dubbed the "reactionary internationale" by Macron—all arguing that one of their own was being persecuted by the liberal-left establishment to keep her out of power. Donald Trump condemned the trial as a "'Witch Hunt" and likened Le Pen's legal battles to his.[5] Viktor Orbán, Hungary's authoritarian prime minister, said "Je suis Marine!" (I am Marine) in solidarity, while Matteo Salvini, Italy's far-right deputy prime minister, compared the Le Pen verdict to Romania's decision to cancel the first attempt at its 2024 presidential election and exclude the extreme-right front-runner

Călin Georgescu. Putin's spokesman weighed in as well, complaining shamelessly that "more and more European capitals are going down the path of trampling democratic norms".[6]

Other far-right nationalists who voiced support for Le Pen included Geert Wilders in the Netherlands, Brazil's former president Jair Bolsonaro and MPs of the AfD.[7] The newsletter of Coda Media, a non-profit group that studies authoritarians and disinformation, said the "synchronised" international response immediately after the Le Pen verdict showed how effectively authoritarians now operated across borders. "Despite their nationalist rhetoric, these leaders function as a cohesive bloc defending each other against democratic accountability," it said.[8]

There were several problems with the argument that she was unfairly targeted. The proof of guilt was persuasive (among other evidence, the judges cited a damning email exchange between an MEP and the party treasurer about the embezzlement scheme), and the court had applied the punishments dictated by the laws—laws, furthermore, that Marine Le Pen and her party had vigorously supported; she had even said that politicians guilty of such crimes should be banned for life.[9] Nor was she by any means the first politician either to be disqualified from elections or to be convicted of crimes such as corruption, influence-peddling, embezzlement and misuse of state funds. Previous convictions included those of former presidents Jacques Chirac and Nicolas Sarkozy, and former prime minister François Fillon.[10]

More helpful for Le Pen than the embarrassing support from the Kremlin or the convicted felon in the White House were the reservations expressed by French politicians about the court's decision to disqualify her from elections. They included Jean-Luc Mélenchon, leader of the far-left LFI party; then centrist prime minister François Bayrou; Gérald Darmanin, the hard-line justice minister from the centre-right; and François-Xavier Bellamy, an MEP and senior figure in the Gaullist Les Républicains party.

EMBEZZLEMENT

Cynics might say that some of these people had skin in the game: Mélenchon was put under judicial investigation in 2018, following accusations of EU parliamentary assistants' salaries being used to fund the LFI at home—he and the party deny all wrongdoing, and the investigation has been frozen since 2022, when two of Mélenchon's former European parliamentary assistants were placed under formal suspicion as "assisted witnesses". Bayrou was one of a dozen figures from his party Mouvement démocrate to go on trial in October 2023, again for alleged embezzlement of EU parliamentary assistant salaries; Bayrou denies all wrongdoing and was acquitted with two others in February 2024 (the rest, and the party itself, received a variety of suspended jail sentences, fines and terms of ineligibility).[11] But there was also a broader concern about the credibility of the democratic process if the most popular candidate found herself excluded from the race.

"Whatever you think of the RN or the case judged today, this will remain a very dark day for French democracy," Bellamy said on the day of the verdict. "The candidate who was leading in the opinion polls for the presidential election has been prevented from competing by a court decision: this unprecedented event will leave deep marks."[12] Even *The Economist* published an editorial entitled "Why Marine Le Pen should be allowed to run for president", arguing that "the aim should be to punish the offender without also punishing French democracy".[13]

Until the Marine Le Pen case, the most politically consequential prosecution of this kind involved Fillon. Back in 2017, Fillon, the former French prime minister, who was at the time the leading candidate to win the presidential election, saw his popularity fall sharply after press allegations that he had used government money to pay his wife for a French parliamentary assistant's work that she never did. Prosecutors immediately started investigating before the vote. Fillon, the candidate for Les

Républicains, did not win enough votes to qualify for the second round, which was contested by Macron and Le Pen and won by Macron, a newcomer to politics. At the end of a scandal that became known as Penelopegate after the name of his British wife, Fillon was convicted of embezzlement for paying her more than €1 million, sentenced to prison for five years, fined €375,000 and barred from elected office for ten years. Fillon had developed a habit of "grabbing public money by breaking the rules", the prosecutors said, but his supporters among Les Républicains complained of a "witch hunt" and questioned the independence of the judiciary over its unusually rapid decision to place Fillon under formal investigation just before the election.[14] The court of appeal and the court of *cassation* subsequently upheld the guilty verdict, though Fillon continues to appeal against his sentence.[15]

* * *

Le Pen's supporters reacted with fury to the verdict in her trial, condemning the "red judges" of a supposedly leftist judicial system and the shadowy figures of the establishment deemed to be behind what Le Pen called "an extremely serious attack on democracy and the electoral process".[16] Christophe Soulard, who heads France's highest court, the Cour de cassation, retorted by explaining the years-long process of investigation and trial that had led to the verdict. "It's a complete process that is very protective of the rights of the defence. If that is a threat to democracy, I don't know what the words mean." For Soulard, it was the attacks on the justice system—including worrying personal attacks against judges on social media—that were threatening to undermine democracy.[17]

The far right's vociferous attacks on French institutions were out of character for Le Pen and Bardella and a sign of how shocked she, her lawyers and her party were at the unexpected harshness of the sentence imposed on her. She had spent years trying to demonstrate that the party respected the French Republic and its laws, which she wanted rigorously enforced. She told her MPs in the National Assembly to dress conservatively—suits and ties for the men—and to avoid disruptive behaviour, in order to demonstrate that the RN was a potential party of government rather than an opposition faction dedicated to protest.

The intemperate outbursts over the verdict did not last long, and there was a sense that neither Le Pen nor her colleagues had the heart for an extended campaign to try to mobilise reluctant citizens to take part in street protests against the judge's decision. At a rally of a few thousand supporters in Paris less than a week later, Bardella called the verdict "unjust and scandalous", and Le Pen condemned it as "a political decision". But—in a rather forced attempt to liken herself as the white leader of a far-right European party to the black martyr of the US civil rights movement—she also promised "peaceful resistance" like that of "the pastor Martin Luther King in defence of the civil rights of Americans who were at the time oppressed and deprived of their rights".[18]

An opinion poll on the day of the verdict suggested that the French people as a whole were not greatly upset by her plight, with views expressed largely along party lines. According to the survey, 68 per cent thought that the rule disqualifying her from elections was "fair", against 31 per cent who thought it "unfair", while 57 per cent reckoned the verdict was normal given the accusations and 42 per cent thought it had been influenced by the desire to prevent Le Pen standing in the next presidential election.[19] "Today Marine Le Pen has been caught up by her own demagoguery and double standards," said Jean-François Copé, a centre-right politician and former minister. "When applying the law suits her, she is in favour, but as soon as it constrains her it becomes political oppression. Fortunately the French are not deceived."[20]

But was this really the end of Marine Le Pen's political career? Many thought she was finished after her botched television debate against Macron during the 2017 campaign. Others decided that the 2022 contest that Macron won again was going to be her last. But she has always returned to the fray. "Today, they have dropped the nuclear bomb because we are close to power," she told the newspaper *Le Parisien* the day after the verdict. "That's what this demonstrates. The higher you climb, the stronger you are, the heavier the attacks against you. That doesn't bother me, it motivates me. Injustice has always motivated me anyway, and when the injustice is perpetrated by the justice system, it gives me steely, granite-like determination." She rejected the idea of implementing the party's "Plan B"—replacing her as presidential candidate with another such as Bardella—before exhausting all the options for "Plan A", her own candidacy. Le Pen did however hesitate over her long-term future. Asked whether she would finally bow out if she competed and lost in the 2027 presidential election, she said: "It seems that in politics you should never say 'never'. But yes, I think it will be the last. Unless I am elected."[21]

After the trial verdict, Le Pen, herself a lawyer by training, did have some options to extract herself from the politically crippling disqualification that would stop her from becoming president. "The path is narrow, but I think there is a path," she told the Club de l'Hémicycle, a parliamentary video programme on YouTube.[22] She could win her appeal in the summer of 2026, an unlikely but not impossible outcome. Or the appeal judges could confirm the verdict but shorten, remove or suspend the disqualification while she appealed again to the highest court, which would take long enough to allow her to compete in 2027. She also said she would call for a ruling by France's Constitutional Council to decide as a "priority question of constitutionality" whether the sentence of immediate disqualification, even when an appeal was under way, conflicted with the rights of voters to choose their candidates. Lastly, she said she wanted to refer the case to the European Court of Human Rights, although it can only intervene when all avenues under French law have already been exhausted. Asked whether the appeal court was not likely simply to confirm the original decision of the lower court, she said: "So what are you suggesting? That I should commit suicide before being assassinated? No, I won't do that, so I will fight to the end."[23]

The RN party now faced a double danger for its plan to win elections and govern France. The first and most obvious obstacle was that its experienced and popular figurehead, with the most recognisable name in right-wing politics, would probably be prevented from running. But the second difficulty was that the party risked wasting its energy and losing momentum for more than a year while Le Pen tried to overturn the judgment that disqualified her from standing. The result was rising tension within what had previously been a harmonious double act between Le Pen and her chosen successor Bardella, in which he would become her prime minister if she was elected president. She and her supporters argued that to avoid weakening the RN or undermining her chances of success the party should proceed on the assumption that she would indeed be the presidential candidate in 2027; they argued that although Bardella was at least as popular as her in opinion polls at the time of the verdict in mid-2025, he would be too young at the time of the election (just thirty-one years old) to attract widespread support from the French electorate or make an effective president.

Bardella's backers demurred, pointing to his undoubted popularity among the young and his social media skills, and suggesting he would benefit from an early endorsement as the unchallenged representative of the French far right. Bardella himself was in the awkward position of trying simultaneously to express loyalty to Le Pen and fulfil his own ambitions. "At this moment, it is imperative that we stay united and cohesive," he said. "There is not the slightest ambiguity in the fact that Marine Le Pen is my candidate, and that if she is prevented from standing in the future, I think I can tell you that I will be her candidate. I can't be clearer than that."[24]

Before Le Pen's trial verdict, Bardella had always brushed off questions about whether he could stand for president by saying he was confident Le Pen was innocent and would win in court. His acknowledgement after she was disqualified that he might end up replacing her after all irritated Le Pen's camp, but it was the truth, and it was hard to see what else he could have said without ducking the question altogether. A more important matter was whether Bardella's youth and inexperience would discourage voters and prevent him winning the Élysée. He ran two very successful European election campaigns for the RN, in 2019 and 2024, and oversaw the best result in the party's history in 2024's snap French parliamentary election. As Marine Le Pen likes to point out, however, in a French presidential election the voters elect a person, not a party. That is why Bardella's youth might count against him in his attempt to occupy the quasi-monarchical presidency of the Fifth Republic devised by Charles de Gaulle for himself in 1958.

At the age of thirty-nine, Macron was the youngest president in French history and the youngest head of state since Napoleon when he first took office in 2017, but he had at least worked as an investment banker, a government adviser and as finance minister by the time he occupied the Élysée. Bardella would be eight years younger, and his only serious work experience is as a political activist for the RN. Not everyone thought it mattered much, given that Le Pen and Bardella were neck-and-neck in the polls before the verdict against her. One RN politician even told me Bardella would be more likely to win than Le Pen because voters would be so angry about her disqualification. "I think it would make the campaign for the presidential elections a doddle. Bardella has given our party something incredible—a direct line to the younger generations." Hervé Marseille, a senator who leads the centrists in the upper house, thought either would do. "They [the RN] have the advantage of a solid electorate," he said. "The polls are all the same, it's six of one and half a dozen of the other. The outlook isn't so bad for Jordan Bardella."[25]

CONCLUSION

FAR-RIGHT FUTURE

Two years before the next scheduled presidential election, the disqualification of Marine Le Pen immediately shook French politics, forcing the dozen or more presidential hopefuls from far left to far right who were already starting to position themselves for the race to re-calculate their chances for 2027. The probable elimination of the candidate who had been expected to win one of the largest vote shares in the first round, and thereby to qualify for the second-round run-off, obviously makes a potentially decisive difference to the outcome under the hard-to-predict French election system, especially when the incumbent is finishing his second term and cannot stand again in the coming election. To understand the system's potential to produce surprises, it is worth remembering how Jean-Marie Le Pen shocked France in 2002 by eliminating the Socialist prime minister Lionel Jospin and qualifying for the run-off against President Jacques Chirac. One should also recall that in the first rounds of voting in both 2017 and 2022, the far-left candidate Jean-Luc Mélenchon came within two percentage points of qualifying for the run-off; in both elections, there was the real possibility of French voters having a final choice between a far-left candidate and a far-right one, although in the end the centrist Macron qualified and won the run-off both times. If Marine Le Pen—who in 2022 scored more than 23 per cent of the first-round vote and more than 41 per cent in the run-off—cannot run in 2027, it will be the first time in fifteen years that she has not been a candidate.

A definitive disqualification of Marine Le Pen—who was described as "a tragic figure" by one of her MPs after prosecutors announced the harsh sentences they were demanding in the EU embezzlement trial[1]—has implications not only for the RN but also for other parties of the far right. The RN, under the leadership of Jordan Bardella, who is the party's "Plan B", is overwhelmingly the dominant movement in this part of the political spectrum. Among other prominent parties and individuals on the far right with political ambitions are Marion Maréchal, Marine Le Pen's niece who previously called herself Marion Maréchal-Le Pen. She was an RN MP but resigned in 2017 and, the following year, dropped the "Le Pen" from her surname to found a right-wing college in Lyon called the Institut des sciences sociales, économiques et politiques (Issep). She then defected to Éric Zemmour's rival Reconquête! (Reconquest!) party and became an MEP, before being expelled from that party after calling on French voters to support the RN in the 2024 National Assembly elections. She remained in the European Parliament, and in October 2024 took over a far-right party that she renamed Identité–Libertés (Identity and Freedoms); it was previously called the Mouvement conservateur (Conservative Movement) and before that Sens commun (Common Sense). Zemmour himself, a popular television commentator and writer who for a moment nearly overtook Le Pen in the opinion polls during the 2022 presidential campaign, is another prominent possible candidate on the far right, as is his partner Sarah Knafo, who was previously his adviser and campaign manager. "The power of the extreme right is no longer limited to Marine Le Pen," said left-

CONCLUSION

wing MP François Ruffin. "There is a Plan B as in Bardella, a Plan R as in Retailleau, a plan Z as in Zemmour."[2]

Bruno Retailleau, who was appointed interior minister in 2024, is one of several presidential hopefuls from the traditional right whose ambitions raise a fundamental question about the future of all the right-wing and far-right movements in France: will the RN of Le Pen and Bardella end up cooperating in some way with the traditional right-wing republicans, either to win elections, or to govern the country after they have been won, or both? Marine Le Pen's probable elimination from the presidential race makes such an alliance more likely, because she has opposed the watering-down of the RN's hostility to immigration and the EU and been wary of closer ties with big business or proponents of economic liberalisation, whereas Bardella has been more open to collaborating with the rest of the French right to broaden the RN's support base and more willing to listen to private investors. The RN has already formed an electoral alliance with defectors from Les Républicains, whose former leader Ciotti was ousted after he rebelled and decided to cooperate with the RN in 2024; the sixteen MPs of his Union des droites pour la République (Union of the Right for the Republic) are in a joint group with the RN in the National Assembly. As in many other countries, the policies of the far right and the old centre-right in France have begun to converge on certain crucial issues such as immigration, largely because the centre-right has become increasingly hard line in response to public opinion.

The two conservative Catholic French tycoons who most vigorously deploy their media power and their money to try to ensure that France is governed by the far right or at least the right in future—Vincent Bolloré and Pierre-Édouard Stérin—are opposed to mass immigration but supportive of liberal economic policies that would serve their business interests. The stands taken by Bolloré's media outlets and the public statements of

Stérin suggest that neither would mind who wins the next presidential election as long as they implement the policies they want. Among politicians on the traditional right, Retailleau is clearly a favourite for these big beasts of business because he is on the right of the right, while some other putative candidates—for example Édouard Philippe, Macron's former prime minister and mayor of Le Havre, and Dominique de Villepin, the flamboyant former foreign minister and prime minister under Chirac—are closer to the moderate centre.

With populists and right-wing nationalists in the ascendant across the world, the likelihood is that they will triumph in France as well in the years ahead after decades of diligent preparation. Jean-Marie Le Pen and Marine Le Pen have steadily increased their movement's popularity and influence since it was founded in 1972, and until the pronouncement of the verdict against her in March 2025 she was favoured to win the presidency two years later. But even if she is definitively excluded, the far right will probably attain political dominance in one way or another. It could be Jordan Bardella, or another as-yet-unknown choice from within the party, who takes on the task of running for president and wins the Élysée. If Bardella were to stand, and if he were to win the presidency, he might appoint Le Pen as his prime minister in a "Medvedev–Putin" arrangement, because the unelected post of prime minister would not be covered by the judicial disqualification, and Bardella would be free to name her. (When Vladimir Putin was unable to stand legally for a third consecutive presidential term, he installed his colleague Dmitry Medvedev as president with himself as prime minister, before returning as president four years later.)[3] Or an outsider could do what Donald Trump did to the Republicans in the US: take over an established party, bend its ideology and its policies to his personal whims and use it to seize power in a national election. In mid-2025, it emerged that Cyril Hanouna, the star of the TV

CONCLUSION

channel C8, which was shut down by the regulator, was considering a bid for the Élysée in 2027.[4]

What would a far-right government actually be like for France? Left-wingers and liberals are certainly worried. Pierre-Yves Bocquet, who worked at the Élysée for the Socialist president François Hollande, has warned that it would take less than 100 days to transform France into an authoritarian, xenophobic state at the heart of the EU. "That's all that is needed today for the RN or any other party motivated by the same authoritarian intentions to transform France into an illiberal democracy and to take the lead in this European club already joined by Viktor Orbán's Hungary and Robert Fico's Slovakia, two nations transformed in a few years into authoritarian states that defy the principles of the European Union and are radically hostile to foreigners," he wrote in a pamphlet.[5] Published in early 2025, it called for an urgent change to the French constitution to make it harder for the RN to implement its own radical constitutional changes to discriminate against foreigners by means of the referendum it has said it will call as soon as it wins presidential and parliamentary power.

Bocquet said the RN's programme, endorsed by the will of the people in such a plebiscite,[6] would eliminate the universal freedoms for which France has been known since the Revolution, because *liberté*, *égalité* and *fraternité* would only be for French citizens. "It would be a change of regime. That's why it is not an exaggeration to talk of revolution, a new national, authoritarian, plebiscitary and xenophobic Revolution. The Sixth Republic of the RN."[7] In an epilogue to his book on the trial of Marshal Philippe Pétain, the historian Julian Jackson issued a similar warning about the political strategy of the French far right and its allies, saying that it was very much in the Pétainist tradition—"racism, inward-looking nationalism, stigmatisation of domestic enemies, discrimination against French citizens (not

Jewish this time but north African), all while shamelessly claiming to be following in the footsteps of General de Gaulle".[8]

RN leaders do indeed like to quote de Gaulle—Marine Le Pen does it all the time, and Bardella did so twice during his interview with me in May 2025—and they agree that they have revolutionary plans for France that would include reducing immigration to a trickle of skilled workers for temporary jobs, re-imposing border controls with EU neighbours, implementing "national priority" for French citizens over foreigners, cracking down on crime, completely resetting the country's relationship with the EU, introducing more trade protectionism and slashing wasteful public spending. "The reality is that for the past thirty years we have moved towards more laxity, a culture of excuses and a policy of allowing immigration in unprecedented numbers which is changing the nature of our country, changing its values and changing its identity," Bardella said in the interview at the party's unassuming headquarters in western Paris.[9] He called for a complete change of direction after three decades of rule by the right, the left and a mixture of the two under the centrist Macron, saying that the RN's aims were to strengthen French national pride and the defence of the nation state and protect people from the consequences of "savage and ultraliberal globalisation, deindustrialisation, massive immigration, the loss of our values".[10] Echoing the key slogan of the UK's Brexiters, he said the idea was to "take back control" (he used the English phrase) of the country.

When I asked Bardella what would have changed a year into an RN administration in France, he replied that they would have already held the immigration referendum to change the constitution, ended the *droit du sol* allowing those born on French soil to claim citizenship, negotiated deals with other countries to stem the flow of migrants to Europe and introduced "national priority" to give French citizens exclusive access to social security

CONCLUSION

benefits. On the economy, he wants to help businesses by reducing red tape and the charges levied on employers, reduce foreign development aid and France's net contribution to the EU and set up what he called a "DOGE *à la française*" that would emulate Elon Musk's attempt to cut public spending in the United States. The RN no longer needed to lead France out of the EU (a policy it abandoned nearly a decade ago), he said, because more and more member states from Denmark to Italy and Hungary were now defending their national sovereignty against the federally minded bureaucrats of Brussels. "These days there is every reason to take power from within [the EU]," he said. "What I mean is that when you're winning the match, you don't suddenly leave the pitch."[11]

The RN, despite being the most popular party in France, has so far been kept out of power by a combination of its pariah status in national politics and the country's two-round electoral system, but if and when it does take control of France, the effect on the EU will be profound because Paris and Berlin dominate the twenty-seven-member union. "We may be last in line [of the European nationalist parties to win power], but we'll get there," said Bardella. "A victory in France is also a victory for Europe, because I know that a lot of European countries and European partners see us as the only country along with Germany that can change the way the European project works."[12] At the time of the last presidential election in 2022, in which Macron eventually beat Le Pen, analysts pointed out the dangers to the EU of a hypothetical Le Pen presidency given that many of her economic, social and migration policies would be in breach of EU law. Mujtaba Rahman of Eurasia Group said if Le Pen's policies were implemented, they would cause "the greatest crisis in the EU's history" and would amount to Frexit by stealth or at least emulate the disruption and disobedience already shown by Hungary. "For Budapest to break EU law systematically is a dangerous challenge to Brussels," he wrote. "For France to do so, a founder member and second largest economy in the EU27, would make the Union unworkable—and raise the prospect of its collapse in its current form."[13]

Not everyone thinks either the domestic or the international effects of an RN administration in France would be quite so dramatic, and some French commentators point hopefully to the example of Giorgia Meloni, the radical-right Italian prime minister from the Brothers of Italy party (of fascist origins), who has cooperated with EU leaders since taking office, moderated her migration policies and seems to have been constrained by the realities of government. "My own personal view is that if the party [the RN] comes into power—and it's a guess, it's only a guess—it will be much more like Italy with Meloni," Jean-Yves Camus, an expert on the European far right, told me:

> Of course Marine Le Pen [whether president or prime minister] will have a difficult time because she will need to restrain the real extremists within her party, those who will say, "Now that we are in power we must be like Donald Trump and do everything we please and immediately shut down universities, shut down liberal newspapers."[14]

In early 2025, the authors of a satirical French novel set during a future Le Pen presidency imagined a scenario in which the RN has done what it set out to do: the new administration has managed to "take back control", discriminating against immigrants, undermining the justice system and the establishment media, ditching rules and subsidies designed to limit global warming and reducing transfers to Paris and other irritatingly *bobo* (bourgeois-bohemian) big cities. Then it all starts to go wrong. Tourism declines. Climate disasters proliferate. Immigrants emigrate again, leaving hospitals short of doctors and nurses. A severe debt crisis triggers economic disaster, forcing Le Pen to go cap in hand to German chancellor Friedrich Merz for a bailout,

CONCLUSION

which comes at the price of an even greater humiliation: the absorption of France into a protective European superstate that previous French leaders said they wanted but actually did not. The RN leadership resists, suggesting instead that France suspend debt payments and withdraw from the euro currency and that the president declare a state of emergency. The book, whose authors are no fans of the far right, ends with Le Pen wondering which of the two equally unpalatable solutions she will choose. "The RN," they write, "had of course deep down never really considered what sovereignty really meant in an interdependent world and for an indebted nation."[15]

The far right's reluctance to come to terms with globalisation and modern life—because its ideology is essentially inward-looking and backward-looking—is a political vulnerability that will probably make it harder for parties such as the RN to exercise power even if it does not prevent them from being elected in the first place. One of the most striking sentences in the nostalgic, cantankerous autobiography of the right-wing polemicist, politician and entrepreneur Philippe de Villiers (who is not in the RN but shares many of its views) was about his childhood in the "harmony" of the rural Vendée in the 1960s. "The society in which I grew up had barely changed in a thousand years," he wrote, implying that it would have been better if it had changed equally little in the six decades that followed. Yet no one can turn the clock back, in France, the US, China or anywhere. Yes, Donald Trump has triumphed twice at the ballot box by convincing tens of millions of the most prosperous and privileged consumers the world has ever seen that Americans are victims in the twenty-first century—victims of foreigners, especially Chinese and Europeans, and victims of the American elite. In office, however, he has struggled through a chaotic series of trade wars, foreign aid cuts, immigrant and student expulsions and half-hearted diplomatic initiatives to unravel the innumerable international connections that underpin US prosperity—and this in a vast, continental nation that is better positioned than most for some kind of glorious self-sufficiency. If his project fails to deliver the improvements promised, a similar project for France, with fewer resources and a much smaller economy, risks meeting with even greater failure.

When I asked Bardella whether it made sense to complain about globalisation when each of us depends on the rest of the world—after all, we spend our days looking at the output of American social media platforms on phones made in China using US and Korean software—he agreed that globalisation was an unavoidable reality but insisted that France needed to emulate the other "great powers" in standing up for its own national interests. This raises the question of whether the far right in France, like the British politicians who promoted Brexit, are deluding themselves in thinking that in a world of jostling superpowers they are stronger without the benefit of the pooled negotiating power of twenty-seven EU member states.

For the next election, these theoretical considerations about the state of the world may not matter much. What will count is the mood in France. Le Pen, Bardella and the RN have been on a roll for years—with increasing popularity and improving election results—and are ready to cash in their investment in the popular anger that erupted in the *gilets jaunes* demonstrations during Macron's first term and has continued to simmer ever since. If Le Pen is prevented from standing for president, Bardella is ready and eager to take her place. Either way, says Le Pen, "there is a genuine collective realisation, even among our own voters who didn't necessarily use to believe it, that we can win. In a way, our victory is inevitable."[16]

ACKNOWLEDGEMENTS

My thanks go to all the people who made this book possible. First, the French people, including the many voters, ministers, politicians and analysts who took the time to talk to me over the years, sometimes at great length and on many different occasions; there were a few Front National-Rassemblement National politicians who refused to speak to a foreign journalist such as myself, but others, including the party's leaders, were more forthcoming, and I hope I have given them the same fair hearing I aimed to give to all my interlocutors. Second, my dynamic agent Kelly Falconer ("Agent K") of Asia Literary Agency, and the team at Hurst, including Michael Dwyer and my brilliantly rigorous editor Lara Weisweiller-Wu. Third, all my colleagues at the *Financial Times*, which goes from strength to strength as one of the world's great newspapers because of the quality of its global coverage. And finally, Michèle, Natasha and Geneviève, who tolerated my months-long occupation of the living-room table in Paris while I wrote the book and gave me the love and strength to complete it.

NOTES

PREFACE

1. "Le mot extrême droite fut bien utile en France après la seconde guerre mondiale: fasciste, colonialiste, impérialiste, raciste, intégriste ou réactionnaire, l'extrême droite désignait toujours le méchant du théâtre politique, l'infréquentable, celui qui ne doit pas accéder au pouvoir. L'adjectif extrême est négatif, il suggère un excès, où tout excès est un défaut par rapport à l'idéal de l'équilibre. Par convention, il frappe plus la droite que la gauche: on dit un gauchiste, mais un extrémiste de droite, pas un droitiste." Jean-Marie Le Pen, *Mémoires: Tribun du peuple*, Muller, 2019, p. 18.
2. "Répartition des groupes politiques dans l'hémicycle, XVIIe législature", Répartition des groupes politiques dans l'hémicycle XVIIe legislature, https://www2.assemblee-nationale.fr/instances/liste/groupes_politiques/effectif/(hemi)/true
3. Pierre-Henri Tavoillot, "Je dirais qu'il s'agit d'un parti de droite radicale, populiste et illibérale: Le Rassemblement national est-il encore d'extrême droite?", *Le Figaro*, 11–12 Nov. 2023.
4. Catherine Fieschi, *Populocracy*, Agenda Publishing, 2019, p. 30.
5. Fieschi, *Populocracy*, pp. 36, 162.

INTRODUCTION: AFTER EMMANUEL MACRON

1. Conversation with the author, Jan. 2022. The word used was *basculer*.
2. Victor Mallet, "The meaning of Macron", *Financial Times*, 23 July 2021.
3. "'Tu m'appelles monsieur le Président': Macron recadre un collégien lors des commémorations du 18-Juin", franceinfo, 18 June 2018, https://

www.franceinfo.fr/politique/emmanuel-macron/video-tu-m-appelles-monsieur-le-president-macron-recadre-un-collegien-lors-des-commemorations-du-18-juin-1940_2808179.html

4. Emmanuel Macron, *Revolution*, trans. Jonathan Goldberg & Juliette Scott, Scribe, 2017.
5. Victor Mallet and Roula Khalaf, "FT Interview: Emmanuel Macron says it is time to think the unthinkable", *Financial Times*, 16 Apr. 2020.
6. Roula Khalaf, Ben Hall and Victor Mallet, "Emmanuel Macron: 'For me, the key is multilateralism that produces results'", *Financial Times*, 18 Feb. 2021.
7. Ben Ansell, "Twilight of the populists?", Political Calculus/Substack, 10 Mar. 2025, https://benansell.substack.com/p/twilight-of-the-populists
8. As the historian Julian Jackson said in an interview in *Le Monde*: "All liberal democracies today are living through a crisis of legitimacy, arising from the financial crisis and the fact that their populations are not benefitting from globalisation. People who feel like social rejects ponder the decline of their country and search for scapegoats to explain these problems. As for the stability and solidity of institutions, there is today a grave, profound crisis of liberal democracy. Some of the symptoms can be seen in the voters who chose Donald Trump, Brexit or the Rassemblement National, who share the same fears about being left behind." Jackson added a warning: "We too often forget that in the aftermath of the second world war, liberal democracy as we know it today is a recent phenomenon. Nobody would have said after the crises of the 1930s in Europe that liberal democracy was safe and sound" (*Toutes les démocraties libérales vivent aujourd'hui une même crise de légitimité, provenant de la crise financière et du fait que des populations ne profitent pas de la mondialisation. Ce sont des laissés-pour-compte qui pensent au déclin de leur pays et cherchent des boucs-émissaires pour expliquer ces problèmes. Pour en revenir à la stabilité et la solidité des institutions, il y a aujourd'hui une grave et profonde crise de la démocratie libérale. Les symptômes se trouvent en partie dans l'électorat de Donald Trump, du Brexit et du Rassemblement national (RN), qui ont en commun les mêmes peurs de déclassement. On oublie trop souvent que depuis la seconde guerre mondiale,*

la démocratie libérale comme nous la vivons actuellement est récente. Personne n'aurait dit après les crises des années 1930 en Europe que la démocratie libérale fut saine et sauve. Dans un sens, nous vivons sur un temps long quelque chose d'assez court.) From "Le plus grand danger pour la démocratie et la République est que leurs valeurs sont de plus en plus minées de l'intérieur", interview by Gaïdz Minassian, *Le Monde*, 8 Mar. 2025.

9. Jeremy Black, *France: A Short History*, Thames & Hudson, 2021, pp. 166–7. The name of the left-wing Nouveau Front Populaire, the largest alliance in the National Assembly after the 2024 election, is a deliberate echo of the 1930s Front Populaire.
10. Philip M. Williams, *Crisis and Compromise: Politics in the Fourth Republic*, Longman, 1972, p. 27.
11. See Reuters Institute's "Digital Media Report 2025": https://reutersinstitute.politics.ox.ac.uk/digital-news-report/2025/dnr-executive-summary
12. "[J]e crois être au milieu d'eux. Je suis eux ... Très souvent, j'ai le sentiment de ressentir la même chose que ce que ressentent les Français. Je réagis comme réagit la moyenne des Français. Je partage leur indignation quand ils sont indignés ... J'ai les mêmes élans d'enthousiasme, les mêmes inquiétudes. Et, surtout, les mêmes espérances." "Nous ne devons rien à personne", interview by Tugdual Denis and Sébastien Lignier, *Valeurs Actuelles*, 11 Dec. 2024.
13. Seuil, 2019.
14. Flammarion, 2014. He followed up in 2025 with a fictionalised version, a kind of fable of elitist political incompetence called *Métropolia et Périphéria: Un voyage extraordinaire*, Flammarion, 2025.
15. *Producteurs et parasites: L'imaginaire si désirable du Rassemblement national*, La Découverte, 2024.
16. "En cinquante ans, nous avons connu d'énormes bouleversements économiques: il y a des franges de la population qu'on n'a jamais inscrites dans le processus de mondialisation, qui se sentent tenues à l'écart depuis des années de ce monde-là, qui n'ont d'ailleurs pas forcément envie de l'intégrer." "La notion de travail est au coeur du vote RN", interview by Céline Delbecque on the appearance of Jarousseau's book

Dans les âmes et les urnes: Dix ans à la rencontre de la France qui vote RN, Arènes, 2025.

17. "On ne peut plus écarter une victoire du RN en 2027", interview by Jérôme Béglé, *Le Journal du Dimanche*, 17 July 2022.
18. Ivanne Trippenbach, "Why Serge Klarsfeld, the renowned Nazi hunter, says he's ready to vote RN", *Le Monde* (English edn), 23 June 2024.
19. Jeanne Belanyi, "RN dans les Outre-mer: Symbole d'une extrême droite au dernier stade de sa 'dédiabolisation'?", Fondation Jean Jaurès, 26 June 2024.
20. "L'ambition que nous portons avec le président Ciotti est celle d'une rupture responsable, respectueuse des corps intermédiaires et des partenaires sociaux, soucieuse de la stabilité des institutions", quoted in Barthélémy Philippe and Alexandre Chauveau, "Auditionné par le Medef, Jordan Bardella veut rassurer les patrons sur son projet", Europe 1, 20 June 2024, https://www.europe1.fr/economie/auditionne-par-le-medef-jordan-bardella-veut-rassurer-les-patrons-sur-son-projet-4253718
21. Robin d'Angelo, "Au Rassemblement national, les Horaces peinent à conserver leur place", *Le Monde*, 17 May 2025.
22. "Les Horaces", https://les-horaces.fr
23. "[O]n est d'accord avec vous, finalement, mais il y a toujours cette question de ne pas sortir du bois pour ne pas être stigmatisé", Les Horaces news conference, Paris, 16 May 2025.
24. Les Horaces news conference, Paris, 16 May 2025.
25. "Les Horaces", https://les-horaces.fr
26. Sarah White and Leila Abboud, "How France's far right built a national movement", *Financial Times*, 4 July 2024.
27. "Ils ont un vrai talent pour satisfaire la demande de fierté locale, les fêtes traditionnelles et tout ce qui témoigne de l'ancrage dans un territoire", quoted in Luc Bronner, "RN, la grande accoutumance", *Le Monde*, 13 Apr. 2024.
28. Conversation with the author, 11 Feb. 2025.
29. Interview by Anne Rosencher, "Rappelez-vous ce qui se disait dans le milieu intellectuel et journalistique avant le victoire de Trump", *L'Express*, 23–9 Jan. 2020.

NOTES

1. YELLOW-VEST REBELLION

1. "La macronie a fait feu à boulets rouges sur l'ennemi public numéro un, le populisme, le nationalisme haï: sans l'apport des gilets jaunes, c'en était fini du RN." Le Pen, *Mémoires: Tribun*, p. 411.
2. "Les gilets jaunes un moment ont semblé montrer que le peuple peut encore se lever. Mais les tuniques bleues du système nous ramènent toujours à coups de matraque dans notre réserve de Peaux Rouges." Le Pen, *Mémoires: Tribun*, p. 474.
3. Jérôme Fourquet, *Métamorphoses françaises: État de la France en infographies et en images*, Seuil, 2024, p. 170.
4. "Le mouvement des Gilets jaunes est anti-urbain, anti-élites, anti-intellectuels, anti-parlementaires, anti-mondialisation, antilibéral, et occasionnellement antisémite, ce qui va avec le reste—mais cela, le RN a eu l'intelligence de ne pas le laisser trop prospérer. Toujours est-il que les leaders du mouvement qui ont fait ensuite de la politique—à l'exception notable de Priscillia Ludosky et d'un ou deux mélenchonistes moins connus—sont allés du côté de l'extrême droite." Guillaume Hannezo, Hakim El Karoui and Thierry Pech, *Marine Le Pen présidente: Dystopie politique 2026–2029*, Les Petits matins, 2025, p. 27.
5. "*Ni … ni …*", neither one nor the other, or "a plague on both your houses", is a common sentiment among French voters, especially when only two candidates remain in the second round of an election.
6. These descriptions and interviews are taken from my reports at the time, including "The gilets jaunes are marching to a different beat", *Financial Times*, 29 Jan. 2019, and "France's gilets jaunes protests keep heat on Macron", *Financial Times*, 23 Mar. 2019.
7. "Figureheads emerge among France's 'gilets jaunes' protesters", *Financial Times*, 11 Jan. 2019; "Lunch with the FT: Priscillia Ludosky: 'Things are boiling over everywhere'", *Financial Times*, 2–3 Nov. 2019; see also Giuliano da Empoli, *Les ingénieurs du chaos*, Lattès, 2019, 2023, p. 189.
8. "Europe Express: Macron's popular touch", *Financial Times*, 15 Feb. 2019; "Cahiers de doléances: Un abandon démocratique et un trésor d'informations inexploité", Radio France, 5 Sep. 2024.
9. "France set to ban Champs Élysées protests in wake of riots", *Financial Times*, 18 Mar. 2019.

10. "Year of 'gilets jaunes' leaves angry mark on France", *Financial Times*, 14 Nov. 2019.
11. Fourquet, *Métamorphoses françaises*, pp. 167–71 (the categories do not add up to 100 per cent because they sometimes overlap).
12. Published in France as *Sérotonine*, Flammarion, 2019.
13. Da Empoli, *Les ingénieurs du chaos*, pp. 155–6.

2. THE TRUMP EFFECT

1. John Burn-Murdoch, "What makes the Maga mindset different?", *Financial Times*, 7 Mar. 2025.
2. "[M]on ami Fischer dit que j'ai encore des fans en Amérique, ils me voient en grand frère de Trump, en père du populisme; ... Trump a réussi au contraire en se radicalisant, en devenant le diable qu'on l'accusait d'être, que l'eau que les nationalistes suédois ont mise dans leur vin les éloigne du pouvoir alors que le Chianti Classico de Salvini lui réussit à merveille." Le Pen, *Mémoires: Tribun*, p. 405.
3. Conversation with the author and others after Jordan Bardella's news conference, 27 Jan. 2025.
4. "J'ai beaucoup de respect et d'admiration pour le patriotisme de Donald Trump, pour la volonté de défendre les intérêts de son pays d'abord et avant tout." Conversation with the author, Paris, 27 Jan. 2025.
5. "Jordan Bardella annule son discours au CPAC après le salut nazi de Steve Bannon", HuffPost France, 21 Feb. 2025.
6. Interview with the author, Mar. 2025.
7. Via Elon Musk's X account (@elonmusk), on 4 Apr. 2025, https://x.com/elonmusk/status/1908013951113195741?t=l3QILDJEaRR7PJ22EzvlgQ&s=03
8. Interview with the author, 11 Feb. 2025.
9. "Donald Trump met le populisme sous une lumière négative. J'ai toujours pensé qu'il était toxique et qu'il fallait prendre nos distances, expliquer en quoi nous sommes différents." "Le RN embarrassé par le trumpisme", *Le Monde*, 13–14 Apr. 2025.
10. By Christophe Blain and Abel Lanzac, Dargaud, 2010.
11. De Villepin speaking to Anglo-American Press Association in Paris, 14 Feb. 2025.

12. Mark Mazower, "The exceptional nation", *Financial Times*, 16–17 Nov. 2024.
13. Conversation with the author, 7 Mar. 2025.
14. "How Donald Trump is shaping other countries' politics", *The Economist*, 5 Apr. 2025.
15. Andrew Higgins, "With Trump's victory, Europe's populist right sees return of a fellow believer", *New York Times*, 8 Nov. 2024; Gideon Rachman, "Trump's European allies think history is turning in their direction", *Financial Times*, 11 Nov. 2024.
16. "Europe's far-right leaders applaud Trump and downplay threat of possible US tariffs", Associated Press, 8 Feb. 2025; David Latona, "Orban, Le Pen hail Trump at far-right 'Patriots' summit in Madrid", Reuters, 8 Feb. 2025.
17. @elonmusk, X, 22 Feb. 2025, https://x.com/elonmusk/status/1893436853665308706
18. "Munich Security Conference as it happened: JD Vance says he fears Europe's 'threat from within'", FT blog, 14 Feb. 2025, https://www.ft.com/content/3af08b74-9432-4183-8e95-a1dc7dd16bbb
19. See for example Marco Margaritoff, "Polish cold war hero slams 'insulting' Trump–Zelenskyy meeting: 'We are shocked'", HuffPost, 4 Mar. 2025, https://www.yahoo.com/news/polish-cold-war-hero-slams-145238935.html
20. Ivan Krastev, "Europe must hijack Trump's revolutionary plans for the world", *Financial Times*, 1–2 Mar. 2025.
21. "Comme aux États-Unis, tous les ferments d'une victoire de l'extrême droite sont implantés dans notre pays, de la constitution d'un empire médiatique acquis à sa cause au sentiment de déclassement d'une partie grandissante de la population et à la focalisation obsessionnelle sur les questions migratoires. Sans être encore officiellement au pouvoir, le national-populisme a déjà conquis les esprits, alimenté par la polarisation à outrance de notre débat public." Cécile Prieur, "Trump 2, le défi aux progressistes", *Le Nouvel Obs*, 14 Nov. 2024, p. 3.

3. IN THE BEGINNING WAS THE FATHER

1. Christiane Chombeau, *Le Pen: Fille & père*, Panama, 2007, p. 46.

2. Jean-Yves Camus and Nicolas Lebourg, *Far-Right Politics in Europe*, Belknap Press of Harvard University Press, 2017, pp. 2–3.
3. "Haïr le juif et le métèque, c'est aimer la France"; "C'est la revanche de Dreyfus." Quoted in Jacques de Saint Victor, "Le drame en trois actes de la droite française depuis 1789", *Revue des deux mondes: Les droites conquérantes*, Mar. 2025, pp. 21–2.
4. "On n'insistera jamais assez sur le poids du processus de fascisation de la droite intellectuelle, à partir de son noyau maurrassien, ainsi que sur le rôle des intellectuels dans la création d'un climat qui a permis l'emprise du fascisme ... Les hommes arrivés au pouvoir en été 1940 étaient moralement et intellectuellement prêts à se mettre à l'œuvre autant que les nazis en 1933, et peut-être plus que les fascistes italiens en 1921 ... Ni Franco, ni Salazar, ni Mussolini ne sont allés aussi loin." Zeev Sternhell, *Ni droite ni gauche: L'idéologie fasciste en France*, Fayard, 1987, 2000, pp. 14, 48, 51.
5. Michel Eltchaninoff, *Inside the Mind of Marine Le Pen*, Hurst, 2017, pp. 104–6.
6. Camus and Lebourg, *Far-Right Politics in Europe*, p. 7.
7. "Au fil des deux dernières siècles s'est constituée, par strates successives, une extrême droite très plurielle. Il en reste aujourd'hui une branche réactionnaire, l'Action française, sans doute la mieux structurée intellectuellement; une extrême droite néofasciste; et une extrême droite national-populiste, dont le Rassemblement national est l'héritier ... Il est avant tout un parti anti-immigrés, c'est ainsi qu'il naît et qu'il rencontre le succès. Par la suite, il devient une formation vraiment populiste." Interviewed in Franck Johannes, "L'institutionnalisation du RN a partiellement échoué", *Le Monde*, 24–5 Jan. 2021.
8. Conversation with the author, 11 Feb. 2025.
9. "En attendant, n'ayez pas peur de rêver. Vous, les petits, les sans grade, les exclus, ne vous laissez pas enfermer dans les vieilles divisions de la gauche et de la droite. Vous qui avez supporté depuis vingt ans toutes les erreurs et les malversations des politiciens, vous, les mineurs, les métallos, les ouvrières et les ouvriers de toutes ces industries ruinées par l'euro mondialisme de Maastricht, vous, les agriculteurs aux retraites de misère et acculés à la ruine et à la disparition, vous aussi, qui êtes les

premières victimes de l'insécurité dans les banlieues, les villes et les villages ... Je suis socialement à gauche, économiquement à droite et plus que jamais nationalement de France." "Déclaration de Jean-Marie Le Pen", L'INA éclaire l'actu, 21 Apr. 2005, https://www.ina.fr/ina-eclaire-actu/video/2004466001018/declaration-de-jean-marie-le-pen; "'Don't be afraid to dream,' Le Pen tells jubilant far-right supporters", *Financial Times*, 22 Apr. 2002.

10. "Le Pen's star on the wane as rivals step in", *Financial Times*, 20 Mar. 2002.
11. "Business leaders round on Le Pen", *Financial Times*, 30 Apr. 2002.
12. "Friends of Chirac attacker questioned", *Financial Times*, 16 July 2002.
13. "Embittered Le Pen plots his return in political backlash", *Financial Times*, 1 Oct. 2002.
14. Fieschi, *Populocracy*, p. 3.
15. Jean-Marie Le Pen, *Mémoires: Fils de la Nation*, Muller, 2018, pp. 46–7.
16. Philip Williams, *Crisis and Compromise: Politics in the Fourth Republic*, Longman, 1972, pp. 168–9.
17. Le Pen, *Mémoires: Tribun*, p. 221.
18. Le Pen, *Mémoires: Tribun*, p. 347.
19. Laurent de Boissieu, "Les 'front national' de Jean-Marie Le Pen", iPolitique, 8 Feb. 2013, http://www.ipolitique.fr/archive/2013/02/07/front-national-jean-marie-le-pen.html; Le Pen, *Mémoires: Fils*, p. 301.
20. "La nation est la communauté de langue, d'intérêts, de race, de souvenirs où l'homme s'épanouit. Il y tient par ses racines, ses morts, le passé, l'hérédité ou l'héritage ... Dans cette protection de la communauté, l'immigration et l'assimilation des étrangers sont un des soucis majeurs. Rien ne sert de veiller aux frontières si une invasion pacifique et légale change la nature et le particularisme du peuple français." "La Déclaration d'intention du Front national en 1972", Fragments sur les Temps Présents, https://tempspresents.com/2022/10/07/la-declaration-dintention-du-front-national-en-1972/
21. "Je m'honorais de réunir communistes, démocrates chrétiens, monarchistes, sympathisants du nazisme, de même que je rassemblais juifs, chrétiens, musulmans, païens, noirs, arabes, jaunes et Français de souche. Je voulais attirer à moi les Français de toute origine, pourvu qu'ils fussent patriotes." Le Pen, *Mémoires: Tribun*, p. 32.

22. Camus and Lebourg, *Far-Right Politics in Europe*, p. 47.
23. "On a été jusqu'à parler de l'absurde égalité des races, mais si maintenant il y a en plus l'égalité des civilisations, je ne sais pas jusqu'où nous ne descendrons pas." RTL interview, Sept. 1996, quoted in Michel Soudais, *Le Front National en Face*, Flammarion, 1996.
24. "Aux Jeux olympiques, il y a une évidente inégalité entre la race noire et la race blanche ... c'est un fait. Je constate que les races sont inégales." Christiane Chombeau, "M. Le Pen récidive sur 'l'inégalité des races'", *Le Monde*, 11 Sept. 1996.
25. "Le monde blanc est en train de mourir." Le Pen, *Mémoires: Fils*, pp. 283–5.
26. "Et puis regardons une carte. Paris avait jadis une ceinture rouge, elle est verte aujourd'hui. La capitale est encerclée et pénétrée par la racaille Islamiste ... Si les pays du Sud continuent à déverser leurs 'migrants pacifiques', que ferons-nous? Quand ils arriveront, coulera-t-on leurs bateaux? Si on ne les coule pas, c'est foutu." Le Pen, *Mémoires: Tribun*, pp. 427–32.
27. There are multiple sources for Jean-Marie Le Pen's racial and antisemitic comments, including his own memoirs, because most of them were published in the media and several were litigated in court. Many of them are collected in the obituary in *Libération*: "Mort de Jean-Marie Le Pen, voyage au bout de l'extrême", *Libération*, 7 Jan. 2025.
28. "S'il faut user de violence pour découvrir un nid de bombes, s'il faut torturer un homme pour en sauver cent, la torture est inévitable, et donc, dans les conditions, anormales où l'on nous demande d'agir, elle est juste"; "Je n'ai rien à cacher. J'ai torturé parce qu'il fallait le faire." Details of many of the cases can be found in "Les Exactions du Lieutenant Le Pen", *Le Monde*, 2 Mar. 2024, a review of the book *Le Pen et la Torture: Alger 1957, l'histoire contre l'oubli*, Le passager clandestin, 2024.
29. Le Pen, *Mémoires: Tribun*, pp. 248–57.
30. "Entre nous, le courant est passé. Il y a eu quelque chose. Une sympathie naturelle entre deux parias qui refusent de courber l'échine devant la puissance injuste et cherchent des solutions humaines à des conflits humains." Le Pen, *Mémoires: Tribun*, p. 302.

31. Le Pen, *Mémoires: Tribun*, p. 12.
32. "Le Pen pose parfois les bonnes questions même s'il y apporte de mauvaises réponses." Quoted in "Mort de Jean-Marie Le Pen, voyage au bout de l'extrême", *Libération*, 7 Jan. 2025.
33. "C'était le choix entre le blanc clair et le blanc foncé, Jean-Marie Le Pen: 'Les députés RN sont silencieux'", *Le Journal du Dimanche*, 28 Aug. 2022.
34. "La mort d'un homme, fût-il un adversaire politique, ne devrait inspirer que de la retenue et de la dignité. Ces scènes de liesse sont tout simplement honteuses ... Rien, absolument rien ne justifie qu'on danse sur un cadavre", "Mort de Jean-Marie Le Pen: Des manifestants célèbrent, Retailleau dénonce des 'scènes de liesse honteuses'", HuffPost, 8 Jan. 2025.
35. "Figure historique de l'extrême droite, il a ainsi joué un rôle dans la vie publique de notre pays pendant près de soixante-dix ans, qui relève désormais du jugement de l'Histoire", Élysée statement, 7 Jan. 2025.
36. RN statement, 7 Jan. 2025.
37. Catherine Fieschi, *Fascism, Populism and the French Fifth Republic*, Manchester University Press, 2004, p. 146. Fieschi cites Edwy Plenel and Alain Rollat's book *L'Effet Le Pen*, La Découverte, 1984.

4. POLITICAL PATRICIDE

1. Victor Mallet, "Strongwoman with a smile", *Financial Times*, 23–4 Feb. 2022.
2. Macron's approval ratings fell from over 60 per cent when he was first elected in 2017 to a low of 23 per cent at the end of 2018, before recovering to just above 40 per cent at the time of his re-election in 2022, according to Ifop polling. "Les indices de popularité", Ifop, July 2022, https://www.ifop.com/wp-content/uploads/2022/07/118722-Indices-de-popularite-Juillet-2022.pdf
3. Vivienne Walt, "Why France's Marine Le Pen is doubling down on Russia support", *Time*, 9 Jan. 2017, https://time.com/4627780/russia-national-front-marine-le-pen-putin/
4. Victor Mallet, "Resurgent Marine Le Pen revels in Macron's woes", *Financial Times*, 30 Jan. 2020.

5. "Mineurs isolés: Eric Zemmour condamné en appel à 10 000 euros d'amende pour provocation à la haine", *Le Nouvel Obs*/AFP, 12 Sept. 2024.
6. "Une enquête ouverte après des propos de Jean-Marie Le Pen sur les chambres à gaz", franceinfo, 2 Apr. 2015, https://www.francetvinfo.fr/politique/front-national/derapage-de-jean-marie-le-pen/ouverture-d-une-enquete-pour-contestation-de-crime-contre-l-humanite-apres-des-propos-de-jean-marie-le-pen_866691.html
7. "C'est le moment le plus difficile de ma vie après l'accouchement", interview with Karine Le Marchand, "Une ambition intime", M6, 9 Oct. 2016.
8. "[A]vec les excès que l'on peut connaître, évidemment ça emportait en quelque sorte une image d'un mouvement qui était à l'époque de surcroît un mouvement plus contestataire qu'un gouvernement. J'ai beaucoup lutté pour montrer le mouvement tel qu'il était et non pas tel qu'on pouvait le caricaturer en raison du comportement de Jean-Marie Le Pen et je crois avec un certain succès." Interview with the author, 22 Jan. 2020.
9. "Ce n'est pas cosmétique comme changement, c'est un changement de philosophie, c'est une révolution culturelle. Le 'Front', on fait front contre quelque chose. Passer du Front au Rassemblement ... c'est vraiment une modification totale de la philosophie, il a effectivement rassemblé, il a rassemblé les gens comme Thierry Mariani qui est un ancien ministre de Nicolas Sarkozy, comme Jean-Paul Garraud. Il est dans une dynamique de rassemblement, il est dans une dynamique d'implantation locale, il apparaît de plus en plus comme étant plus lucide et plus capable de faire face aux difficultés de notre temps et de notre pays ... Et vous verrez que ce sont des gens profondément raisonnables, pragmatiques, nous ne souhaitons pas effectuer une révolution quelconque mais revenir dans le bon sens. Faire du patriotisme économique, baisser les impôts, faire des économies, arrêter l'immigration massive qui aujourd'hui déstabilise notre sécurité, nos comptes sociaux." Interview with the author, 22 Jan. 2020.
10. "Il y a des êtres humains, ils ont des droits, on ne va pas leur reprocher à eux la politique de l'immigration." And on the question of a

Muslim: "Est-ce qu'il met sa foi avant les lois du pays, est-ce qu'il est français avant d'être musulman, est-ce qu'il va chercher à influencer, à imposer sa manière de voir, ses valeurs, est-ce qu'il va traiter ma fille à égalité comme l'exige notre culture ou est-ce qu'il va chercher à imposer la sienne?" Interview with Karine Le Marchand, "Une ambition intime", M6, 9 Oct. 2016.

11. Marine Le Pen, *À contre flots*, Grancher, 2006. The words written were "père fasciste", p. 55.
12. "Je pense que la politique est un virus que vous avez en vous", interview with Karine Le Marchand, "Une ambition intime", M6, 9 Oct. 2016.
13. Née Lalanne.
14. "[C]'était un couple bohème, très amoureux l'un de l'autre, mais très couple, peut-être même couple avant d'être parents ... Notre père était fort, notre mère était belle, et quand on est enfant, c'est un peu l'image idéale, quoi", "Une ambition intime", M6, 9 Oct. 2016. She has frequently referred to her childhood nicknames "Miss bonne humeur" and "Miss trompe-la-mort", including in her autobiography *À contre flots*, p. 28.
15. "J'ai huit ans et réalise brutalement que mon père est quelqu'un de connu et qu'on lui en veut. Je comprends aussi que mon père peut mourir, qu'il risque de mourir, et ce qui est pire encore, de mourir parce-qu'on veut le tuer"; "Je vis donc vraiment, depuis ce moment, avec la conscience du danger. Je sais que nous avons face à nous des gens qui n'hésitent pas et qui n'ont pas hésité, par cet attentat, à risquer la vie de dix familles pour tuer une seule personne." Le Pen, *À contre flots*, pp. 17, 21.
16. "La maison était envahie par la politique or Pierrette n'est pas une femme politique. Au moment des élections européennes de 1984, tout le staff de campagne s'est retrouvé à Montretout. Elle n'avait plus d'espace. Jean-Marie, lui, faisait campagne à travers la France." Chombeau, *Le Pen: Fille & père*, p. 120.
17. "Madame Le Pen fait le ménage, Monsieur est servi ...", *Playboy*, June 1988.
18. "Y compris en faisant des ménages, ce qui n'est pas déshonorant." Chombeau, *Le Pen: Fille & père*, p. 135.

19. "De ces photos dans *Playboy*, j'en ai énormément voulu à ma mère car ce fut une violence psychologique inouïe qu'elle nous infligea." Le Pen, *À contre flots*, pp. 119–20.
20. "C'est une fille libre, honnête, qui ne renie pas sa famille ... Elle porte un amour fou a son père. Elle l'adore. Elle a une vue juste de ce qu'il est ou n'est pas, et, quand il fait des conneries, elle le lui dit, mais elle l'admire ... Marine, je ne l'ai jamais entendu dire 'sale Arabe' or 'sale Juif' et tenir des propos racistes." Chombeau, *Le Pen: Fille & père*, pp. 153–4.
21. Interview with Karine Le Marchand, "Une ambition intime", M6, 9 Oct. 2016.
22. "Je ne pensais pas du tout à votre cliente, j'étais en train de me dire: 'est-ce que ça n'est pas la fille de Jean-Marie Le Pen?'" Le Pen, *À contre flots*, pp. 157–9.
23. In Reims on 5 Feb. 2022.
24. Le Pen, *À contre flots*, p. 264.
25. "La France s'est transformée en camp de rééducation psychologique. Les Français ont eu peur parce qu'on leur a fait peur. On a dit que si Jean-Marie Le Pen était élu, les rivières s'arrêteraient de couler, le soleil ne se lèverait plus, ce serait le début de l'ère glaciaire." On France 3, 5 May 2002, quoted in Caroline Fourest and Fiammetta Venner, *Marine Le Pen*, Grasset, 2011, p. 115, and Chombeau, *Le Pen: Fille & père*, p. 262.
26. "Catholiques intégristes et païens, antijuifs et antiarabes, ouvriéristes et grands patrons", Fourest and Venner, *Marine Le Pen*, p. 143.
27. Eltchaninoff, *Inside the Mind of Marine Le Pen*, pp. 35–6.
28. Camus and Lebourg, *Far-Right Politics in Europe*, p. 200.
29. "Marine est bien gentille mais sa stratégie de dédiabolisation ne nous a rien apporté. Les médias nous ignorent. Un Front gentil, ça n'intéresse personne! Je n'ai pas cherché un scandale pour briser l'omerta. Mais reconnaissez que cela marche!", *Nouvel Observateur*, 17 Jan. 2005, quoted widely in French media. For a full account of the incident, see Chombeau, *Le Pen: Fille & père*, pp. 299–305.
30. "Marine Le Pen estime que la rafle du Vel d'Hiv a été ordonnée par 'les autorités françaises'", AFP, 16 July 2024, https://www.lagazette-

france.fr/article/marine-le-pen-estime-que-la-rafle-du-vel-d-hiv-a-ete-ordonnee-par-les-autorites-francaises

31. "Législatives: L'historien Serge Klarsfeld votera pour le Rassemblement national en cas de duel face à La France insoumise", franceinfo/AFP, 16 June 2024; "Pourquoi Serge Klarsfeld, figure de l'antinazisme, se dit prêt à voter RN", *Le Monde*, 19 June 2024; Stéphanie Trouillard, "En cas de duel, Serge Klarsfeld votera RN 'qui soutient les Juifs', face à LFI 'résolument antijuif'", France 24, 17 June 2024, https://www.france24.com/fr/france/20240617-serge-klarsfeld-rn-soutient-les-juifs-face-%C3%A0-lfi-r%C3%A9solument-antijuif
32. Chombeau, *Le Pen: Fille & père*, p. 211.
33. Eltchaninoff, *Inside the Mind of Marine Le Pen*, pp. 117–18, 128–9.
34. Camus and Lebourg, *Far-Right Politics in Europe*, pp. 202, 169.
35. Decision of the Cour de cassation, 23 June 2009, https://www.legifrance.gouv.fr/juri/id/JURITEXT000020821426/
36. Fourest and Venner, *Marine Le Pen*, p. 339.
37. Le Pen, *À contre flots*, p. 257.
38. "[J]e lui passe le relais d'un Front national en parfait état et hop, elle me fout à la porte"; "Pour être à même de capter l'extraordinaire mouvement qui soulève l'Europe et le monde, il faut qu'elle le sente, le comprenne, et comprenne ses propres erreurs qui l'ont jusqu'à présent empêchée de mieux le faire." Le Pen, *Mémoires: Tribun*, pp. 435, 438–9.
39. "'Mère à chats', Marine Le Pen confie avoir pleuré le décès de sa chatte", *Le Figaro*, 23 Apr. 2015; "Le doberman de son père tue son chat, Marine Le Pen déménage", BFM TV, 1 Oct. 2015, updated 20 Dec. 2015, https://www.bfmtv.com/politique/le-doberman-de-son-pere-tue-son-chat-marine-le-pen-demenage_AN-201410010040.html
40. "C'est, précisément, sur le sujet des ambiguïtés de Jean-Marie Le Pen, que je considérais comme étant une faute politique rendant impossible la continuité d'un combat commun, que nous avons rompu ... J'ai pris une décision, elle a été difficile et elle m'a coûté sentimentalement. ... [mais] il ne peut exister en matière d'antisémitisme aucune ambiguïté." "Marine Le Pen: 'La classe politique manque malheureusement de grandeur'", *Le Journal du Dimanche*, 12 Nov. 2023.
41. The debate was broadcast live on TF1 and France 2 on 3 May 2017.

42. "Emmanuel Macron accuses Marine Le Pen of dependence on Vladimir Putin", *Financial Times*, 21 Apr. 2022.
43. "Macron domine, Le Pen tient le choc" was the *Figaro* headline. "Présidentielle: La presse donne l'avantage à Emmanuel Macron après le débat face à Marine Le Pen", *Ouest-France*/AFP, 21 Apr. 2022.

5. THE ROAD TO POWER

1. "Je ferai donc une analyse du projet mondialiste, du rôle joué dans sa réalisation par nos élites politiques, médiatiques et financières, de la guerre qu'elles mènent au peuple, à la République et à la Nation, et de la violence contre la démocratie à laquelle elles sont résolues pour se maintenir en place ... Vous comprendrez alors, je l'espère, pourquoi ces élites militent pour le libéralisme économique extrême et la financiarisation, le libre-échange, l'Europe supranationale et l'immigration, en un mot pour l'accomplissement du projet mondialiste." Marine Le Pen, *Pour que vive la France*, Grancher, 2012, pp. 15–16.
2. "Les oubliés pour qui je me bats, ce sont les petits salariés, les employés, les fonctionnaires, les ouvriers, les classes moyennes, les retraités, les jeunes ou les seniors sans emploi, c'est cette France qu'on a dédaigneusement qualifiée de 'France d'en bas', parfois de 'France moisie.'" Le Pen, *Pour que vive la France*, p. 18.
3. "En imposant aux Français le multiculturalisme, fruit de l'immigration de masse, on les a progressivement coupés de leur culture, cherchant à affaiblir la conscience nationale, rempart à l'édification du 'village global'. L'arrivée de millions d'immigrés en quelques décennies, une première dans notre Histoire, secoue bien sûr un peuple dans ses profondeurs, et crée un malaise naturel. Elle affaiblit les anciennes solidarités et rend plus perméable le corps social au discours mondialiste. L'immigration a facilité le travail de déracinement des Français, sommés de se réjouir de cette nouvelle société, aux couleurs Benetton. Le métissage, qui devrait relever d'un choix personnel tout à fait privé, a été institutionnalisé." Le Pen, *Pour que vive la France*, p. 86.
4. Quoted by Le Pen in *Pour que vive la France*, p. 179.
5. According to official statistics. "Comparateur de territoires: Commune de la Ricamarie (42183)", Insee, https://www.insee.fr/fr/statistiques/1405599?geo=COM-42183

6. Victor Mallet, "France votes: Macron's frontrunner status conceals deep rifts in society", *Financial Times*, 29 Mar. 2022.
7. "Nous ne sommes pas un plus que la droite, ou à la droite de la droite, nous sommes ailleurs que la droite ... nous sommes les défenseurs du peuple et les défenseurs de tous les peuples. Pour tous les peuples du monde, nous appelons au respect des identités. L'identité recouvre deux réalités: 1) L'identité c'est ce qui fait au plus profond de nous les individus que nous sommes; Mais 2) L'identité c'est aussi ce qui nous rend identiques, dans la culture reçue, adoptée et transmise, proches les uns des autres et nous fait considérer tous les compatriotes, quels qu'ils soient, d'où qu'ils viennent, comme les membres d'une même grand famille." "Mon message aux adhérents du Rassemblement National", speech at eighteenth RN Congress, Paris, 5 Nov. 2022.
8. "[P]arce que je souhaite mettre en place un gouvernement d'union nationale et que, par conséquent, les ministres auxquels je confierais des responsabilités ne seront pas obligatoirement tous issus du Rassemblement National et certains seront amenés évidemment à me rejoindre." Victor Mallet, "Marine Le Pen touts national unity government for France", *Financial Times*, 30 Mar. 2021. She was speaking at a video meeting with the Anglo-American Press Association.
9. "[T]oute une partie de l'électorat de gauche a voté pour M. Johnson, tout un électorat qui avant jamais aurait pu voter pour un candidat comme M. Johnson. Pourquoi? Parce que encore une fois ces électeurs de gauche ont vu en Johnson le candidat capable de réguler la mondialisation et de cesser de faire d'eux les perdants systématiques de la mondialisation." "Marine Le Pen touts national unity government for France", *Financial Times*, 30 Mar. 2021.
10. "Mais je pourrais très bien avoir des gens qui viennent par exemple de la gauche chevènementiste, c'est-à-dire d'une gauche souverainiste, d'une gauche qui défend la réindustrialisation, la défense de nos grandes industries." RTL Radio, quoted in Victor Mallet, "Marine Le Pen open to appointing leftists if she wins French presidency", *Financial Times*, 7 Apr. 2022; also "Marine Le Pen n'exclut pas de gouverner avec 'des gens d'une gauche souverainiste'", *Paris Match*/AFP, 7 Apr. 2022, https://www.parismatch.com/Actu/Politique/Marine-Le-Pen-n-

exclut-pas-de-gouverner-avec-des-gens-d-une-gauche-souverainiste-1798911

11. "La marée monte. Elle n'est pas montée assez haut cette fois-ci, mais elle continue à monter et, par conséquent, notre victoire n'est que différée." "Législatives 2024: 'La marée continue à monter', 'notre victoire n'est que différée', assure Marine Le Pen", Europe 1/AFP, 7 July 2024, https://www.europe1.fr/politique/legislatives-2024-la-maree-continue-a-monter-notre-victoire-nest-que-differee-assure-marine-le-pen-4257084

12. Victor Mallet, "France's forgotten chamber makes its political comeback", *Financial Times*, 23 July 2024.

13. "Monsieur le Premier ministre, vous avez fait le choix de prolonger l'hiver technocratique dans lequel est plongée la France depuis l'élection d'Emmanuel Macron en 2017: la déconnexion des attentes démocratiques, la verticalité des décisions, le refus des consultations et des compromis, en somme le respect de la volonté du peuple français en matière migratoire, sécuritaire ou fiscale, ou en matière de construction européenne, et ce malgré les résultats sans appel des élections de juin et juillet dernier." Speech on no-confidence motion, National Assembly, 4 Dec. 2024.

14. "Voilà la grande leçon de ces dernières semaines. Rien ne peut se faire sans nous ... Nous ne devons rien à personne. Rien aux banques, rien à la grande distribution, rien à telle ou telle grande entreprise ou agence de conseil. Rien. Nous sommes libres." Interview in *Valeurs Actuelles*, 11 Dec. 2024.

6. WHO IS JORDAN BARDELLA?

1. "Je comprendrai plus tard que mon prénom est un marqueur au fer rouge, la carte d'identité de ma classe sociale. Il raconte mes origines et il signe mon appartenance à une décennie ... Admettons-le: donner un prénom issu du calendrier des saints est une déférence a l'égard de la patrie, mais il serait réducteur d'en faire un baromètre de 'francité'. S'il faut le préciser, le prénom Jordan est d'origine hébraïque, inspire du fleuve Jourdain qui traverse Israël et la Jordanie, là ou Jésus-Christ fut baptisé. Il apparaît en France au Moyen Âge avec les croisades, puis

tombe dans l'oubli avant de reparaître à l'aube des années 1990." *Ce que je cherche*, Fayard, 2024, pp. 120–1.
2. "Au sein de la cité, nous sommes tous fils et filles d'immigrés. Le 'Français de souche' est rare. Les 'petits Européens' viennent d'Italie, d'Espagne, du Portugal, de Pologne ou de Serbie ... L'afflux important de populations venue d'ailleurs, la lâcheté de l'État pour ses missions régaliennes, le renoncement à l'autorité et à la fierté nationale, et bien sur l'enracinement d'un islam conquérant ont constitué les ingrédients d'un cocktail explosif et d'une situation hors de contrôle. Beaucoup de nouveaux arrivants ont rejoint la cité en tournant le dos à l'assimilation. Le deal est monté en puissance et il a pris le pas sur le climat d'entente cordiale qui régnait entre les familles." *Ce que je cherche*, pp. 140–1.
3. These details, including some later confirmed by Bardella, appeared in Pierre-Stéphane Fort, *Le Grand Remplaçant: La face cachée de Jordan Bardella*, StudioFact, 2024. The book's title is a pun about Bardella possibly replacing Marine Le Pen—it alludes to the "great replacement theory" beloved by the far right about a supposed conspiracy to replace white populations with Muslim immigrants.
4. "Le Pen protégé vows to reclaim sovereignty from EU", *Financial Times*, 20 Jan. 2019, https://www.ft.com/content/1e110d78-19ba-11e9-b93e-f4351a53f1c3
5. "[Il] apparaît aux yeux de beaucoup comme un homme neuf, propre et lisse. Bien qu'adhérent du parti depuis l'âge de 17 ans et pur apparatchik du RN, il a la faculté de faire tomber les dernières préventions contre le lepénisme. Grâce à ses talents de communicant—sur lui glissent attaques et reproches—il incarne l'ultime banalisation de l'extrême droite. Et suscite un engouement collectif qui, en démocratie, peut mener aux plus hautes responsabilités." Sylvain Courage, "Le piège Bardella", *Le Nouvel Obs*, 16 May 2024.
6. "Mon combat, c'est la normalisation du RN. Je souhaite que tous les Français qui partagent nos idées, ou du moins notre amour pour la patrie, puissent l'exprimer ouvertement, sans craindre les caricatures ou le prêt-à-penser. Mon objectif est de rendre banal le soutien à un parti politique qui croit dans le destin français et au génie de son peuple", "Ma plus grande peur serait de décevoir", interview by Jules Torres, *Le Journal du Dimanche*, 21 Apr. 2024.

7. "En France, pour remporter une élection présidentielle, il faut convaincre tant ceux qui nous soutiennent que ceux qui sont en désaccord avec nous et qui n'ont pas voté pour nous au premier tour. La France valorise la raison: dans une élection a deux tours, le candidat le plus excessif est toujours éliminé. C'est pourquoi je crois fermement en cette stratégie et rejette toute forme de retour en arrière, de provocation. La normalisation est une étape vers la maturité d'un mouvement politique." "Ma plus grande peur serait de décevoir", interview by Jules Torres, *Le Journal du Dimanche*, 21 Apr. 2024.
8. "France's conservative Republicans kick out party chief Ciotti", Reuters, 12 June 2024, https://www.reuters.com/world/europe/frances-conservative-republicans-kick-out-party-chief-ciotti-2024-06-12/
9. "Les victoires futures passeront par l'unité du camp patriote, par une capacité à agréger les orphelins d'une droite plus orléaniste. Je veux aller plus loin dans cette direction et tendre la main. La France n'attend pas!", Bardella, *Ce que je cherche*, p. 59. An *orléaniste* originally meant a supporter of the claim to the French throne by the House of Orléans but now suggests someone who is a conservative but constitutionalist republican.
10. "Ma vision repose sur les 'trois R': une Rupture Raisonnable et Rassurante. La France est à un tournant sur les questions économiques, migratoires, sécuritaires et industrielles. Les choix faits aujourd'hui détermineront si la France reste une puissance capable de relever les défis du XXIe siècle ou si elle s'enfonce dans le déclin." "La politique est un virus", *Le JDNews*, 19 Nov. 2024.
11. "La ferveur des fans de Bardella: 'On dirait un influenceur'", *Le Monde*, 26 Nov. 2024.
12. "Il était surtout la coalition contre nature de convictions divergents et de programmes opposés, l'alliance monstrueuse entre M. Mélenchon et M. Macron!" Bardella, *Ce que je cherche*, p. 101.
13. "Derrière l'échec relatif du RN aux législatives, les limites de la 'génération Bardella'", *Le Monde*, 8 July 2024.
14. "Législatives 2024: Ces candidats, qualifiés de 'Brebis Galeuses' par Jordan Bardella, qui embarrassent le RN", LCP, Assemblée Nationale, 27 Aug. 2025, https://lcp.fr/actualites/legislatives-2024-ces-candidats-qualifies-de-brebis-galeuses-par-jordan-bardella-qui

15. "Vidé de toute substance idéologique et de toute sincérité, réduit à une alliance fatiguée de contraires, affaibli, le 'front républicain' fonctionne toujours. Je gage qu'il s'agit de sa dernière réussite." Bardella, *Ce que je cherche*, p. 102.
16. "Non, non, je ne me sens pas trop jeune. Je fais à 29 ans, bientôt 30, ce que l'on fait normalement dans la vie quand on a 50 ans. Donc j'ai grandi très vite sur le champ de bataille et à l'âge que j'ai aujourd'hui, je suis président d'un parti politique qui compte 130,000 adhérents, qui a des dizaines de salariés, qui compte 170 parlementaires et donc malheureusement je ne me sens pas jeune dans ma tête et je suis écrasé par les responsabilités. Donc non, je pense qu'en politique, l'âge n'est pas nécessairement un gage d'efficacité." Interview with the author, Paris, 28 May 2025.
17. "Sans doute, notre duo a permis de convaincre davantage de Français. Mais ce bilan est d'abord le sien, le fruit de ses choix, de sa détermination, de sa pugnacité, de son instinct, de son envie de quitter les bancs de l'opposition pour rejoindre la salle des commandes ... Partout où elle se déplace, Marine suscite l'intérêt et l'émotion. C'est une rock star ... Entre nous, le lien de confiance est absolu. Elle connait mes doutes et mes craintes; je lui fais part de chacune de mes hésitations. Rien ni personne ne parviendra à semer la moindre discorde. Elle connaît ma loyauté, je sais l'étendue de ma dette envers elle. Le reste n'est que bavardage." Bardella, *Ce que je cherche*, pp. 27, 45, 310.
18. "[J]'ai toujours rejeté l'opposition peuple–élite. Je n'aime pas ça." Interview with the author, 28 May 2025.
19. Bardella, *Ce que je cherche*, p. 175.
20. "Jordan Bardella: Marion Maréchal, la bataille qui vient à l'extrême droite", *Le Parisien*, 10 Sept. 2023; "Jordan n'est pas cosette", *Le Nouvel Obs*, 16 May 2024.
21. "Les mémoires courtes de Jordan Bardella", *La Tribune Dimanche*, 10 Nov. 2024; "L'enfant gâté de l'extrême droite", *Le Nouvel Obs*, 16 May 2024; "Ma plus grande peur serait de décevoir", *Le Journal du Dimanche*, 21 Apr. 2024.
22. "La politique est un virus", interview in *Le JDNews*, 27 Nov. 2024.
23. "Je dois aussi avouer que la politique engloutit toute mon existence, la

recouvre, me donne le vertige, m'enivre, m'écrase, telle une vague insubmersible. L'engagement politique est un don, un sacerdoce. On entre en politique comme en religion." Bardella, *Ce que je cherche*, p. 10.

24. "Raphaël Llorca: Chez Jordan Bardella, l'insignifiance est un acte de discours", *Le Monde*, 3 Dec. 2024.
25. "C'est un très bon politicien, mais ça n'est pas un homme politique." Quoted in Fort, *Le Grand Remplaçant*, p. 48.
26. "En fait, ce que mes parents ne vous disent pas, c'est que je voulais être tout. Je voulais être Superman, James Bond, en première ligne du GIGN." Interviewed in "Une ambition intime", M6, 1 June 2025.
27. Bardella's connections with identitarians are detailed in the chapter "La 'GUD Connection'", in Fort, *Le Grand Remplaçant*, pp. 199–220; his obsession with neatness, including the way he folds his shirts and wipes down the shower to remove calcareous marks, is discussed by himself, and by Marine Le Pen, with Karine Le Marchand in "Une ambition intime", M6, 1 June 2025.
28. Bardella, *Ce que je cherche*, p. 12.
29. "Je crois aussi que les Français recherchent aujourd'hui davantage des personnalités fortes que des programmes figés. Il est essentiel de rassembler classes populaires, moyennes, et même une partie des élites autour de valeurs de bon sens: travail, mérite, défense de l'identité et rétablissement de l'autorité. Je suis convaincu que ces principes peuvent unir une majorité de Français." "Je veux porter le discours du 'Ce sera mieux demain!'", *Le Journal du Dimanche*, 10 Nov. 2024.

7. NORTH AND SOUTH

1. This section is based on reporting by the author from Beaucaire in November 2024.
2. Pierre Bousquet, the first treasurer of the party, and Léon Gaultier were former Waffen-SS members who co-founded the FN with Jean-Marie Le Pen in 1972.
3. Political advertising is banned in public service locations such as stations, but books by politicians are a grey area since the book covers shown are not always overtly political. See Pierrick Gardien, "Peut-on faire de la publicité pour un livre politique dans une gare ou un métro?",

Village de la Justice, 29 Oct. 2024, https://www.village-justice.com/articles/peut-faire-publicite-pour-livre-politique-dans-une-gare-metro,51288.html

4. "Il y a une tétanie des gens."
5. See for example "L'insécurité n'augmente pas en France", Centre d'observation de la société, 2 Oct. 2023, https://www.observationsociete.fr/modes-de-vie/divers-tendances_conditions/evolutioninsecurite/
6. "La France va basculer."
7. This section is based on reporting by the author in December 2024.
8. See for example Bernardette Sauvaget, "L'électorat musulman et son plébiscite de la gauche: 'Ce qui arrive en tête, c'est la question palestinienne'", *Libération*, 18 June 2024.

8. FAR-RIGHT FIEFDOM

1. "Brigitte Bardot renvoyée en correctionnelle pour injures raciales envers les Réunionnais", Europe 1/AFP, 7 May 2020, https://www.europe1.fr/societe/brigitte-bardot-renvoyee-en-correctionnelle-pour-injures-raciales-envers-les-reunionnais-3966948
2. "A côté d'elle, Marilyn Monroe faisait serveuse de bar ... Elle aime les animaux, elle a la nostalgie d'une France propre." Le Pen, *Mémoires: Tribun*, p. 98.
3. This chapter is based largely on reporting from Hénin-Beaumont and the surrounding area by the author in early 2025.
4. "Comparateur de territoires", Insee, https://www.insee.fr/fr/statistiques/1405599?geo=COM-62427
5. Coal mine museums in the Pas-de-Calais display histories of the industry in the region. See also "Le déclin du charbon et la conversion dans le Nord-Pas-de-Calais", Mineurs du Monde, https://fresques.ina.fr/memoires-de-mines/fiche-media/Mineur00181/le-declin-du-charbon-et-la-conversion-dans-le-nord-pas-de-calais.html
6. Francine Aizicovici, "Les ex-Samsonite se rendent à Boston défendre leurs droits", *Le Monde*, 4 Mar. 2014, https://www.lemonde.fr/economie/article/2014/03/04/les-ex-samsonite-contre-le-fonds-d-investissement-bain-capital_4377037_3234.html
7. Le Pen, *À contre flots*, p. 195.

8. "Aussi s'applique-t-elle à s'afficher régulièrement avec cette class populaire pauvre, à se mêler à elle, à ne pas hésiter à l'embrasser, la toucher, rire, boire avec elle, bref, à engranger un capital de sympathie dans un univers où les politiques sont perçus comme étant éloignés des préoccupations des gens 'ordinaires'. D'apparatchik parisienne et fille de millionnaire, elle parvient à apparaître comme la porte-parole des gens 'simples' du Nord. Un sérieux pied de nez à la gauche, socialiste ou communiste, qui a largement contribué à façonner l'identité ouvrière dans la région en prenant la défense des travailleurs pauvres." Sylvain Crépon, *Enquête au coeur du nouveau Front National*, Nouveau Monde, 2012, p. 114.
9. "Marine Le Pen a trouvé dans le Pas-de-Calais une légitimité tant sociale que politique portée par une population souvent issue des rangs de la gauche." Crépon, *Enquête au coeur du nouveau Front National*, p. 164.
10. "Des villes vont devenir demain des villes Front national, nous allons enfin pouvoir montrer aux Français ce que nous sommes capables de faire." Quoted in Haydée Sabéran, *Bienvenue à Hénin-Beaumont: Reportage sur un laboratoire du Front national*, La Découverte, 2014, p. 17.
11. "Effectivement, le combat contre le Front national s'est trop souvent éloigné du champ politique pour rejoindre celui de la démonologie. Certains tentent de combattre ce parti comme ils organiseraient une séance collective d'exorcisme. Les dommages de cette stratégie, humiliante pour les électeurs et inefficace pour ceux qui tentent de les convaincre, sont aujourd'hui connus de tous. Le phénomène est international. Mais les habitudes sont tenaces et l'extrême droite me semble avoir encore de belles heures devant elle." Marine Tondelier, *Nouvelles du Front*, Les liens qui libèrent, 2024, pp. 21–2.
12. "C'était une citadelle imprenable. C'était comme si le Front de gauche avait voulu créer quelque chose à Neuilly-sur-Seine! Ça forge le caractère." Quoted in Sabéran, *Bienvenue à Hénin-Beaumont*, p. 24.
13. "Ce qui me choquait, c'est que des gens de ma génération parlent arabe entre eux ... Ça me mettait hors de moi." Quoted in Sabéran, *Bienvenue à Hénin-Beaumont*, p. 23.
14. "[U]ne messe bolcho-tiers-mondiste, politicienne", Tondelier, *Nouvelles du Front*, p. 167.

15. "Hénin-Beaumont vote une motion anti-migrants alors qu'aucun projet de centre d'accueil n'est prévu", TF1, 7 Oct. 2016, https://www.tf1info.fr/politique/henin-beaumont-vote-une-motion-anti-migrants-alors-qu-aucun-projet-de-centre-d-accueil-n-existe-2006605.html
16. "[E]lle pense avoir 'une chance sur deux de tomber sur un facho'. Les stéréotypes collent désormais à la peau des habitants de la ville. Hénin-Beaumont n'est pourtant ni un ghetto, ni un coupe-gorge, ni un repaire de crânes rasés ... Hénin-Beaumont est une petite ville de 27,000 habitants, d'où ressort un sentiment d'abandon. Une ville de gens ordinaires." Sabéran, *Bienvenue à Hénin-Beaumont*, pp. 216–17.

9. THE BIG ISSUES: IMMIGRATION AND THE ECONOMY

1. "Bayrou met en péril son entente avec le PS", *Le Monde*, 30 Jan. 2025; "Bayrou fait sauter les digues contre l'extrême droite", *Le Monde*, 31 Jan. 2025.
2. "Assassinat de Samuel Paty: Huit personnes sur le banc des accusés", Radio France, 4 Nov. 2024, https://www.radiofrance.fr/franceculture/podcasts/le-reportage-de-la-redaction/assassinat-de-samuel-paty-huit-personnes-sur-le-banc-des-accuses-4171556
3. "Nicolas Sarkozy a-t-il vraiment utilisé le mot kärcher?", *Libération*, 21 Mar. 2018, https://www.liberation.fr/checknews/2018/03/21/nicolas-sarkozy-a-t-il-vraiment-utilise-le-mot-karcher_1653412/
4. "France 'to take back control' of immigration policy", *Financial Times*, 6 Nov. 2019.
5. "Macron's interior minister confronts Le Pen on her own territory", *Financial Times*, 15 Mar. 2021.
6. Bardella quoted the Institut Montaigne for this figure, but the institute's own conclusions are more nuanced. See for example "L'immigration transforme la France, mais son impact économique est limité", 9 Nov. 2021, https://www.institutmontaigne.org/expressions/limmigration-transforme-la-france-mais-son-impact-economique-est-limite
7. Jordan Bardella, speech for *voeux à la presse* and news conference, Paris, 27 Jan. 2025.
8. "German frontrunner vows permanent border controls after knife attack", BBC, 23 Jan. 2025, https://www.bbc.com/news/articles/ce9nvllzn7ko;

"Germany: Far right decide vote on anti-migration proposal", DW, 29 Jan. 2025.

9. "Rede des Bundesministers für Wirtschaft und Klimaschutz, Dr. Robert Habeck", Die Bundesregierung, 29 Jan. 2025, https://www.bundesregierung.de/breg-de/service/newsletter-und-abos/bulletin/rede-des-bundesministers-fuer-wirtschaft-und-klimaschutz-dr-robert-habeck--2332920

10. "Friedrich Merz's flirtation with German far right condemned by Angela Merkel", *Financial Times*, 30 Jan. 2025, https://www.ft.com/content/58e77cd4-58ef-4230-8309-c9fe888f84c9; "En Allemagne, la radicalisation de la droite sur l'immigration", *Le Monde*, 28 Jan. 2025.

11. Conversation with the author, 27 Jan. 2025.

12. "What is 'ordo amoris?' Vice President JD Vance invokes this medieval Catholic concept", AP, 6 Feb. 2025, https://apnews.com/article/jd-vance-catholic-theology-migration-e868af574fb2e742c6ed3d756c569769

13. "Je préfère ma fille [ou ma famille] à mes amis, mes amis à mes voisins, mes voisins à mes compatriotes, mes compatriotes aux Européens." Citation Célèbre, https://citation-celebre.leparisien.fr/citations/97215

14. "Read: JD Vance's full speech on the fall of Europe", *The Spectator*, 14 Feb. 2025, https://www.spectator.co.uk/article/jd-vance-what-i-worry-about-is-the-threat-from-within/

15. Camus and Lebourg, *Far-Right politics in Europe*, p. 7.

16. "Aigues-Mortes", Musée de l'histoire de l'immigration, https://www.histoire-immigration.fr/aigues-mortes#

17. These numbers are derived from the author's reporting at the time, but there are multiple sources giving similar figures for the composition of the diverse population of Marseille. See for example *Le Temps des Italiens* in the departmental archives of Les-Bouches-du-Rhône or Sylvia Poggioli, "Diverse Marseille spared in French riots", NPR, 10 Dec. 2005, https://www.npr.org/2005/12/10/5044219/diverse-marseille-spared-in-french-riots

18. "Marseilles: A city of foreigners who take badly to newcomers", *Financial Times*, 22 July 2002; "Southern racism buoys National Front as it casts about for votes", *Financial Times*, 1 June 2002.

19. "L'essentiel sur ... les immigrés et les étrangers", Insee, 22 May 2025, https://www.insee.fr/fr/statistiques/3633212
20. Fourquet, *Métamorphoses françaises*, p. 81.
21. "L'essentiel sur ... les immigrés et les étrangers", Insee.
22. "International Migration Outlook 2024", OECD, 14 Nov. 2024, https://www.oecd.org/en/publications/2024/11/international-migration-outlook-2024_c6f3e803.html
23. "Sur l'immigration, avant de parler de submersion, il faut tenir compte des faits", *Le Monde*, 13 Feb. 2025.
24. Michel Soudais, *Le Front National en Face*, Flammarion, 1996.
25. "La menace terroriste d'extrême droite est-elle suffisamment prise au sérieux?", France Culture, 5 June 2025, https://www.radiofrance.fr/franceculture/podcasts/questions-du-soir-le-debat/la-menace-terroriste-d-extreme-droite-est-elle-suffisamment-prise-au-serieux-5268337
26. "Étrangers détenus: Derrière les chiffres de la sur-représentation", Observatoire international des prisons, 3 Feb. 2021, https://oip.org/analyse/etrangers-detenus-derriere-les-chiffres-de-la-sur-representation/
27. Fourquet, *Métamorphoses françaises*, pp. 82–5.
28. Franck Johannès, "Marine Le Pen revendique la 'brutalité' contre l'islamisme", *Le Monde*, 31 Jan.–1 Feb. 2021.
29. "The 2011 Time 100", *Time*, 21 Apr. 2011, https://content.time.com/time/specials/packages/article/0,28804,2066367_2066369_2066134,00.html
30. Comments at a news conference in the National Assembly, 28 Jan. 2025.
31. There was a controversy over a nativity scene in the RN-controlled Beaucaire in December 2024, which the municipality was ordered to move under the 1905 *laïcité* law, and then fined €103,000 when it failed to do so. "Crèche de Beaucaire: Le juge des référés condamne la commune de Beaucaire à payer 103 000 euros d'astreinte", Tribunal administratif de Nîmes, https://nimes.tribunal-administratif.fr/decisions-de-justice/dernieres-decisions/creche-de-beaucaire-le-juge-des-referes-condamne-la-commune-de-beaucaire-a-payer-103-000-euros-d-astreinte

32. Senate Avis no. 134 of 2023–4 session, https://www.senat.fr/rap/a23-134-2/a23-134-21.pdf
33. Liz Alderman, "France desperately needs workers, but the fixes could anger left and right", *New York Times*, 23 Dec. 2022, https://www.nytimes.com/2022/12/23/business/france-jobs.html; Alderman, "In an industrial corner of France, 18,000 jobs are on offer: Why aren't people taking them?", *New York Times*, 27 July 2019, https://www.nytimes.com/2019/07/27/business/labor-manufacturing-france.html
34. "Législatives 2024: Le coût de l'immigration, une idée fausse, mais une vraie recette électorale", *Le Monde*, 3 July 2024, https://www.lemonde.fr/societe/article/2024/07/03/legislatives-2024-le-cout-de-l-immigration-fausse-idee-et-vraie-recette-electorale-du-rn_6246189_3224.html; "L'impact budgétaire des immigrés dans les pays de l'OCDE, 2006-18", OECD, 28 Oct. 2021, https://www.oecd.org/fr/publications/perspectives-des-migrations-internationales-2021_da2bbd99-fr/full-report/component-8.html#section-d1e28625
35. Amy Pope, "Migration can work for all", *Foreign Affairs*, Jan.–Feb. 2025.
36. Pope, "Migration can work for all".
37. "The European elections will be a rough ride for the political mainstream", *Financial Times*, 31 May 2024.
38. "Macron's interior minister confronts Le Pen on her own territory", *Financial Times*, 15 Mar. 2021.
39. "Revenue Statistics 2024: France", OECD, https://www.oecd.org/content/dam/oecd/en/topics/policy-sub-issues/global-tax-revenues/revenue-statistics-france.pdf; "Public finance and budgets", OECD, https://www.oecd.org/en/topics/policy-issues/public-finance-and-budgets.html
40. "Effectifs dans la fonction publique par versant et ministère", Insee, 27 May 2025, https://www.insee.fr/fr/statistiques/2493501#tableau-figure1; Nicolas Lecaussin, "Fonction publique: 59 000 postes supplémentaires en 2023 !", Iref, 29 Feb. 2024, https://fr.irefeurope.org/publications/les-pendules-a-lheure/article/fonction-publique-59-000-postes-supplementaires-en-2023/
41. "In 2024, the public deficit reached 5.8 % of GDP, the public debt 113.0 % of GDP", Insee, 27 Mar. 2025, https://www.insee.fr/en/statistiques/8542247

42. "CheckNews: Est-il vrai que les Français n'ont pas perdu en pouvoir d'achat ces dernières années, comme l'affirme le directeur de l'Insee?", *Libération*, 26 Dec. 2024.
43. Fractures françaises poll by Ipsos for *Le Monde*, reported in Gilles Finchelstein, "'Comment vivent les Français?', un portrait à 'échelle humaine'", *Le Monde*, 3 Dec. 2024.
44. Conversation with the author, 11 Feb. 2025.
45. "Chiffrage du programme présidentiel Marine Le Pen", official campaign document 2022; "Marine Le Pen: Synthèse des chiffrages", Institut Montaigne, https://www.institutmontaigne.org/presidentielle-2022/marine-le-pen/synthese/
46. "Je veux bien qu'on parle de crédibilité, si vous voulez, mais qui est crédible exactement dans les quarante dernières années? Quand vous me dites qu'on était crédible, ceux qui sont les champions du monde de la dette, les champions du monde des déficits, les champions du monde, le déficit du commerce extérieur, les champions du monde du chômage, des champions du monde de la pauvreté qui n'ont eu de cesse d'augmenter dans notre pays. Le moins qu'on puisse dire, c'est que si tous ces gens là sont crédibles, alors j'ai presque envie de dire que c'est rassurant de ne pas l'être." Marine Le Pen at Anglo-American Press Association, 30 Mar. 2021.
47. Victor Mallet, "France's national auditor sounds alarm over public finances", *Financial Times*, 15 July 2024.
48. John Springford, "The economic impact of Brexit, nine years on: Was the consensus right?", Constitution Society, 23 June 2025, https://consoc.org.uk/publications/the-economic-impact-of-brexit
49. "'Pognon de dingue': Comment les Français veulent-ils dépenser l'argent public?", *Hexagone*, 27 Nov. 2024, https://observatoire-hexagone.org/index.php/2024/11/27/depense-publique/
50. Sarah White, Adrienne Klasa and Leila Abboud, "Why France's far right is spooking markets", *Financial Times*, 13 June 2024; Leila Abboud, Adrienne Klasa and Sarah White, "French businesses court Le Pen after taking fright at left's policies", *Financial Times*, 18 June 2024.
51. Marylou Magal, "Le RN aux portes des cercles de pouvoir", *L'Express*, 28 Nov. 2024.

52. Eugénie Bastié, "Cible obsessionnelle de la gauche: Pierre-Edouard Stérin, le patron catholique qui veut mettre la droite au pouvoir", *Le Figaro Magazine*, 19 Apr. 2025.
53. "Périclès", https://periclesfrance.org/

10. ENVIRONMENTAL BATTLES AND CULTURE WARS

1. "Où sont-ils, Vierge souveraine, mais où sont les bêtes d'antan? ... Chez moi en Bretagne, la chimie de l'agriculture et le remembrement destructeur de haies ont fait grand mal. Quand j'étais enfant, les oiseaux étaient si nombreux et si divers que nos activités prédatrices et dénicheuses avaient une incidence insignifiante sur leur population. La campagne bruissait de leurs chants, de leurs appels, du bruit de leurs ailes. Mésanges, pinsons, chardonnerets, rouges-gorges (en breton *rouzicoet*, le petit rouge des bois), roitelets, moineaux, bruants, rossignols, alouettes, qui chantaient tant qu'elles étaient en vol, fauvettes, bergeronnettes qui nichaient souvent dans les bateaux hivernants." Le Pen, *Mémoires: Fils*, p. 367.
2. Le Pen, *Mémoires: Tribun*, p. 414.
3. Philippe de Villiers, *Mémoricide*, Fayard, 2024, pp. 81, 83, 137.
4. "Rendre aux ménages les 5 milliards de subventions versées notamment aux éoliennes, M la France: 22 mesures pour 2022."
5. "Je crois vital que nous, le camp national, ne nous comportions pas comme la gauche se comporte à l'égard de l'immigration depuis trente ans, c'est-à-dire dans une forme de déni." Quoted from a *Valeurs Actuelles* debate in Apr. 2023 in Clément Guillou, "L'inaction climatique, la ligne assumée du RN", *Le Monde*, 24–5 Nov. 2024.
6. "Les populistes s'emparent de tous les problèmes pour les braquer contre les élites. En ce sens, l'écologie, éclairée par la science et qui nécessite des nouvelles normes décidées par des dirigeants, est un magnifique terrain d'opportunités pour eux, surtout si les classes populaires et moyennes s'estiment lésées." Quoted in Matthieu Goar, "La transition écologique, cible des populismes", *Le Monde*, 29 Jan. 2025.
7. Tony Barber, "Europe Express Weekend: Populists seek dividends from a climate change backlash", *Financial Times*, 25 Nov. 2023.
8. Anses is the Agence nationale de sécurité sanitaire de l'alimentation, de

l'environnement et du travail; Ademe is the Agence de la transition écologique; and OFB is the Office français de la biodiversité.
9. Victor-Isaac Anne, "Les combats liberticides de l'écologisme", *Le JDNews*, 5 Mar. 2025.
10. "L'écologie c'est bien … mais si demain on ne peut plus se déplacer, qu'on ne peut plus prendre l'avion, qu'on ne peut plus construire parce qu'il y a une petite plante verte à coté qu'il faut sauvegarder, eh bien c'est très beau mais on sera tous morts." Quoted from BFMTV, 18 Nov. 2024, in Clément Guillou, "L'inaction climatique, la ligne assumée du RN", *Le Monde*, 24–5 Nov. 2024.
11. "[L]e Green Deal est probablement l'un des plus grands plans de décroissance qu'ait connu notre continent ces 50 dernières années … Les dirigeants de l'UE sont des ayatollahs prêts aux manœuvres les plus malsaines pour imposer un projet de société au caractère presque religieux." "Jordan Bardella demande la 'suspension immédiate' du Green Deal [interview]", *Le Journal du Dimanche*, 23 Jan. 2025.
12. "Je regarde la #cérémoniedouverture des JO avec mes enfants. Difficile d'apprécier les rares tableaux réussis entre les Marie-Antoinette décapitées, le trouple qui s'embrasse, des drag queens, l'humiliation de la Garde républicaine obligée de danser sur du Aya Nakamura, la laideur générale des costumes et des chorégraphies. On cherche désespérément la célébration des valeurs du sport et de la beauté de la France au milieu d'une propagande woke aussi grossière." Marion Maréchal (@MarionMarechal), X, 26 July 2024, https://x.com/MarionMarechal/status/1816915105117770025
13. "Ils veulent nous imposer une vision de l'Homme qui n'est pas la nôtre. Une vision de la France qui n'est pas la nôtre, que nous rejetons, que les étrangers eux-mêmes découvrent avec stupéfaction, ou tristesse." Éric Zemmour (@ZemmourEric), X, 27 July 2024, https://x.com/ZemmourEric/status/1817129520203252139
14. "Elle a été travaillée, mûrie, ruminée. Ce fut une affaire réfléchie en haut lieu. Elle trace un nouveau sillage dans les boucles de la Seine: nous changeons de société, nous changeons de culture, nous changeons de civilisation. Rien de moins." De Villiers, *Mémoricide*, p. 15.
15. Claire Legros, "Entre racisme et masculinisme, des liaisons ordinaires", *Le Monde*, 28 Mar. 2025.

16. "Qu'on soit homme ou femme, hétérosexuel ou homosexuel, chrétien, juif, musulman ou non-croyant, on est d'abord français!" Quoted in Sylvain Crépon, *Enquête au cœur du nouveau Front national*, Nouveau Monde, 2012, p. 241.
17. "'Une gourgandine sans foi ni loi', et son entourage 'composé d'invertis notoires'". This was Jérôme Bourbon, head of the extreme-right journal *Rivarol*, quoted in Crépon, *Enquête au coeur du nouveau Front national*, p. 243.
18. "Marine Le Pen veut interdire les langues étrangères dans la publicité", AFP, 15 Feb. 2022, https://www.ouest-france.fr/elections/presidentielle/presidentielle-marine-le-pen-veut-interdire-les-langues-etrangeres-dans-la-publicite-1b4268a2-8f10-11ec-91ef-c5100846ffb2
19. Marylou Magal, "'Déconstruire la déconstruction': Le RN veut lutter contre le 'wokisme'", *Le Figaro*, 24 Apr. 2023, https://www.lefigaro.fr/politique/deconstruire-la-deconstruction-le-rn-veut-lutter-contre-le-wokisme-20230423
20. David Smith, "'Not what we signed up for': Inside Trump's 'shocking' Kennedy Center takeover", *The Guardian*, 24 Feb. 2025.
21. Allan Kaval, "Entre l'Italie et la France, itinéraire du 'gramscisme de droite'", *Le Monde*, 19 Apr. 2025.

11. FRANCE'S FOX NEWS AND THE BATTLE FOR PUBLIC OPINION

1. "Les Français n'attendent pas qu'on leur dise quoi penser ou qu'on leur désigne un 'camp du Bien' ... Censurer des plateformes numériques, interdire la promotion d'un livre, se réjouir de la disparition d'un adversaire politique, appeler à la fermeture de chaînes de télévision après un harcèlement ciblé: je veux aussi vous appeler, journalistes intègres, à ne pas laisser l'obscurantisme abîmer ou restreindre notre démocratie." Bardella is referring to his own autobiography, against which trade unions protested; to rejoicing over the death of party founder Jean-Marie Le Pen; and to complaints of bias against TV channels CNews and C8. *Voeux à la presse*, 27 Jan. 2025.
2. "Plus globalement, si la défiance s'est installée entre une grande partie du peuple français et les médias, ce n'est pas en raison des 'mauvais

instincts', des 'dérives' d'une liberté d'expression qui irait trop loin sur les réseaux sociaux, c'est principalement parce que trop de Français ont le sentiment que la presse chercher à prescrire l'opinion plutôt qu'à informer." *Voeux à la presse*, 27 Jan. 2025.
3. Barbara Moens, "Hungary accused of illegal subsidies for pro-government media", *Financial Times*, 28 Apr. 2025.
4. Alex Loftus, "EU investigates TikTok over alleged Russian meddling in Romanian vote", BBC, 17 Dec. 2024.
5. Chombeau, *Le Pen: Fille & père*, pp. 122–3. Chombeau dates Le Pen's letter to May 1982. There is controversy about the dates and the nature of the exchange, although the arguments are less about the merits of Le Pen's complaint than whether Mitterrand was deliberately promoting the FN for political reasons to divide the right. See "Controverse autour d'un soutien de François Mitterrand au Front national", Wikipedia, https://fr.wikipedia.org/wiki/Controverse_autour_d%27un_soutien_de_Fran%C3%A7ois_Mitterrand_au_Front_national#:~:text=Jean%2DMarie%20Le%20Pen%20lui,dont%20Jean%2DMarie%20Le%20Pen
6. "Voter Front national relève de la facilité. Ce geste aggrave la situation au lieu de résoudre les problèmes. Ceux qui choisissent quand même de voter FN ont une pointe d'infantilisme dans le cœur. Il faut être un grand enfant pour croire que l'on peut tout avoir: la sécurité d'un État fort et payer moins d'impôt, l'immigration zéro et la retraite à 60 ans." From the chapter "Comment résister au 'nouveau' FN" in Fourest and Venner, *Marine Le Pen*, p. 420.
7. "Chiffres clés, statistiques de la culture: 2022", Ministère de la Culture, https://www.culture.gouv.fr/Media/medias-creation-rapide/Chiffres-cles-2022-Presse-ecrite-Fiche.pdf
8. Éric Aeschimann and Sébastien Billard, "Alerte à la désinformation climatique", *Le Nouvel Obs*, 10 Apr. 2025.
9. Adrienne Klasa, "French regulator pulls licence for Vincent Bolloré's channel C8", *Financial Times*, 24 July 2024; Émilie Garcia and Loïse Delacotte, "Cyril Hanouna donne sa version sur son altercation avec Louis Boyard: 'J'ai été trahi par mon pote en direct'", HuffPost, 14 Mar. 2024, https://www.huffingtonpost.fr/culture/video/cyril-hanouna-

donne-sa-version-sur-son-altercation-avec-louis-boyard-j-ai-ete-trahi-par-mon-pote-en-direct_231230.html; Leila Abboud, "The maverick TV host amping up France's far right", *Financial Times*, 6 July 2024.

10. See for example Vincent Isore, "Vincent Bolloré, parrain d'une alliance entre la droite et l'extrême droite", *Le Monde*, 20 Dec. 2023.
11. "Le journal du RN du dimanche", *Le Canard enchaîné*, 24 Jan. 2024.
12. Vincent Thobel, "Audiences TV: TF1 domine en janvier 2025, France 2 et M6 en progression", Media Leader, 4 Feb. 2025, https://fr.themedialeader.com/audiences-tv-tf1-domine-en-janvier-2025-france-2-et-m6-en-progression/; "Classement radios juin 2025", ACPM, https://www.acpm.fr/Les-chiffres/Frequentation-Radios/Classement-des-Radios-Digitales/Par-marque/Classement-France
13. Adel Miliani and Anne-Aël Durand, "L'Arcom a pris 52 sanctions contre les chaînes C8 et CNews en douze ans, dont 16 pendant la seule année 2024", *Le Monde*, 15 Nov. 2024.
14. Julien Labarre, "French Fox News? Audience-level metrics for the comparative study of news audience hyperpartisanship", *Journal of Information Technology & Politics*, 21:4, 16 Jan. 2024, pp. 510–27, https://doi.org/10.1080/19331681.2023.2300845
15. Marine Le Pen, *Pour que vive la France*, Grancher, 2012, pp. 184–5; de Villiers devoted more than two pages of his polemical book *Mémoricide* about the decline of France (pp. 357–9) to syrupy praise of Bolloré, one of whose companies was the book's publisher; *Paris Match* was subsequently sold on to LVMH, the conglomerate controlled by Bernard Arnault, France's richest man.
16. "La Présidence de la République dément avoir employé les termes 'faire peur' qui lui sont prêtés dans l'édition du jour du JDD. Il ne s'agit ni de son expression ni de son intention. En cette période grave où, face à la menace russe, la quasi-totalité des chefs d'État et de gouvernement prend des mesures inédites pour assurer leur défense, chacun doit veiller au respect de la parfaite véracité des faits. Le moment exige lucidité, patriotisme et sens de l'unité nationale." Élysée (@Elysee) post on X, 9 Mar. 2025, https://x.com/Elysee/status/1898766688448823630
17. Conversation in Montretout, 10 Sept. 1997, quoted in Fieschi, *Populocracy*, pp. 54–5.

18. Quoted in Andy Bounds, "Europe Express: Anti-social media", *Financial Times*, 18 Mar. 2024; "These European parliamentarians shape the political conversation on Facebook", Common Consultancy, https://static1.squarespace.com/static/649acb8ca646a90b8742e9d4/t/65f83c9e3bb91000431b5452/1710767269061/MEP_analyse_altPDF.pdf
19. Catherine Fieschi, "Why Europe's new populists tell so many lies—and do it so shamelessly", *The Guardian*, 30 Sept. 2019; Fieschi, *Populocracy*.
20. Gallimard, 2019, 2023.
21. "Colère + algorithmes = chaos"; "En créant des contradictions, des clashs, ils font émerger de nouvelles majorités qui ne naissent plus d'une convergence vers le centre, comme dans la politique classique, mais d'une attraction vers les extrêmes." Xavier de la Porte, Nathalie Funès and Grégoire Leménager, "Le décodeur du chaos", *L'Obs*, 4 Jan. 2024.
22. See for example Tamás Matura, "Sino-Russian convergence in foreign information manipulation and interference: A global threat to the US and its allies", Center for European Policy Analysis, 30 June 2025, https://cepa.org/comprehensive-reports/sino-russian-convergence-in-foreign-information-manipulation-and-interference/
23. Sheelah Delestre, "Les fake news en France: Faits et chiffres", Statista, 5 Jan. 2024, https://fr.statista.com/themes/5481/les-fake-news-en-france/#topicOverview
24. "Giuliano da Empoli: 'Le combat contre la barbarie se renouvelle avec chaque génération'", interviewed by Nicolas Truong, *Le Monde*, 23 Apr. 2025.
25. "Il faut lutter contre la ridicule soumission du politique à la technologie, et rétablir une cohérence entre le fonctionnement des plateformes et un débat politique soutenable." De la Porte, Funès and Leménager, "Le décodeur du chaos".

12. TO RUSSIA WITH LOVE

1. Victor Mallet, "'She's radiant': What French voters like about Le Pen this time", *Financial Times*, 20 Apr. 2022.
2. Leila Abboud, "Le Pen's RN party pays back €6mn Russian loan", *Financial Times*, 19 Sept. 2023.

3. Marie-Pierre Bourgeois, "Marine Le Pen assure que la Crimée a voté 'librement' pour être rattachée à Moscou", BFMTV, 24 May 2023, https://www.bfmtv.com/politique/front-national/marine-le-pen-assure-que-la-crimee-a-vote-librement-pour-etre-rattachee-a-moscou_AV-202305240631.html; the RN also produced a 2022 campaign leaflet featuring a photo of her shaking hands with Vladimir Putin at the Kremlin to show her statesmanship. Anthony Cuthbertson, "Marine Le Pen's far-right party orders 1.2 million election leaflets showing her with Putin to be 'binned'", *The Independent*, 2 Mar. 2022, https://www.independent.co.uk/news/world/europe/france-elections-le-pen-putin-b2025791.html

4. "Et je le dis avec beaucoup de gravité ce soir parce que pour notre pays c'est une mauvaise nouvelle, parce que vous dépendez du pouvoir russe et que vous dépendez de M. Poutine ... vous parlez à votre banquier quand vous parlez avec la Russie. C'est ça le problème Mme Le Pen." "Débat télévisé entre M. Emmanuel Macron, président de la République, et Mme Marine Le Pen, députée du Rassemblement national, candidats à l'élection présidentielle, le 20 avril 2022, sur les programmes des deux candidats", Vie publique, https://www.vie-publique.fr/discours/285127-debat-televise-20042022-emmanuel-macron-marine-le-pen-candidats

5. "[N]otre intérêt national est de renouer l'alliance traditionnelle avec la Russie pour contrebalancer l'impérialisme exacerbé d'une Amérique aujourd'hui sans contrepoids, cherchant à obtenir l'endiguement de cette puissance renaissante. S'appuyer sur la Russie aujourd'hui c'est créer le véritable espace européen de l'Atlantique à l'Oural, l'Europe des patries poursuivant leurs intérêts nationaux et associées dans une communauté de civilisation, bien éloignée du modèle communautariste ultralibéral Americain vers lequel l'Union européenne nous conduit." Le Pen, *Pour que vive la France*, p. 225.

6. Camus and Lebourg, *Far-Right Politics in Europe*, p. 228.

7. "Russia's foreign ministry says France 'killed democracy' with Le Pen conviction", Reuters, 3 Apr. 2025, https://www.reuters.com/world/europe/russias-foreign-ministry-says-france-killed-democracy-with-le-pen-conviction-2025-04-03/

8. Eltchaninoff, *Inside the Mind of Marine Le Pen*, pp. 77, 142, 147.

9. "The 2011 Time 100", *Time*, 21 Apr. 2011, https://content.time.com/time/specials/packages/article/0,28804,2066367_2066369_2066134,00.html

10. "Je ne crois absolument pas qu'il y a eu une annexion illégale: il y a eu un référendum, les habitants de Crimée souhaitaient rejoindre la Russie", Marie-Pierre Bourgeois, "Marine Le Pen assure que la Crimée a voté 'librement' pour être rattachée à Moscou", BFMTV, 24 May 2023, https://www.bfmtv.com/politique/front-national/marine-le-pen-assure-que-la-crimee-a-vote-librement-pour-etre-rattachee-a-moscou_AV-202305240631.html

11. "Marine Le Pen évoque des 'crimes de guerre' en Ukraine", *Le Point*/AFP, 4 Apr. 2022, https://www.lepoint.fr/politique/marine-le-pen-evoque-des-crimes-de-guerre-en-ukraine-04-04-2022-2470801_20.php#11; Marie-Pierre Bourgeois, "Ukraine: Marine Le Pen 'ne regrette rien' de ses propos sur Poutine mais estime qu'il a 'franchi la ligne rouge'", BFMTV, 1 Mar. 2022, https://www.bfmtv.com/politique/elections/presidentielle/ukraine-marine-le-pen-ne-regrette-rien-de-ses-propos-sur-poutine-mais-estime-qu-il-a-franchi-la-ligne-rouge_AV-202203010652.html; "Le Pen réclame l'abandon des sanctions contre la Russie, qui 'ne servent à rien'", Europe 1/AFP, 2 Aug. 2022, https://www.europe1.fr/politique/le-pen-reclame-labandon-des-sanctions-contre-la-russie-qui-ne-servent-a-rien-4126228

12. "La Russie est évidemment une menace aujourd'hui multidimensionnelle pour la France et pour les intérêts européens." Jordan Bardella to France Inter radio, cited in Marie-France Bourgeois, "'Deux sensibilités différentes': Le Pen et Bardella pas parfaitement alignés sur la guerre en Ukraine", BFMTV, 12 Mar. 2025, https://www.bfmtv.com/politique/front-national/deux-sensibilites-differentes-le-pen-et-bardella-pas-parfaitement-alignes-sur-la-guerre-en-ukraine_AN-202503120044.html

13. "On est tout près de la résolution du conflit ... Dans un conflit il y a des vainqueurs et des vaincus, et qui sont les vainqueurs et qui sont les vaincus? Les vainqueurs sont les Américains, les premiers vainqueurs de cette guerre sont les Américains ... Du côté des Français, des Européens c'est une défaite ... Nous, on a tout perdu dans cette guerre,

dans une guerre entre deux peoples Slaves." "Face à Philippe de Villiers", CNews, 28 Feb. 2025, https://www.cnews.fr/emission/2025-02-28/face-philippe-de-villiers-emission-du-28022025-1642822

14. Isabelle Mandraud, "L'égérie russe du Groupe Bolloré", *Le Monde*, 26 Mar. 2025; Ariane Chemin and Ivanne Trippenbach, "Les médias Bolloré défendent ouvertement la Russie", *Le Monde*, 9–10 Mar. 2025.

15. Catherine Belton, *Putin's People: How the KGB Took Back Russia and Then Took on the West*, HarperCollins, 2020, Loc7910 on Kindle version.

16. Angelique Chrisafis/Agencies, "France says Russian hackers behind attack on Macron's 2017 presidential campaign", *The Guardian*, 29 Apr. 2025, https://www.theguardian.com/world/2025/apr/29/france-says-russian-hackers-behind-attack-on-macrons-2017-presidential-campaign

17. Hugh Schofield, "Star of David graffiti in Paris: The Russian connection", BBC, 8 Nov. 2023, https://www.bbc.com/news/world-europe-67360768; Antoine Albertini, Damien Leloup and Florian Reynaud, "Stars of David graffiti in Paris: Russian interference suspected", *Le Monde* [English], 7 Nov. 2023, updated 23 Nov. 2023, https://www.lemonde.fr/en/france/article/2023/11/07/stars-of-david-graffiti-in-paris-russian-interference-suspected_6235378_7.html

18. Romain Gubert, "Comment Poutine déstabilise l'Europe", *Le Point*, 6 June 2024.

19. "'Psychose des punaises de lit en France': Pourquoi le gouvernement accuse-t-il la Russie?", TF1, 1 Mar 2024, https://www.tf1info.fr/international/psychose-des-punaises-de-lit-en-france-pourquoi-le-ministre-delegue-charge-de-l-europe-jean-noel-barrot-accuse-t-il-la-russie-doopelganger-2287905.html

20. Jacques Follorou, "L'ombre de Moscou sur le scrutin européen", *Le Monde*, 2 Mar. 2024.

21. Carmen Paun, "Romania's presidential front-runner Georgescu benefited from Russia-style booster campaign, declassified docs say", Politico, 5 Dec. 2024, https://www.politico.eu/article/romanias-presidential-frontrunner-benefited-from-russia-style-booster-campaign-declassified-docs-say/

22. Laura Pitel, "Senior German MP says vote was 'successfully' manipulated by foreign actors", *Financial Times*, 28 Feb. 2025.

13. EMBEZZLEMENT: "UNBELIEVABLE"—BUT TRUE

1. "Marine Le Pen affirme que 'le système a sorti la bombe nucléaire'", *Le Parisien*/AFP, 1 Apr. 2025; "[U]n coup de tonnerre dans la vie politique française." "Condamnation de Marine Le Pen: De l'application des lois votées", *Le Monde*, 2 Apr. 2025.
2. "Ainsi, à l'été 2014, alors que 23 députés du RASSEMBLEMENT NATIONAL étaient élus au Parlement européen, le système était destiné à constituer une véritable manne financière pour le parti. Avec 23 députés élus, les frais d'assistance parlementaire représentaient en effet désormais plus de 6,5 millions d'euros par an, soit environ le double de la masse salariale du RN à l'époque, de l'ordre de 3 millions d'euros sur un budget de 10,2 millions d'euros. Les contrats conclus au cours de la 8ème législature étaient donc susceptibles de contribuer de façon de plus en plus significative au financement des charges de personnel du parti. Le système élaboré mis en place n'a trouvé de limite que dans la dénonciation des faits et l'ouverture de la présente procédure judiciaire." "Délibéré dossier dit des assistants fictifs du RN" (official court summary of judgment, 31 Mar. 2025, p. 28).
3. See note 95 of the 154-page judgement: "Sur un montant total de 4,4 millions d'euros de fonds publics détournés, les députés ont été poursuivis et déclarés coupables en leur qualité d'auteurs principaux à hauteur d'environ 3 170K€. D'autres contrats représentant un montant total de 1 224K€ sont visés à la prévention, pour lesquels les eurodéputés concernés, (essentiellement Jean-Marie LE PEN et Marine LE PEN) n'ont pas été mis en examen ni poursuivis comme auteurs principaux. Le président du parti à l'époque des faits, Jean-Marie LE PEN jusqu'au 16 janvier 2011 et Marine LE PEN après cette date, est néanmoins renvoyé pour complicité de ces détournements. Le RN, dont la responsabilité est engagée par le président du parti, est déclaré coupable, à l'exception de quelques relaxes partielles intervenues, sur la totalité de la période et des contrats, au titre de la complicité et du recel, soit pour un montant total de 4,4 millions d'euros."

4. "Aujourd'hui, ce n'est pas seulement Marine Le Pen qui est injustement condamnée: c'est la démocratie française qui est exécutée." #JeSoutiensMarine, Jordan Bardella (@J_Bardella) post on X, 31 Mar. 2025, https://x.com/J_Bardella/status/1906659577174589915
5. "Trump and Vance support Marine Le Pen after her conviction", *Le Monde*/AFP, 4 Apr. 2025.
6. Salvini and Dmitry Peskov were both quoted in Leila Abboud, Adrienne Klasa, Ian Johnston and Guy Chazan, "Marine Le Pen banned from standing for office for 5 years", *Financial Times*, 1 Apr. 2025.
7. Philippe Ricard et al., "L'"internationale réactionnaire' s'associe au Kremlin pour critiquer la justice française", *Le Monde*, 2 Apr. 2025.
8. "The Le Pen verdict: Authoritarians rally worldwide", Coda Currents, 3 Apr. 2025.
9. "VIDEO: Quand Marine Le Pen demandait 'l'inéligibilité à vie' pour les élus condamnés pour 'détournement de fonds publics'", Public Sénat TV, 5 Apr. 2013, https://www.publicsenat.fr/actualites/politique/video-quand-marine-le-pen-demandait-lineligibilite-a-vie-pour-les-elus-condamnes-pour-detournement-de-fonds-publics
10. Victor Mallet and David Keohane, "Former French PM sentenced to jail for embezzlement", *Financial Times*, 29 June 2020.
11. The Mélenchon/LFI investigation has been frozen since 2022, when two of Mélenchon's former European parliamentary assistants were designated as "assisted witnesses". "Soupçons d'emplois fictifs: Deux ex-assistants parlementaires de Mélenchon au Parlement européen placés sous le statut de témoin assisté", *Le Monde*/AFP, 15 Nov. 2022, https://www.lemonde.fr/societe/article/2022/11/15/soupcons-d-emplois-fictifs-deux-ex-assistants-parlementaires-de-melenchon-au-parlement-europeen-places-sous-le-statut-de-temoin-assiste_6149945_3224.html; Samuel Laurent and Clément Guillou, "François Bayrou relaxé dans l'affaire des assistants parlementaires du MoDem, faute de preuves", *Le Monde*, 5 Feb. 2024, https://www.lemonde.fr/societe/article/2024/02/05/affaire-des-assistants-parlementaires-du-modem-francois-bayrou-relaxe-faute-de-preuves_6214865_3224.html
12. "Quoiqu'on pense du RN et de l'affaire jugée aujourd'hui, cette date restera un jour très sombre pour la démocratie française. La candidate

que les sondages placent de fait en tête à l'élection présidentielle est empêchée de concourir par une décision de justice: cet événement inédit laissera des traces profondes." Statement from Bellamy's office, 31 Mar. 2025.
13. *The Economist*, 1 Apr. 2025.
14. Victor Mallet and David Keohane, "Former French PM sentenced to jail for embezzlement", *Financial Times*, 29 June 2020.
15. "François Fillon dépose un nouveau pourvoi en cassation dans l'affaire des emplois fictifs de son épouse", *Le Monde*/AFP, 30 June 2025, https://www.lemonde.fr/politique/article/2025/06/30/francois-fillon-depose-un-nouveau-pourvoi-en-cassation-dans-l-affaire-des-emplois-fictifs-de-son-epouse_6617018_823448.html
16. "Condamnation de Marine Le Pen: 'Il existe' des 'juges rouges', dénonce Sébastien Chenu", BFM-RMC, 7 Apr. 2025, https://rmc.bfmtv.com/actualites/politique/condamnation-de-marine-le-pen-il-existe-des-juges-rouges-denonce-sebastien-chenu_AV-202504070339.html; "[C]'est une atteinte gravissime à la démocratie et au processus électoral." Interview in *Le Parisien*, "Ça ne m'atteint pas, ça me motive", 2 Apr. 2025.
17. "C'est un processus complet, très protecteur des droits de la défense. Si cela est une mise en cause de la démocratie, je ne sais pas quel sens il faut donner aux mots ... Attaquer l'institution judiciaire, ce n'est pas seulement porter atteinte aux juges mais aussi aux fondements de notre démocratie. J'observe que les juges, aujourd'hui, sont eux-mêmes attaqués à titre personnel, notamment sur les réseaux sociaux, ce qui est un phénomène nouveau." "Nous vivons une forme de fragilisation de la démocratie", interview of Christophe Soulard by Grégoire Biseau and Jérôme Lefilliâtre, *Le Monde*, 3 Apr. 2025.
18. "La famille de Martin Luther King dénonce la référence de Marine Le Pen à cette figure de la lutte contre le racisme, 'une distorsion inappropriée de l'histoire'", franceinfo, 14 Apr 2025, https://www.franceinfo.fr/politique/marine-le-pen/la-famille-de-martin-luther-king-denonce-la-reference-de-marine-le-pen-au-pasteur-afro-americain-une-distorsion-inappropriee-de-l-histoire_7189767.html
19. Elabe poll for BFMTV, "Les Français et la condamnation de Marine

Le Pen", 31 Mar. 2025, https://elabe.fr/wp-content/uploads/2025/04/31032025_elabe-bfmtv_les-francais-et-la-condamnation-de-marine-le-pen.pdf

20. "L'État de droit? Sauf pour le Rassemblement national!", opinion column in *L'Express*, 10 Apr. 2025.
21. "Aujourd'hui, on utilise la bombe nucléaire parce que nous sommes proches du pouvoir. C'est ça que ça révèle. Plus vous êtes haut, plus vous êtes fort, plus les attaques contre vous sont lourdes. Ça ne m'atteint pas, ça me motive. L'injustice m'a toujours motivée de manière générale. Quand elle est commise par la justice, ça me donne une motivation d'airain, de granit ... Il paraît qu'en politique il ne faut jamais dire jamais. Mais oui, je pense que ce sera la dernière. Sauf si je suis élue." "Ça ne m'atteint pas, ça me motive", interview by Olivier Beaumont, Quentin Laurent and Marion Mourgue, *Le Parisien*, 2 Apr. 2025.
22. Club de l'Hémicycle via YouTube, 10 Apr. 2025, https://www.youtube.com/watch?v=NbyCQ1v-mWQ
23. Club de l'Hémicycle via YouTube, 10 Apr. 2025, https://www.youtube.com/watch?v=NbyCQ1v-mWQ
24. "Dans le moment actuel, nous avons l'impérieuse nécessité de rester unis et soudés. Il n'y a pas d'ambiguïté sur le fait que Marine Le Pen est ma candidate, et que si elle devait être empêchée demain, je pense pouvoir vous dire que je serai son candidat. Je ne peux pas être plus clair que ça", quoted in "Si elle est empêchée, je serai le candidat de Marine Le Pen", *Le Parisien*, 27 Apr. 2025.
25. "Ils ont la chance d'avoir un électorat solide: les études sont toutes les mêmes, c'est bonnet blanc et blanc bonnet. La situation n'est pas si inconfortable pour Jordan Bardella." Quoted in "Le RN en plein dilemme stratégique", *Le Monde*, 4–5 May 2025.

CONCLUSION: FAR-RIGHT FUTURE

1. "Marine est une figure tragique", quoted in "Marine Le Pen, la malédiction et les secousses, Solenn de Royer", *Le Monde*, 2 Apr. 2025.
2. "[L]a puissance de l'extrême droite ne se limite plus à la figure de Marine Le Pen. Il y a un plan B comme Bardella, un plan R comme Retailleau, un plan Z comme Zemmour", quoted in Sandrine Cassini, Mariama

Darame, Claire Gatinois and Alexandre Pedro, "Le procès du RN bouscule la présidentielle", *Le Monde*, 4 Apr. 2025.

3. The far-right, Russia-sympathetic newspaper *Le Journal du Dimanche* quoted an unnamed centre-right MP on this. "'Le RN pourrait tres bien nous faire une 'Medvedev–Poutine'", *Le Journal du Dimanche*, 17 Nov. 2024.

4. The left-wing magazine *Marianne* broke the story in Feb. 2025, and the far-right magazine *Valeurs Actuelles* obtained what it said was his presidential programme: the front cover was headlined "2027: Le candidat Hanouna!", 30 Apr.–6 May 2025.

5. "Moins de cent jours. C'est tout ce qu'il faut aujourd'hui au RN, ou à tout autre parti mû par une même intention autoritaire, pour transformer la France en démocratie illibérale, et lui faire prendre la tête de ce club européen où figurent déjà la Hongrie de Viktor Orbán et la Slovaquie de Robert Fico—transformées en quelques années en États autoritaires, défiants à l'égard des principes de l'Union européenne et radicalement hostiles aux étrangers. La 'révolution nationale' en 100 jours, et comment l'éviter", Pierre-Yves Bocquet, *Tracts Gallimard*, no. 64, 2025, p. 3. Bocquet argues that the only method for changing the constitution should be via its restrictive Article 89, not via the simpler method of Article 11, which was used by de Gaulle to call referendums that bypassed parliament.

6. "'Nous l'organiserons dès notre arrivée au pouvoir': Bardella pousse l'idée d'un référendum sur l'immigration", BFMTV/AFP, 2 Feb. 2025, https://www.bfmtv.com/politique/front-national/nous-l-organiserons-des-notre-arrivee-au-pouvoir-bardella-pousse-l-idee-d-un-referendum-sur-l-immigration_AD-202502020172.html; Justine Faure, "LR et RN souhaitent organiser des référendums sur l'immigration, mais est-ce possible?", TF1, 30 Aug. 2023, https://www.tf1info.fr/politique/referendum-immigration-lr-et-rn-le-souhaitent-en-organiser-mais-est-ce-possible-que-dit-la-loi-droit-2268084.html

7. "C'est un changement de régime. Voilà pourquoi il n'est pas exagéré de parler de révolution—une nouvelle révolution nationale, autoritaire, plébiscitaire et xénophobe. La VIe République du RN. La 'révolution nationale' en 100 jours, et comment l'éviter", Pierre-Yves Bocquet, *Tracts Gallimard*, no. 64, 2025, p. 51.

8. "[L]e racisme, le répli national, la stigmatisation d'ennemis de l'intérieur, la discrimination envers des citoyens français (en l'occurence d'origine non pas juive mais maghrébine)—tout en se réclamant sans vergogne de l'héritage et de l'action du général de Gaulle." Julian Jackson, *Le Procès Pétain*, trans. Marie-Anne de Béru, Seuil, 2024, p. 416.
9. "Ça fait 30 ans qu'en réalité on va vers plus de laxisme, de culture de l'excuse et de politique d'immigration au nombre sans précédent, qui change aujourd'hui le visage de notre pays, qui en change les valeurs et qui en change l'identité", interview with the author, 28 May 2025.
10. "[L]a mondialisation sauvage et ultralibérale, la désindustrialisation, l'immigration massive, la perte de nos valeurs", interview with the author, 28 May 2025.
11. "Maintenant, il y a toutes les raisons pour prendre le pouvoir de l'intérieur. Je veux dire, quand on est en train de gagner la partie, on ne quitte pas la table de jeu", interview with the author, 28 May 2025.
12. "Là, on fermera peut-être le banc, mais on y arrivera. Et en réalité, une victoire en France, c'est ça aussi, c'est une nouveauté. Une victoire en France est aussi une victoire pour l'Europe, parce que je sais que beaucoup de pays européens et beaucoup de partenaires européens nous regardent dans la mesure où le seul pays qui peut changer le fonctionnement de la construction européenne, c'est, je l'ai dit, l'Allemagne ou la France", interview with the author, 28 May 2025.
13. Mujtaba Rahman, "Le Pen would try to destroy the EU from within", Eurasia Group, 12 Apr. 2022.
14. Conversation with the author, 11 Feb. 2025.
15. "Le RN, bien sûr ... Il n'avait au fond jamais vraiment réfléchi au contenu réel de la souveraineté, dans un monde interdépendant ou pour un État endetté." Guillaume Hannezo, Hakim El Karoui and Thierry Pech, *Marine Le Pen présidente: Dystopie politique 2026–2029*, Les petits matins, 2025, p. 249.
16. "Il y a une réelle prise de conscience collective, au sein même de notre électorat qui n'y croyait pas forcément, que nous pouvons gagner. Notre victoire est en quelque sorte inévitable. Marine Le Pen interviewed in Tugdual Denis and Sébastien Lignier, "Notre victoire est en quelque sorte inévitable", *Valeurs Actuelles*, 18 July 2024.

SELECT BIBLIOGRAPHY

Bardella, J., 2024. *Ce que je cherche*. Fayard.
Belton, C., 2020. *Putin's People: How the KGB Took Back Russia and Then Took On the West*. HarperCollins.
Black, J., 2021. *France: A Short History*. Thames & Hudson.
Blain, C. and Lanzac, A., 2010. *Quai d'Orsay*. Dargaud.
Bocquet, P.-Y., 2025. *La "Révolution Nationale" en 100 jours, et comment l'éviter*. Tracts Gallimard.
Camus, J.-Y. and Lebourg, N., 2017. *Far-Right Politics in Europe*. Belknap Press of Harvard University Press.
Chombeau, C., 2007. *Le Pen: Fille & père*. Panama.
Crépon, S., 2012. *Enquête au cœur du nouveau Front National*. Nouveau Monde.
Da Empoli, G., 2023. *Les ingénieurs du chaos*. Lattès.
De Villiers, P., 2024. *Mémoricide*. Fayard.
Eltchaninoff, M., 2017. *Inside the Mind of Marine Le Pen*. Hurst.
Feher, M., 2024. *Producteurs et parasites: L'imaginaire si désirable du Rassemblement national*. La Découverte.
Fieschi, C., 2004. *Fascism, Populism and the French Fifth Republic*. Manchester University Press.
—— 2019. *Populocracy*. Agenda Publishing.
Fort, P.-S., 2024. *Le Grand Remplaçant: La face cachée de Jordan Bardella*. StudioFact.
Fourest, C. and Venner, F., 2011. *Marine Le Pen*. Grasset & Fasquelle.

SELECT BIBLIOGRAPHY

Fourquet, J., 2019. *L'Archipel français: Naissance d'une nation multiple et divisée*. Seuil.

—— 2024. *Métamorphoses françaises: État de la France en infographies et en images*. Seuil.

Granville, B., 2021. *What Ails France?* McGill–Queen's University Press.

Guilluy, C., 2014. *La France périphérique: Comment on a sacrifié les classes populaires*. Flammarion.

—— 2025. *Métropolia et périphéria: Un voyage extraordinaire*. Flammarion.

Hannezo, G., El Karoui, H. and Pech, T., 2025. *Marine Le Pen présidente: Dystopie politique 2016–2019*. Les Petits matins.

Houellebecq, M., 2015. *Soumission*. Flammarion.

—— 2019. *Sérotonine*. Flammarion.

Jackson, J., 2019. *A Certain Idea of France: The Life of Charles de Gaulle*. Penguin.

—— 2024. *Le procès Pétain* [French edn]. Translated by M.-A. de Béru. Seuil.

Jarousseau, V., 2025. *Dans les âmes et les urnes: Dix ans à la rencontre de la France qui vote RN*. Arènes.

Kepel, G., 2012. *Quatre-vingt-treize*. Gallimard.

Le Pen, J.-M., 2018. *Mémoires: Fils de la nation*. Muller.

—— 2019. *Mémoires: Tribun du peuple*. Muller.

Le Pen, M., 2006. *À contre flots*. Grancher.

—— 2012. *Pour que vive la France*. Grancher.

Maddow, R., 2024. *Prequel: An American Fight against Fascism*. Penguin.

Mak, G., 2023. *The Dream of Europe: Travels in a Troubled Continent*. Vintage.

Peel, M., 2019. *The Fabulists: The World's New Rulers, Their Myths and the Struggle against Them*. Oneworld.

Perrineau, P., 2021. *Le populisme*. Que sais-je?/Humensis.

Plenel, E. and Rollat, A., 1984. *L'effet Le Pen*. La Découverte/Le Monde.

Roque, F. (ed.), 2008. *Les droites en France 1789–2008*. Foreword by J. Daniel. Ed. Claude Weill. Saint-Simon/Nouvel Observateur/CNRS Éditions.

Sabéran, H., 2014. *Bienvenue à Hénin-Beaumont: Reportage sur un laboratoire du Front national*. La Découverte.

SELECT BIBLIOGRAPHY

Schlink, B., 2024. *The Granddaughter*. Translated by C. Collins. Weidenfeld & Nicolson.

Soudais, M., 1996. *Le Front National en Face*. Flammarion.

Sternhell, Z., 1987. *Ni droite ni gauche: L'idéologie fasciste en France*. Fayard.

Szelényi, Z., 2022. *Tainted Democracy: Viktor Orbán and the Subversion of Hungary*. Hurst.

Tondelier, M., 2024. *Nouvelles du Front*. Les Liens qui libèrent.

Vigogne Le Coat, C., 2023. *Les rapaces*. Les Arènes.

Williams, P.M., 1972. *Crisis and Compromise: Politics in the Fourth Republic*. Longman.

INDEX

À contre flots (Le Pen), 94
Abdeslam, Salah, 151
abortion, 42, 81, 85
Académie française, 182
Achilli, Jean-François, 117
Action française, 49, 50
activists, 16
Ademe, 178
Afghanistan, 155
Agency for Fundamental Rights, 166
agriculture, 53, 110, 114, 128, 133–4, 163
   environmental policies and, 11, 175–6, 177, 178
   food imports and, 133–4, 177
aide médicale d'État, 163
Aigues-Mortes, Occitania, 158
air pollution, 29
Albania, 166
Albrechtsen, Thomas, 191
alcoholism, 139
Algeria, 47, 63, 102, 125, 127, 142, 150, 158
   War of Independence (1954–62), 51, 60, 61, 62, 63, 65–6, 129, 138, 153
Algerian migrants, 26, 99, 127, 151
Aliot, Louis, 80, 82
Alleanza Nazionale, 184
Alstom, 88
Alternative für Deutschland (AfD), 8, 42, 43, 154–5, 178, 205, 210
Amman, Naella, 98–9
anarchism, 27, 30
And God Created Woman (1956 film), 137
Anglo-American Press Association, 40
Ansell, Ben, 10
Anses, 178
anti-Americanism, 199
anti-fascism, 14, 18, 72, 122–3, 131, 145, 183, 197
antisemitism, 48–9, 50, 61, 63, 74, 83, 204
   Le Pen Marine and, xiv, 14, 25, 78, 82, 83, 84, 87

INDEX

Le Pen Jean-Marie and, xiv, 14, 35, 57, 64–5, 83, 87
Arabic, 128, 142
Arc de Triomphe, Paris, 30
L'Archipel français (Fourquet), 12–13
Arcom, 190
Argentina, 4, 41
Armenian migrants, 158
Artificial Intelligence (AI), 193
al-Assad, Bashar, 66, 135
assimilation, 107, 128, 143–4, 150, 158, 160–62
astrology, 193
asylum seekers, 97, 135, 142, 151, 154–5, 165–6
Attac, 133
Attal, Gabriel, 117, 161
Auray, 60
Australia, 8
Austria, 9, 96, 113

Bain Capital, 139
Baltic states, 198
Bannie (Fedorova), 191
Bannon, Steve, 36–7, 192
Barbara, Saint, 142
Bardella, Guerino, 106
Bardella, Jordan, xi, xiii, 3, 4, 5, 11, 15, 73, 99, 105–19, 214, 220, 222
  Barnier no-confidence vote (2024), 134
  Beaucaire visit (2024), 121–9
  Berber heritage, 106, 116, 161
  Briois and Bilde removals (2022), 116

Ce que je cherche (2024), 105, 117, 121–9
centre right, cooption of, 111–12, 116
charisma, 109–10
childhood, 5, 106–8, 116, 117, 118, 160
class background, 5, 108, 116, 126
cleanliness, 118–19
CPAC cancellation (2025), 36–7
culture wars, views on, 181, 182–3
economic policies, 116, 118, 169, 172, 221, 224
education, 108, 117, 126
embezzlement ruling (2025), 209, 213, 215–17
environmental policies, 8, 176, 177, 178
Étrépagny rally (2024), 130–36
EU, stance on, 110, 179, 224, 225
European elections (2019), 101, 108–9, 216
European elections (2024), 101, 109, 216
French language, views on, 182–3
de Gaulle, references to, 47, 118, 224
girlfriends, 116–17
globalisation, views on, 228
government efficiency dept proposal, 38, 225
homosexuality rumours, 117

280

INDEX

identitarianism, 118
immigration, views on, 106, 107, 110, 154, 159–60, 224
inexperience, 19, 114, 117, 118, 169
Islam, views on, 135
Italian heritage, 106, 161
Le Pen, relations with, 115–16
legislative elections (2024), 3–4, 10, 101–3, 111, 112–14, 172
media, relations with, 18, 116–18, 134–5, 185, 189
name, 106
personality, primacy of, 119
Plan B, 115, 214, 220
revolution, views on, 111–12
Russia, relations with, 202
social media, 109, 191
Trump, comparisons with, 118, 119, 121
Trump, relations with, 33–4, 36, 44, 45
welfare, views on, 116, 224–5
Bardella, Olivier, 106, 107
Bardella, Réjane, 106
Bardot, Brigitte, 137–8, 144–5, 146
Bariki, Salah, 158
Barnier, Michel, 103, 132, 134, 150
Barreau, Frédéric, 133
Barrot, Jean-Noël, 204
Barthomeuf, Rémy, 197
Bataclan theatre attack (2015), 107–8, 151
Battle of Algiers (1956–7), 65
Battle of Berlin (1945), 62

Battle of Điện Biên Phủ (1954), 59
Bayeux, Normandy, 130
Bayrou, François, 132, 149–50, 152, 153, 157, 159, 210, 211
Beaucaire, Occitania, 121–9
bedbugs, 204
Bellamy, François-Xavier, 210
Belton, Catherine, 203
Benetton, 96
Bengal cats, 80, 86–7
de Benoist, Alain, 184
Berbers, 106, 116
Berlin, Germany
    Battle of Berlin (1945), 62
    Berlin Wall, fall of (1989), 7
Bertelli, Luisa, 106
Biden, Joseph, 7, 10, 39, 88, 203
Bigot, Guillaume, 15
Bilde, Bruno, 116, 139, 142
black bloc, 30
black French people, 14, 84
Blanchard, Olivier, 172
Blum, Léon, 11
BNP Paribas, 28
bobo society, 14, 226
Bocquet, Pierre-Yves, 223
Boëll, Lise, 117
Bolloré, Vincent, 110, 117, 123, 173, 188–91, 203, 221
Bolsonaro, Jair, 133, 210
Bonnefoy, Cyrille, 97–8
Bonnet, Florelle, 70
Bossard, Sarah, 161
Boucheron, Patrick, 180
Boulanger, Georges Ernest, 48
Bousquet, Pierre, 62

INDEX

Bouygues, 106, 190
Brands, Hal, 33
Braun-Pivet, Yaël, 102
Brazil, 133, 210
Brexit, xi, xii, xiv–xv, 4, 97, 103, 108, 135, 171, 228
  anti-establishment sentiment and, 25
  immigration and, 152, 156–7
  imperial nostalgia and, 2
  liberal establishment and, 10, 41, 135, 141
  media and, 18, 192
  populism and, 171
  'take back control' slogan, 152, 224
  wishful thinking and, 41, 53
Briois, Steeve, 116, 139, 140–44
Brittany, 26, 27, 47, 57, 58, 94
Brothers of Italy, 9, 42, 184, 226
Brunerie, Maxime, 56
Bulgaria, 44, 163
burglaries, 124, 129
burkini, 162
Burn-Murdoch, John, 35
Bush, George Walker, 40, 66
businesses, 14, 15, 54, 82, 164, 172–4, 199, 221–2
  big business, 169, 172–4, 221–2
  small businesses, 24, 60, 126

C8, 188–9, 190, 223
cahiers de doléance, 30
Caigneaux, Charles, 133
Call of Duty, 109
Cambodia, 176
Cameron, David, 25

Camus, Jean-Yves, 17–18, 38, 50, 51, 63, 85, 168, 200, 226
Camus, Renaud, 159–60
Canada, 8, 34–5, 38, 42, 198
Canard enchaîné, Le, 189
cannabis, 99
capitalism, 27, 62, 95, 99, 116, 130, 131, 133–4, 173–4
Caribbean, 14, 28
Carpenter, Michael, 203
Casablanca, Morocco, 106
casseurs, 26–7, 30
Catalonia, 26
Catholicism, xiv, 12, 48, 59, 80, 82, 85, 117, 123, 140, 167, 173, 221
  homosexuality and, 181–2
  immigration and, 142, 156
  names and, 105
  women's rights and, 85
Cauchy, Benjamin, 27
Ce que je cherche (Bardella), 105, 117, 121–9
Cecchinato, Michel, 125
Céline, Louis Ferdinand, 61
centrist politics, 4, 6, 8, 13, 16, 20, 42, 44, 69, 71, 94, 108, 130
  Bardella and, 111–12, 116
  cordon sanitaire and, 101–2, 110–11, 113
  immigration and, 124, 149–50, 152–7
Cercle de l'Union Interalliée, 173
CGT union, 133
Charlemagne Division, 62
Chatillon, Kerridwen, 117
Chaudon, Nelson, 128

INDEX

Chauffroy, Franck, 80
Chauffroy, Jehanne, 80, 81
Chauffroy, Louis, 80, 81
Chauffroy, Mathilde, 80, 81
Chechnya, 151–2
Chevènement, Jean-Pierre, 100–101
Chile, 66
China, 7, 33, 39, 129, 165, 193, 227
Chirac, Jacques, 40, 52, 55, 56, 81, 83, 129, 187, 210, 219
Chombeau, Christiane, 79
Christian Democratic Union (Germany), 109, 154
Christian Social Union (Germany), 109
Christianity, xiv, 12, 48, 59, 80, 82, 85, 117, 123, 140, 167, 173, 180
    homosexuality and, 181–2
    immigration and, 142, 156
    'Judeo-Christian' culture, 85, 162
    names and, 105
    women's rights and, 85
Christmas trees, 178
Chudeau, Roger, 162
Ciotti, Éric, 20, 111, 122, 125, 189, 221
'citizens of nowhere', 5
clandestine migrants, *see* irregular migration
climate change, 2, 7, 8, 11–12, 23–4, 176–9, 183, 188, 190, 193
Clinton, Hillary, 43
Club de l'Hémicycle, 214

CNews, 189–90, 202
Coda Media, 210
cognitive warfare, 193
Cold War (1947–91), 199
Colombia, 154
colonialism, 2, 51, 53, 57, 59, 63, 97, 102, 150
Coluche, 27
Common Agricultural Policy, 179
Communist Party, 6, 12, 16, 49, 50, 55, 59, 61, 63, 82, 94, 97, 133
    RN, support shift to, 127–9, 130, 139–40, 141
Comoros, 149, 158
Conflans-Sainte-Honorine, Île-de-France, 152
Conservative Political Action Conference (CPAC), 36
Constitutional Council, 214
Copé, Jean-François, 213
cordon sanitaire, 103, 110–11
    see also *front républicain*
Corpo, La, 59
Corsica, 26
cost of living, 28, 69, 70, 71, 72, 88, 131, 168
Cour de cassation, 212
Cour des comptes, 171
Coutard, Ghislain, 27
Covid-19 pandemic (2019–23), 4, 6–7, 32, 70, 99, 159, 162, 163
    economic impact, 71, 169, 171
Crépon, Sylvain, 139–40, 182
Creusot-Loire, 98
crime, 53, 54, 55, 70, 124, 129, 143, 152

INDEX

immigration, linking with, 125, 129, 151, 152, 160
Crimea, 71, 197, 199
Croix de Feu, 49
cultural hegemony, 184
culture wars, 16, 34–5, 37, 179–84
   gender, 44, 182, 194
   homosexuality, 85, 181–2
   language, 182–3
   media and, 190, 194
Curie, Marie, 12
currency, 15, 27, 54, 95, 171

Da Empoli, Giuliano, 31, 192, 194
Daily Mail, 189
Dalongeville, Gérard, 140
Darmanin, Gérald, 152–3, 167, 210
Dassault Group, 190
Day of the Jackal, The (Forsyth), 62
de-industrialisation, 6, 97, 101, 129–30, 138–9, 224
Debuchy, Dany, 78
decolonisation, 51, 53, 57, 63
dédiabolisation, xiv, 14, 35, 57, 65, 73, 74–5, 82–5, 86
défrancisation, 106
democracy, 4, 5, 7, 9, 18, 33, 42, 193
   direct, 26
   embezzlement rulings and, 200, 209, 211, 212
   illiberal, 40
   liberal, 5, 9, 33, 42
Democratic Party (US), 124, 135
Denmark, 225

Department of Government Efficiency (DOGE), 38, 225
Dettinger, Christophe, 27
Deville, Delphine, 125
Di Maio, Luigi, 29
Diat, Nicolas, 117
Diaz, Edwige, 16–17
Dion, Céline, 180
Direction générale de la Sécurité intérieure (DGSI), 204
disinformation, 45, 186, 188, 189, 193, 194, 203–5, 210
Djaïz, David, 177
Doppelgänger, 204
Dorgères, Henri, 179
Doriot, Jacques, 50
Dreyfus affair (1894–1906), 48–9, 63
droit du sol, 153–4, 224
Drouet, Éric, 27, 28
Drumont, Édouard, 49
Dupond-Moretti, Éric, 109
Duprat, François, 62
Durafour, Michel, 65
Durvye, François, 174
Dutton, Peter, 35

Eagles of Death Metal, 151
Eat French campaign, 177
Écologistes, Les, 140
Economist, The, 42, 211
economy, 4, 11, 13, 71, 72, 87–8, 100, 126, 133–4, 143, 167–74
   budget deficit, 5, 168, 170, 171, 172
   cost of living, 28, 69, 70, 71, 72, 88, 131, 168

INDEX

Covid pandemic and, 71, 169, 171
free market policies, 27, 62, 95, 99, 116, 130, 133–4, 173–4, 221
globalisation, *see* globalisation
immigration and, 97, 98, 130, 138, 144, 157, 163–4
inequality, 6, 7, 131, 168, 169
poverty, 128, 133, 139
protectionism, 34, 55, 71, 130, 133–4, 170
Russo-Ukrainian War and, 71, 89, 169, 201
taxation, *see* taxation
unemployment, 29, 55, 97, 128, 130, 138, 139, 163–4
welfare, xiv, 98, 116, 116, 131, 163, 164, 167–8, 171–2
Ecuador, 128
education, 139
Egypt, 52, 60, 63, 106
elections, 4, 10, 55, 103, 110–11, 113–14, 203–5
  see also European Parliament; legislative elections; municipal governments; presidential elections
Eltchaninoff, Michel, 82, 84, 200
Élysée Palace, Paris, 1, 6, 18
embezzlement case (2014–25), 1–3, 19–20, 37–9, 73, 114–15, 200, 207–17
  Bardella and, 209, 213, 215–17
  democracy and, 200, 209, 211, 212
  judiciary, attacks on, 212–13

En Marche!, 94
energy
  price inflation, 15, 114, 201
  renewable energy, 2, 177, 178, 183
  Russo-Ukrainian War and, 89, 202
English language, 182
Ennasr mosque, Hénin-Beaumont, 143
environment, 2, 7, 8, 11–12, 175–9
  agriculture and, 11, 175–6, 177, 178
  climate change, 2, 7, 8, 11–12, 23–4, 176–9, 183, 188, 190, 193
  gilets jaunes and, 11–12, 23–5
  media and, 188, 190
  motoring and, 8, 24–5, 176, 177, 178
  renewable energy, 2, 177, 178, 183
Erdoğan, Recep Tayyip, 34, 35
'L'État, c'est moi', 119
Étrépagny, Normandy, 130–36
Eurasia Group, 225
euro, 15, 27, 54, 95, 171
Europe 1 (TV channel), 189, 190
European Central Bank, 169
European Commission, 144–5
European Court of Human Rights, 215
European exceptionalism, 41–2
European Parliament, 3, 24, 58, 69, 118, 142, 155, 166, 201
  1984 elections, 78

INDEX

2019 elections, 24, 101, 108–9, 216
2024 elections, 69, 101 109, 166, 191–2, 204, 216
European Union (EU), xi, xiv, 2, 4, 11, 53, 95, 96–7, 110, 155, 221, 224, 225
  Agency for Fundamental Rights, 166
  asylum and migration pact (2024), 165
  Brexit (2016–20), *see* Brexit
  Common Agricultural Policy, 179
  federalism and, 54
  Frexit proposals, 26, 96, 171, 225
  Green Deal (2020), 166, 179
  Lisbon Treaty (2007), 95, 97
  Maastricht Treaty (1992), 53
  Mercosur trade deal (2024), 134
  RN embezzlement case (2014–25), *see* embezzlement case
  Schengen Zone, 154
  single currency, 15, 27, 54, 95, 171
L'Express, 18
extremism, xii–xv, 35–9

Fabius, Laurent, 67
Facebook, 28, 191
Fages, Yves, 126
fake news, 188, 189, 193, 194, 203–4
far left, xiii, 10, 14, 17–18, 26, 28, 39, 50, 71–2, 98–9, 129, 130, 133
  anti-capitalism, 99, 130, 131, 133
  globalisation and, 71–2, 100, 123
  immigration and, 72, 99, 131
  RN, support shift to, 128–9, 130, 139, 140, 141, 167
  see also Communist Party; La France Insoumise
far right, term, xii–xv
Farage, Nigel, xii, 6, 10
farmers, *see* agriculture
fascism, xii, xiii, xv, 9, 11, 17, 48, 49–51, 54, 56, 62, 74, 82, 127, 179, 184
  anti-fascism, 14, 18, 72, 122–3, 131, 145, 183, 197
  European exceptionalism and, 41–2
Fayard, 117, 123, 191
Federal Communications Commission (US), 190
federal Europe, 54
Fedorova, Xenia, 191
Feher, Michel, 13
feminism, 80, 133
festivals, 17
Fico, Robert, 223
Fieschi, Catherine, xiv, 58–9, 192
Figaro, Le, 89, 190
Fillon, François, 210, 211–12
Financial Times, 6, 108, 167
Finkelstein, Arthur, 192
Firminy, Loire, 98

INDEX

First Czech-Russian Bank, 19, 71, 89, 198–9
fishing, 5, 11, 57, 94, 179
Five Star movement, 29, 203
flat-earthers, 193
Flaubert, Gustave, 6
Fly Rider, 27
football, 56
Foreign Legion, 51–2, 58, 59
foulards rouges, 30
Fourquet, Jérôme, 12–13, 31, 158–9
Fouquet's, Paris, 30
Fox News, 186, 187, 190
franc, 15
français de souche, 59
France
    Dreyfus affair (1894–1906), 48–9
    empire, *see* French Empire
    Fourth Republic (1946–58), 11, 66
    nuclear deterrence forces, 2, 45, 118
    Revolution (1989–99), 48, 50, 63, 95, 162
    Second World War (1939–45), 1, 14, 41, 42, 47, 49–51, 60, 62, 63, 65, 126
    Third Republic (1870–1940), 11, 48–51
    trente glorieuses (1945–75), 50, 98, 129
    UNSC membership, 2, 118, 200
France Inter, 189
France périphérique, La (Guilluy), 13, 25
franceinfo, 189
Francis, Pope, 6, 156
Franco, Francisco, 9, 50, 54
free speech, 186
Freemasonry, 173
French Empire, 2, 51–2, 53, 57, 59, 63, 97, 102, 150
    Algeria (1830–1962), *see under* Algeria
    Indochina (1887–1954), 51, 54, 59
    Morocco (1912–56), 126, 127, 149
    Tunisia (1881–1956), 127, 150
French Guiana, 49
French language, 182–3
Frexit, 26, 96, 171, 225
Front de libération nationale (FLN), 65
Front National (FN), xi, xv, 35, 52–68
    Algeria veterans in, 60, 62
    antisemitism, xiv, 14, 35, 57, 64–5, 74, 82–3, 84
    black French people and, 84
    Catholicism and, xiv, 80, 82, 85
    dédiabolisation, xiv, 14, 35, 57, 65, 73, 74–5, 82–5, 86, 109
    foundation (1972), xi, xv, 62, 123
    Holocaust denial, 62, 64–5, 85
    homosexuality, stance on, 85
    Islamophobia, 82, 83–4
    leadership change (2011), xi, xv, 55, 67, 73, 75, 182
    media and, 187

INDEX

Nazi sympathisers in, 60, 62, 63, 123
presidential election (2002), 52–5, 57, 81, 82, 85, 122, 129, 187
renaming (2018), xi, xv, 35, 55, 86, 109
women and, 85
Front National des Combattants, 61
Front National pour l'Algérie Française, 61
Front Populaire, 11
front républicain, 3–4, 10, 55, 103, 110, 113–14, 140, 225
Frontex, 164

G8, 200
Gabriel-Péri estate, Saint-Denis, 107
Garraud, Jean-Paul, 74
de Gaulle, Charles de, xiv, 26, 38, 51, 60, 61, 63, 102, 111, 168, 216
RN influence on, 47, 118, 134, 224
Gaultier, Léon, 62
Gaza, 102
gender, 44, 182, 194
general elections, *see* legislative elections
Geneva Convention (1951), 165
Gentile, Giovanni, 184
Georgescu, Călin, 186–7, 204–5, 209–10
Germany, 2, 4, 8, 9, 40, 43, 48, 109, 113–14, 129
environmental policies, 178
federal elections (2025), 205
immigration policies, 154–5
Nazi period (1933–45), *see* Nazi Germany
Russia, relations with, 203, 205
United States, relations with, 8, 42
gilets jaunes protests (2018–20), 5–6, 11–12, 20–21, 23–32, 71, 88, 169, 228
casseurs and, 26–7, 30
demographics, 26–8, 31
environmental policies and, 11–12, 23–5, 30
geographic spread, 31
media and, 193
social media and, 29, 30
taxation and, 23–4, 25, 26, 28
Gironde, 16
Giscard d'Estaing, Valéry, 77
globalisation, 4, 6–7, 13, 25, 27, 33, 40, 51, 68, 87, 129, 168, 224, 227–8
first globalisation (c. 1840–1940), 50, 157
gilets jaunes and, 25, 27
left-wing politics and, 71–2, 100, 123
globalism, xiv, 6, 13, 53, 71, 95
Gollnisch, Bruno, 85
Gonzalez, José, 102
Gonzalvo, Laurence, 26
Goodhart, David, 5
Gramsci, Antonio, 133, 183–4
Grare, Yves, 27
Great Depression (1929–39), 11

INDEX

great replacement theory, 64, 159–60
GRECE, 184
Greece, 203
greenfield sites, 178
Greenland, 38, 198
greenshirts, 179
Grillo, Beppe, 25
Groupe Union Défense, 56
Guadeloupe, 14, 126
Guilluy, Christophe, 13, 25
Gulf War (1990–91), 66

Habeck, Robert, 155
Hachette, 123, 190
haemophilia, 80
Haiti, 155
halal food, 84, 160
Hamas, 83
Hammache, Sidi-Ahmed, 152
Hanouna, Cyril, 189, 222–3
Harkis, 153
Harnes, 55
Harris, Kamala, 7, 88
Hassan II mosque, Casablanca, 106
healthcare, 163, 164, 167, 168, 172
Hegel, Georg Wilhelm Friedrich, 133
Helms, Jesse, 66
Hénin-Beaumont, Pas-de-Calais, 55–6, 94, 116, 130, 136, 137–46
herbicides, 175, 176
Hexagone, 171–2
Hidalgo, Anne, 93, 180
Hitler, Adolf, 11, 42, 51, 62, 155
HIV, 80
Holeindre, Roger, 62

Hollande, François, 73, 95, 223
Holocaust (1941–5), 14, 48, 51, 62, 64–5, 83
  denial of, 62, 64–5, 85
homosexuality, 85, 181–2
Hong Kong, 29
Horaces, Les, 15
'Horst Wessel Song', 58
Hôtel de Matignon, Paris, 2
Hôtel le Normandy, Vernon, 69
Houellebecq, Michel, 12, 31, 161
L'Humanité, 127
Hungary, 9, 33, 43, 44, 96, 199, 203, 209, 223, 225–6
  culture wars in, 181
  EU, relations with, 225–6
  media in, 183, 186, 192
  Russia, relations with, 186, 203, 205
Hussein, Saddam, 66

identitarianism, 118
Identité–Libertés, 220
Ifop, 171–2
illiberal democracy, 40
immigration, 11, 13, 27, 34, 38, 43, 100, 127–9, 142–4, 149–67, 181, 183
  assimilation and, 107, 128, 143–4, 150, 158, 160–62
  Bardella and, xiv, 106, 107, 121, 154, 159–60, 224
  crime, linking with, 125, 129, 151, 152, 154–5, 160
  droit du sol, 153–4, 224
  economy and, 97, 98, 130, 138, 144, 157, 163–4

INDEX

great replacement theory, 64, 159–60
irregular, 75, 79, 144, 162–3, 164–6
Islam and, 11, 64, 83, 107, 125, 135, 143, 151–5, 158–9
Le Pen, Marine and, 2, 15, 71, 72, 74–5, 79, 95–6, 100, 153, 159, 221, 224
Le Pen, Jean-Marie and, 54, 57, 62–4, 68, 95–6, 100, 156
left-right divide on, 72, 99, 131, 159
legal migration, 163, 164, 165
media and, 188, 190
names and, 105–6, 160–61
producerist theory and, 13
public perceptions of, 11, 13, 27, 97–9, 100, 121, 124–5, 130, 133, 143–4, 149–67
refugees, 97, 135, 142, 151, 154–5, 165–6
submersion narrative, 149–50, 152, 154, 159, 164
terror attacks and, 107, 143, 151–2, 154–5, 160
welfare and, 98, 154, 163, 224–5
India, 33
Indochina (1887–1954), 51, 54, 59
industry, 6, 97, 101, 129–30, 138–9, 224
inequality, 6, 7, 131, 168, 169
Ingénieurs du chaos, Les (Da Empoli), 192, 194
Insee, 158

Inside the Mind of Marine Le Pen (Eltchaninoff), 82, 84
Instagram, 109
Institut Montaigne, 170
international law, 39, 165
International Monetary Fund (IMF), 95, 172
International Organization for Migration, 164
International Women's Day, 137
'Internationale', 58, 79
internationalism, 4, 12, 44
intersectionality of hate, 181
Iorio, Éric, 80
Iran, 36
Iraq, 40, 41, 66, 107
irregular migration, 75, 79, 144, 162–3, 164–5
Islam, 11, 75, 107, 125, 143–4, 151–5, 158–9, 181
assimilation and, 107, 143–4, 158, 160–62
far left politics and, 131, 173
great replacement theory and, 64, 159–60
Islamophobia, 72, 74, 75, 82, 83–4, 135, 173
terror attacks and, 107, 143, 151–2, 154–5, 160
Islamic State (IS), 107–8, 143, 151
Israel, 14, 34, 83, 102
Issep, 220
Italian migrants, 106, 107, 127, 144, 158
Italy, 9, 25, 29, 33, 35, 108, 133, 184, 192, 209, 225
EU, relations with, 226

INDEX

Fascist period (1922–43), 50, 184
    immigration policies, 165, 166
    Russia, relations with, 203

J'accuse (2019 film), 49
Jackson, Julian, 223
Jacquerie (1358), 6
Japan, 86
Jarousseau, Vincent, 13
Jaurès, Jean, 118, 143
JDNews, Le, 171–2
Jean Jaurès Foundation, 118
Jews, 48–9, 50, 61, 63, 74, 83, 150, 167, 204
    Le Pen Jr and, xiv, 14, 25, 78, 82, 83, 87
    Le Pen Sr and, xiv, 14, 35, 57, 64–5, 83, 87
Joan of Arc, 47, 182
Jobbik, 203
Johnson, Boris, 100
Jolly, Thomas, 180
Jospin, Lionel, 52, 101, 219
Journal du Dimanche, Le, 110, 189, 190
Judeo-Christian culture, 85, 162

Kaczyński, Jarosław, 44
Kagame, Paul, 34
Kennedy Center, 183
Khalaf, Roula, 6
Khmers Rouges, 176
King, Martin Luther, 213
Klarsfeld, Serge, 14, 83
Knafo, Sarah, 36, 37, 189, 220
Krastev, Ivan, 44, 166

Kuwait, 66
Kyrgyzstan, 43, 163

La Courneuve, Seine-Saint-Denis, 152
La France Insoumise (LFI), xiii, 14, 18, 26, 39, 72, 83, 93, 113, 123, 133
    antisemitism accusations, 14
    economic policies, 173
    front républicain, 113
    judicial investigation (2018), 211
    presidential election (2017), 219
    presidential election (2022), 72, 130, 219
    RN, supporter shift to, 130, 167
La Ricamarie, Loire, 97
de La Rocque, François, 49
Labarre, Julien, 190
Labour Party (UK), 4, 10, 124
Lagardère Group, 190
laïcité, 162, 167
Lambert, Hubert, 77
Lasri, Boufeldja, 143
Latin America, 128, 134
Law and Justice (PiS), 9, 44
Le Bourgeois, Robert, 132
Le Bras, Hervé, 159
Le Goff, Jean-Pierre, 18–19
Le Maire, Bruno, 171
Le Marchand, Karine, 75
Le Pen, Jean-Marie, xi, xiv, xv, 9, 11, 35, 51–68, 73, 76, 86–7
    antisemitism, xiv, 14, 35, 57, 64–5, 83, 87
    Bardot, relationship with, 138
    birth (1928), 57

INDEX

bomb attack (1976), 77
Catholicism, views on, 59
death (2025), 57, 67–8
embezzlement, participation in, 3, 208
environment, views on, 175
EU, views on, 54
European elections (1984), 78
expulsion from RN (2015), 57, 65, 67, 73, 86
Foreign Legion service, 51–2, 58, 59, 63, 65–6
de Gaulle, views on, 47
gilets jaunes protests (2018–20), 24
Holocaust denial, 64–5
immigration, views on, 54, 57, 62–4, 68, 95–6, 100, 156
media and, 187, 191
Mémoires (2018), 176
Poujade, association with, 24, 60–61
presidential election (2002), 52–5, 57, 81, 82, 85, 111, 122, 129, 187
pupille de la nation status, 59
racism, 14, 62–4, 74
Russia, relations with, 161, 199, 201
sea, love of, 59, 76, 94
Second World War (1939–45), 60
Serp, 58
taxation, views on, 24, 53, 54
Trump, comparisons with, 35, 52, 53, 54, 58–9

Le Pen, Marie-Caroline, 36, 76, 80, 155
Le Pen, Marine, xi, xiii, xiv, 5, 8, 10, 11, 12, 32, 69–89, 94
À contre flots (2006), 94
abortion, views on, 81, 85
anti-Islamism bill (2021), 161–2
antisemitism, views on, xiv, 14, 25, 78, 82, 83, 84, 87
Bardella, relations with, 115–16
Bardot, relationship with, 137–8
Barnier no-confidence vote (2024), 103, 134, 150
birth (1968), 76
bomb attack (1976), 77
Catholic Church, relations with, xiv, 85, 182
childhood, 75–9
culture wars, views on, 181–4
currency, policies on, 15, 95, 171
dédiabolisation, xiv, 14, 35, 57, 65, 73, 74–5, 82–5, 86, 109
economic policies, 87–8, 100, 169, 170, 221, 224
embezzlement case (2014–25), 1–3, 19–20, 37–9, 73, 114–15, 200, 207–17
environmental policies, 2, 8, 176, 177
Étrépagny rally (2024), 130–34
EU, views on, xiv, 2, 95, 96–7, 171, 221, 224
French language, views on, 182
de Gaulle, quotation of, 47, 134, 224

INDEX

gilets jaunes protests (2018–20), 24
homosexuality, stance on, 85
Hungary, relations with, 199
immigration, views on, 2, 15, 71, 72, 74–5, 79, 95–6, 100, 153, 159, 221, 224
inexperience, 19, 100, 169
Islam, views on, 74, 75, 83–4
Italy, relations with, 29
Joan of Arc celebration (2011), 182
leadership accession (2011), xi, xv, 55, 67, 73, 75, 85, 182
legal career, 74–5, 79, 214
legislative elections (2024), 102–3, 139, 140
media and, 18, 81, 187, 189, 190, 191
Paris municipal election (1983), 76
Pas-de-Calais constituency, 55–6, 94, 116, 130, 136, 137–46
Pour que vive la France (2012), 94, 199–200
presidential election (2012), 70, 72–3, 94
presidential election (2017), *see* presidential election (2017)
presidential election (2022), *see* presidential election (2022)
public office ban (2025), 1–3, 19–20, 37, 73, 114–15, 200, 207–17
Putin, meeting with (2017), 199
race, views on, 74–5, 78

renaming of party (2018), xi, xv, 35, 55, 86
Russia, relations with, 19, 35, 40, 71, 89, 197–205
social media, 8, 191
Trump, relations with, 33–45, 198
welfare, views on, 116
Le Pen, Pierrette, 76, 77–8, 81
Le Pen, Yann, 80
League (Italy), 29, 203
Lebourg, Nicolas, 50, 63, 85, 200
Leclerc supermarkets, 69
Lecornu, Sébastien, 150
left-versus-right structure, 6, 13, 52, 53, 71
left-wing politics, xiii, xiv, 6, 8, 10, 11, 17–18, 71–2, 97–101, 122–4
anti-capitalism, 99, 130, 131, 133
decline of, 14, 122–4, 141
far left, *see* far left
globalisation and, 71–2, 100, 123
immigration and, 72, 99, 131, 159
Le Pen and, 100–101
media and, 18
producerism and, 13
RN, support shift to, 128–9, 130, 139–40, 167
Leggeri, Fabrice, 164
legislative election (1956), 60
legislative election (1986), 55
legislative election (2002), 55–6
legislative election (2022), 8, 69, 93

INDEX

legislative election (2024), xi, 3–4, 10, 39, 83, 101–3, 111–14, 131–2, 139, 220
   Ciotti defection, 20, 111, 122, 125, 189, 221
   economic policies and, 170, 172
   environmental policies and, 8, 176
   front républicain, 3–4, 10, 101–3, 112–14, 140
   media and, 189
Lermet, Gilles, 98
Lescure, Roland, 42
Levavasseur, Ingrid, 27
liberal democracy, 5, 9, 42, 66
Liberal Democrats (UK), 124
liberalism, 4, 8, 18, 25
   wishful thinking and, 10, 41
Libération, 145
Liberté, Egalité, Fraternité, 102, 223
Lidl, 128
Lille, Hauts-de-France, 145
Linke, Die, 203
Lisbon Treaty (2007), 95, 97
Llorca, Raphaël, 118
Loi Veil (1975), 81
Louis XIV, King, 119
low-emission zones, 8, 176, 178
Ludosky, Priscillia, 26, 27–9

Maastricht Treaty (1992), 53
Macron, Emmanuel, xiii, 1–2, 3, 4–8, 18, 19, 27, 31–2, 39, 71, 83, 99, 106, 129
   Bolloré, relations with, 190–91
   Covid-19 crisis (2020–22), 6–7, 99
   economic policies, 99, 114, 131, 169, 171, 172
   environmental policies, 7, 11–12, 23–5, 30
   European elections (2019), 108
   European elections (2024), 69, 101
   foulards rouges, 30
   gilets jaunes protests (2018–20), 5–6, 11–12, 20–21, 23–32, 71, 88, 228
   globalism, 6–7, 87
   immigration, views on, 152
   Le Pen, Jean-Marie death (2025), 67
   legislative elections (2022), 93
   legislative elections (2024), 39, 101–3, 113, 114, 131–2, 176
   Olympic Games (2024), 180
   presidential election (2017), 1, 4, 6, 27, 31, 70, 73, 86–8, 94–6, 171, 203
   presidential election (2022), 1, 13, 14, 17, 67, 69, 70, 88–9, 93, 130
   Révolution (2016), 6, 95
   RN embezzlement rulings (2025), 209
   Russia, relations with, 198, 200, 202
   Trump, relations with, 36
Madrid, Spain, 43
Maginot Line, 42
mainstream media, 18, 81, 87–8, 116–18, 134–5, 185–91

INDEX

Make Europe Great Again conference (2025), 43
Marcos, Ferdinand, 66
Maréchal, Marion, 37, 116, 179, 189, 220
Mariani, Thierry, 74, 201
Marie-Antoinette, Queen consort, 180
Marine Le Pen (Fourest and Venner), 187–8
marinistes, 70
'Marseillaise', 50
Marseille, Hervé, 217
Marseille, 158
Martin, Patrick, 15
Martinique, 14, 28, 126
Maurras, Charles, 49–50
May, Theresa, 5
May Day marches, 54
mayors, 140
Mayotte, 149, 154
Mazower, Mark, 41–2
meat consumption, 178
Medef, 15, 55
media, xii, 18, 29, 116, 183, 185–94, 221
  disinformation, 45, 186, 188, 189, 193, 194, 203–5, 210
  foreign interference, 29, 193–4, 202–5, 210
  mainstream media, 18, 81, 87–8, 116–18, 134–5, 185–91
  social media, 7–8, 18, 29, 30, 109, 186, 191–4, 204
Medvedev, Dmitry, 222
Mégret, Bruno, 56
Mélenchon, Jean-Luc, xiii, 14, 17, 18, 26, 39, 72, 93, 99, 113, 123, 133
  antisemitism accusations, 14
  front républicain, 113
  judicial investigation (2018), 211
  presidential election (2017), 219
  presidential election (2022), 72, 130, 219
  RN embezzlement rulings (2025), 210
  RN, supporter shift to, 130, 167
Meloni, Giorgia, 9, 33, 42, 133, 165, 166, 184, 226
Mémoricide (de Villiers), 181
Mercosur, 134
Merkel, Angela, 4, 155
Merz, Friedrich, 154–5, 226
Métamorphoses françaises (Fourquet), 159
Mexico, 165
middle class, 74, 95, 97, 100, 105, 125
Milei, Javier, 4, 41
Mitterrand, François, 6, 17, 55, 66, 102, 187
Modi, Narendra, 33
Mohammed bin Salman, Saudi Crown Prince, 33
Moldova, 204
Monde, Le, 38, 51, 66, 177, 204, 208
Monroe, Marilyn, 138
Montretout, Saint-Cloud, 56, 77, 86
Morin, Antoine, 54
Moroccan migrants, 112, 126, 127, 129, 151

INDEX

Morocco, 106, 107, 112, 116, 126, 127, 129, 138, 150
Moscovici, Pierre, 171
Mosley, Oswald, 51
motoring, 8, 24–5, 176, 177, 178
Mouraud, Jacline, 27
Mouvement conservateur, 220
Mouvement démocrate, 211
Mouvement National Républicain, 56
Munich Security Conference (2025), 43, 155, 185, 186
municipal governments, 140
    1983 elections, 76
    2014 elections, 140
    2026 elections, 174
Murdoch, Rupert, 18, 188
Musk, Elon, xv, 8, 43, 184, 186, 225
Muslim Brotherhood, 144
Mussolini, Benito, 50, 184

Nakamura, Aya, 180
names, 105–6, 160–61
Napoleon III, Emperor, 48
Narbonne, Occitania, 27
National Assembly, xiii, 1, 3, 8, 10
    1956 election, 60
    1986 election, 55
    2002 election, 55–6
    2022 election, 8, 69, 93
    2024 election, *see* legislative election (2024)
National Front (UK), xv
nationalism, xiv, 6, 12, 18, 24, 34, 44, 50, 53, 71, 96, 124
    economics and, 123, 126
    history and, 181
    sovereigntism, xiv, 101
NATO, 2, 99, 197
natural gas, 89, 177, 178, 202
Nazi Germany (1933–45), 1, 11, 14, 49, 58, 60, 61, 83, 123
    Holocaust (1941–5), 14, 48, 51, 62, 64–5, 83, 85
neo-fascism, xv, 42, 51, 54, 56, 74, 72
neo-Nazism, 8, 36–7, 56, 60, 62, 63
Netanyahu, Benjamin, 34
Netherlands, 9, 43, 97, 178, 210
Neuilly-sur-Seine, Île-de-France, 142
New Order, 62, 82, 200
newspapers, 188
Nicolle, Maxime, 27
Niel, Julie, 69, 70
Noël, Bernadette, 26
non-refoulement, 165
Normandy, 130
Northern League, 203
nostalgia, 2, 11, 54, 98, 125, 138, 143
Notre-Dame cathedral, Paris, 135
von Notz, Konstantin, 205
Nouveau Front Populaire, 101, 113
Nouvel Obs, Le, 45, 109
nuclear deterrence forces, 2, 45, 118
nuclear power, 177

obesity, 139
October 7 attacks (2023), 83
Odoul, Julien, 162

INDEX

OECD, 159, 164, 168
OFB, 178
Officer and a Spy, An (2019 film), 49
Oignies, Pas-de-Calais, 138
Olivier, Nolwenn, 116
Olivier, Philippe, 36, 155
Olympic Games, 64, 179–81, 183, 184, 204
OQTF, 163
Orbán, Viktor, 9, 33, 43, 44, 181, 186, 199, 209, 223
ordo amoris, 156
Ordre Nouveau, 62, 82, 200
Organisation de l'armée secrète (OAS), 62
Orleanists, 111
d'Ormale, Bernard, 138, 144–5
Otium Capital, 174
Oxford University, 10

Palestine, 131
Panama, 198
Paris, France, xii, 5, 11, 13, 14, 18
    antisemitic graffiti campaign (2023), 204
    Arc de Triomphe, 30
    bobo society, 14, 226
    gilets jaunes protests (2018–20), 23–32
    IS attacks (2015), 107–8, 143, 151
    Notre-Dame cathedral, 135
    Olympic Games (2024), 179–81, 183, 184, 204
Paris Match, 190
Paris Saint-Germain, 56
Parisien, Le, 214
Party for Freedom, 178
Pas-de-Calais, 55, 81, 94, 130, 137–46
    Hénin-Beaumont, 55–6, 94, 116, 130, 136, 137–46
Pasteur, Louis, 12
Paty, Samuel, 152
payslips, 168
Pech, Thierry, 17
Pécresse, Valérie, 93, 111
pensions, 26, 53, 167, 169, 172
Perpignan, Occitania, 80
Perrineau, Pascal, 51
de Perthuis, Bénédicte, 3
Pertuis, Provence, 70, 197–8
Peru, 128
pessimism, 11
pesticides, 11, 175, 176
Pétain, Philippe, 47, 49–51, 60, 223
Philippe, Édouard, 152, 222
Philippines, 66
Philippot, Florian, 118
Piaf, Édith, 180
pieds noirs, 125
Pigalle, Paris, 26
Pinochet, Augusto, 66
Playboy, 78
Poilievre, Pierre, 34–5
Poland, 9, 44, 96, 138, 142, 161, 163
Polanski, Roman, 48–9
Pope, Amy, 164
populism, xiii, xiv, 9–10, 24, 40, 45, 50, 53, 54, 70, 71, 85, 123, 124

INDEX

economics and, 171
immigration and, 57, 127, 129, 130–31, 156, 161
media and, 192
Populocracy (Fieschi), 192
Portugal, 9, 50
Poujade, Pierre, 24, 60–61
Pour que vive la France (Le Pen), 94, 199–200
poverty, 128, 133, 139
Praud, Pascal, 189
presidential election (1965), 61
presidential election (2002), 52–5, 57, 81, 82, 85, 111, 122, 129, 187
presidential election (2012), 70, 72–3, 94
presidential election (2017), 1, 4, 6, 27, 31, 70, 73, 86, 87–8, 94–6, 111, 171, 219
    Fillon embezzlement case, 211–12
    Russian interference, 203
    television coverage, 75, 87–8, 214
presidential election (2022), 1, 13, 17, 67, 69–73, 88–9, 93, 97, 111, 130, 219–20, 225
    Caribbean islands and, 14
    economic policies and, 71, 88–9, 170
    environmental policies and, 177
    foreign affairs and, 198
    French language and, 182
    gilets jaunes and, 71
    left v right structure and, 71–2

Zemmour's campaign, 67, 72, 105
presidential election (2027), 1, 3, 14, 39, 73, 89, 115, 189, 207, 214, 220
Prieur, Cécile, 45
producerist theory, 13
Project Périclès, 173–4
proportional representation, 55
protectionism, 34, 55, 71, 130, 133–4, 170
Prussia (1701–1918), 50
public services, 11, 88, 98, 99, 129, 169, 171–2
    healthcare, 163, 164, 167, 168, 172
pupille de la nation, 59
Putin, Vladimir, 4, 10, 19, 33, 34, 35, 40, 66, 188, 197–205, 222
Putin's People (Belton), 203
Puy du Fou, Loire, 181

Quai d'Orsay (de Villepin), 40

racism, 14, 62–4, 73, 74, 82, 109, 112, 113, 124
radicalism, term, xiii, xiv
Radio France, 117
Rahman, Mujtaba, 225
Rassemblement National (RN), xi, xv
    activists, 16
    anti-Islamism bill (2021), 161–2
    antisemitism and, xiv, 14, 25, 82–3, 84

INDEX

Barnier no-confidence vote (2024), 103, 134, 150
Briois and Bilde removals (2022), 116
currency, policies on, 15, 95, 171
dédiabolisation, xiv, 14, 35, 57, 65, 73, 74–5, 82–5, 86, 109
economic policies, 87–8, 100, 116, 118, 169–74, 221
embezzlement case (2014–25), *see* embezzlement case
environmental policies, 2, 8
establishment (2018), xi, xv, 35, 55
EU, stance on, xiv, 2, 95, 96–7, 110, 142, 171, 221, 224, 225
far right status, xii–xv
homosexuality, stance on, 85, 181–2
Horaces, relations with, 15
Hungary, relations with, 199
immigration, stance on, *see under* immigration
inexperience, 19, 113
Islam, stance on, 11, 74, 75, 82, 83–4, 125, 135, 181
Le Pen, Jean-Marie death (2025), 68
Le Pen, Jean-Marie expulsion (2015), 57, 65, 67, 86
legislative election (2022), 8, 69, 93
legislative election (2024), *see* legislative election (2024)
media and, 18, 116–18, 134–5, 185–94

municipal elections (2014), 140
municipal elections (2026), 174
Plan B, 115, 214, 220
presidential election (2012), 70, 72–3, 94
presidential election (2017), *see* presidential election (2017)
presidential election (2022), *see* presidential election (2022)
presidential election (2027), 1, 3, 14, 39, 73, 89, 115
racism and, 14, 73, 74, 82, 109, 112, 113, 124, 133
Russia, relations with, 19, 35, 40, 71, 89, 197–205
taxation, policies on, 24, 114
Trump, relations with, 33–45
welfare, stance on, 116, 154
women and, 85
Reconquête!, 220
Reform UK, 10
refugees, 97, 135, 142, 151, 154–5, 165–6
Renaissance Party, 94
renewable energy, 2, 177, 178
Républicains, Les, xiii, 6, 16, 20, 93, 111, 125, 153, 210, 211–12, 221
Republican Guard, 180
Republican Party (US), 222
République en Marche!, 94
Retailleau, Bruno, 67, 153, 189, 221, 222
retirement age, 169
Reuters, 167
Révolution (Macron), 6, 95
Révolution obligée, La (Djaïz), 177

INDEX

revolution, 95, 111–12
Rhodesia (1965–79), 66
Rivarol, 83
RMC, 189
Roma, 49
Romania, 8, 33, 163, 186–7, 204–5, 209–10
Romanyk, Oksana, 197
Romney, Mitt, 139
Rothschild family, 5, 87
Rouen, Normandy, 130
Rousseau, Jean-Jacques, 12
RT, 29, 191, 203
Ruffin, François, 221
rule of law, 41, 193
rules-based international order, 4
Russian Federation, 7, 10, 19, 33, 34, 35, 39, 43, 99, 188, 197–205
   electoral interference, 203–5
   Hungary, relations with, 186, 203, 205
   international law and, 39, 165
   media and, 29, 188, 190–91, 193, 194, 202–3
   Medvedev-Putin arrangement (2008), 222
   RN, bank loan to (2014), 19, 71, 89, 198–9
   sanctions on, 89, 191, 201, 203, 205
   Trump, relations with, 34, 37, 44, 146
   Ukrainian War (2014–), see Russo-Ukrainian War
Russo-Ukrainian War (2014–), 2, 4, 19, 37, 39, 44, 102, 146, 197
   Crimea invasion (2014), 71, 197, 199, 200, 201
   Donbas invasion (2014), 200, 201
   economic impact, 71, 89, 169, 201
   full-scale invasion (2022), 4, 19, 71, 89, 156, 197, 200, 201
   media and, 191, 203
   peace negotiations, 37, 198, 202
   sanctions and, 89, 191, 201, 203, 205
Rwanda, 34, 75, 166

Sabéran, Haydée, 145
Saint-Cloud, 56, 77, 86
Saint-Denis, Seine-Saint-Denis, 105–6, 107, 160
Saint-Étienne, Loire, 97, 98–9
Salan, Raoul, 61, 62
Salazar, António, 9, 50
Salvini, Matteo, 29, 203, 209
Samsonite, 138
Sanchez, Julien, 121, 127–9
Sardone, Silvia, 192
Sarkozy, Nicolas, 74, 95, 112, 124, 152, 161, 163, 210
Saudi Arabia, 33
Schengen Zone, 154
Scholz, Olaf, 154
science, 12, 193
Sciences Po, 117
Second World War (1939–45), 1, 14, 41, 42, 47, 49–51, 60, 63, 126
   Holocaust (1941–5), 48, 51, 62, 64–5, 83, 85

INDEX

Seigneure, Sandrine, 79
Seillière, Ernest-Antoine, 55
Seine-et-Marne, 26, 27
Seine-Saint-Denis, 105–6, 107
Senegal, 75
Sens commun, 220
September 11 attacks (2001), 143
Serbia, 43, 205
Serotonin (Houellebecq), 31
Serp, 58
Sète, Occitania, 112
SFR, 88
single mothers, 81
Slovakia, 205, 223
Smartbox, 173
Smith, Ian, 66
social media, 7–8, 18, 29, 30, 109, 186, 188, 191–4, 204
Socialist Party, xiii, 6, 16, 17, 52, 55, 93, 95, 101, 126, 130, 139
Société Générale, 132
solar power, 177
'Somewheres' vs 'Anywheres', 5
Sorbonne University, 4
Sorel, Georges, 50
Soulard, Christophe, 212
Soumission (Houellebecq), 161
sovereigntism, xiv, 101
Spain, 9, 43, 50, 54, 127, 142, 165
speed limits, 25
Sputnik, 29, 203
SS (*Schutzstaffel*), 62, 123
Stade de France, Paris, 108, 128, 151
Starmer, Keir, 4
Statista, 194

Stérin, Pierre-Édouard, 173–4, 221–2
Sternhell, Zeev, 49–50
Strasbourg, Alsace
   Christmas market attack (2018), 27
   WWII liberation (1944), 123
submersion narrative, 149–50, 152, 154, 159, 164
Suez Crisis (1956), 52, 60, 63
Sweden, 35
Syria, 66, 135, 151, 155
Syriza, 203

Tahiti, 126
Tanguy, Jean-Philippe, 38–9
Tarascon, 127–8
Tavoillot, Pierre-Henri, xiii
taxation, 24, 54, 114, 131, 133, 167–8, 172
   gilets jaunes and, 23–4, 25, 26, 28
   green taxes, 12, 23–4, 25, 28, 30, 114, 177
   income tax, 114, 167
   Poujadism, 24, 60–61
   value-added tax (VAT), 114, 170, 172, 177
   wealth taxes, 5, 173
television, 81, 87–8, 185–91
Termet, Flavien, 102
Terra Nova, 17
terrorism, 143, 151, 154–5, 160
   Le Pen assassination attempt (1976), 77
   Miraoui murder (2025), 160

INDEX

Paris attacks (2015), 107–8, 143, 151
Paty murder (2020), 151–2
Strasbourg attack (2018), 27
TF1, 102, 187, 189, 190
TikTok, 109, 186, 191
Time, 201
Tixier-Vignancour, Jean-Louis, 61
Tondelier, Marine, 140–41
Touche pas à mon poste!, 189
Toulouse, Occitania, 53
Tour de France, 178
Tourcoing, Hauts-de-France, 152
Tours, Loire, 85
trade unions, 6, 12, 26, 123, 132, 140, 168
trade wars, 34, 37, 38
traditional right, 4, 6, 8, 13, 16, 20, 44, 69, 71, 94, 108, 130
    Bardella and, 111–12, 116
    cordon sanitaire and, 101–2, 110–11, 113
    immigration and, 124, 149–50, 152–7
trente glorieuses (1945–75), 50, 98, 129
Trinité-sur-Mer, Brittany, 57, 67
Trump, Donald, xi, xii, xv, 2, 4, 6, 8–10, 19, 31, 32, 33–45, 52, 96, 124, 133, 198, 227–8
    backlash potential and, 9–10, 34–45, 227–8
    Bardella, comparisons with, 118, 119, 121
    birthright citizenship, views on, 153–4
    Capitol attack (2021), 39
    Colombia deportations (2025), 154
    culture wars, 181, 183, 184
    environmental policies, 176
    immigration policies, 153–4, 164, 227
    Le Pen, Marine, relations with, 33–45, 198
    Le Pen, Jean-Marie, comparisons with, 35, 52, 53, 54, 58–9
    liberal establishment and, 10, 41, 135, 141
    media and, 18, 186, 188
    presidential election (2016), 2, 18, 35, 41, 52, 53
    presidential election (2024), 8, 32, 33, 36, 52, 88, 155, 198
    Republican Party takeover, 222
    RN embezzlement rulings (2025), 209
    Russia, relations with, 34, 37, 44, 146, 202
    trade wars, 34, 37, 38, 227
Trump, Melania, 161
Truss, Liz, 172
Truth Social, 37
Tuileries Palace, Paris, 48
Tunisia, 127, 150, 160
Turgenev, Ivan, 6
Turkey, 34, 35, 97

Ukraine, 2, 4, 19, 37, 39, 44, 71, 89, 102, 146, 169, 197–205
    Crimea invasion (2014), 71, 197, 199, 200, 201

INDEX

Donbas invasion (2014), 200, 201
full-scale invasion (2022), 4, 19, 71, 89, 156, 197, 200, 201
peace negotiations (2025), 37, 198
unemployment, 29, 55, 97, 128, 130, 138, 139, 163–4
Union des droites pour la République, 221
United Colors of Benetton, 96
United Kingdom
Brexit (2016–20), *see* Brexit
empire, nostalgia for, 2
far right in, 33, 51
general election (2019), 100
general election (2024), 10
irregular migration, 144, 166
legal migration, 163, 165
media in, 18, 192
nuclear deterrence forces, 2
retirement age, 169
Trump, relations with, 42
Truss mini-budget (2022), 172
United Nations (UN), 7
International Organization for Migration, 164
Security Council, 2, 118, 200
United Russia, 203
United States
Capitol attack (2021), 39
culture wars in, 181, 183, 184
international law and, 39, 165
Iraq War (2003–11), 40, 41
irregular migration, 165
media in, 186, 189, 190

Munich Security Conference (2025), 43, 155, 185, 186
presidential election (2016), 2, 18, 35, 41, 52, 53
presidential election (2024), 8, 32, 33, 36, 52, 88, 155
Trump administration (2017–21), xi, xii, xv, 2, 4, 10, 18, 19, 33, 41, 53
Trump administration (2025–), xv, 8–10, 32, 33–45, 155, 185, 186, 198, 227–8

Vaffanculo (Grillo), 25
Valeurs Actuelles, 103
value-added tax (VAT), 114, 170, 172
Vance, James David, 8, 43, 155–6, 161, 185, 186, 202
Vance, Usha, 161
Vel' d'Hiv' roundup (1942), 83
Vendée, 227
Vernon, Eure, 69, 70
Vichy France (1940–44), 1, 47, 49–51, 60, 63, 64, 223
Vietnam, 51, 54, 59
Vietnamese migrants, 158
Villeneuve-Loubet, Côte d'Azur, 137
de Villepin, Dominique, 39–40, 222
de Villiers, Philippe, 117, 176, 181, 189, 191, 202–3, 227
Vinther-Jensen, Eske, 191
Vivendi Group, 190
Voltaire, 12
Von der Leyen, Ursula, 145

INDEX

Vox, 43
Vučić, Aleksandar, 43

Waffen SS, 62, 123
Wauquiez, Laurent, 153
Weidel, Alice, 43, 161
welfare, xiv, 98, 116, 116, 131, 154, 163, 164, 167–8, 224–5
Wieviorka, Michel, 30
Wilders, Geert, 43, 178, 210
Williams, Philip, 11, 61
windfarms, 177, 183
'woke', 16, 34–5, 37, 179–84, 188
women; women's rights, 42, 81, 85
working class, 4, 13, 24, 48, 51, 98, 105, 109, 119, 125, 128, 139, 174

Bardella and, 5, 108, 116, 126
World Trade Organization (WTO), 7
World Values Survey, 35

X, 43, 180, 186
Xi Jinping, 33

YouGov, 42
Yugoslavia (1918–92), 97
Zelenskyy, Volodymyr, 19, 44, 202
Zemmour, Éric, 36, 49, 67, 72, 93, 105, 106, 117, 189, 220
Zhirinovsky, Vladimir, 161, 201